Place Advantage

APPLIED PSYCHOLOGY FOR INTERIOR ARCHITECTURE

Place Advantage

APPLIED PSYCHOLOGY FOR INTERIOR ARCHITECTURE

Sally Augustin, PhD

WILEY

JOHN WILEY & SONS, INC.

Copyright © 2009 by John Wiley & Sons, Inc. All rights reserved

Published by John Wiley & Sons, Inc., Hoboken, New Jersey

Published simultaneously in Canada

For general information about our other products and services, please contact our Customer Care Department within the United States at (800) 762-2974, outside the United States at (317) 572-3993 or fax (317) 572-4002.

Wiley also publishes its books in a variety of electronic formats. Some content that appears in print may not be available in electronic books. For more information about Wiley products, visit our web site at www.wiley.com.

Library of Congress Cataloging-in-Publication Data:
Augustin, Sally.
    Place advantage : applied psychology for interior architecture / Sally Augustin.
        p.   cm.
    Includes bibliographical references and index.
    ISBN 978-0-470-42212-0 (cloth : alk. paper)
    1. Interior architecture—Psychological aspects.   I. Title.
    NA2850.A94 2009
    747.01'9—dc22

                                                                    2008045487

Printed in the United States of America
10 9 8 7 6 5 4 3 2 1

This book is dedicated to Stu Oskamp, PhD, and Harv Wichman, PhD, who taught me to be an applied psychologist. I am grateful for their lessons.

It is also dedicated to Sheila Rao and Joann Stock, who have been spurring me onward to expand my horizons since elementary school, and to my sister, Sandy Augustin Sivinski, who has been a positive force in my life for even longer than that.

CONTENTS

A few years ago, a friend of a friend received a coveted design award for a replacement high school within an inner-city public school system. The design press heralded the project for its bold design statement and innovative technology. For the community, the project represented a beacon of hope in this blighted neighborhood. The school board benefited too and was able to boast about bringing in a project within tight budget and schedule constraints. Does this sound like the description of a successful project? Read on.

That fall, when students filed into the new building, expectations, as you'd expect, were very high. One year later, 43 percent of the freshmen through senior classes were still reading below grade level and similar scoring deficiencies were met in math and science. The absenteeism rate among both students and faculty continued to be below state standards, and after the new car smell wore off, low student morale and high rates of vandalism were back in full swing. Does this still sound like a successful project? That depends on how you define success.

For this project team, success was defined by visual appeal and satisfaction with the team's ability to solve issues of space planning, budget containment, and adherence to the project schedule.

This may sound like the correct response on the surface, but here's the flaw in this way of thinking: When space planning, budget, and schedule *alone* become a project's foundation, the project brief lacks ambition and depth and disregards the needs and aspirations of the people who live, work, or use a particular place. A project, no matter how aesthetically innovative, is at risk when the project goals fail to focus on issues of "user" performance.

As the late designer-provocateur Tibor Kalman was famous for saying, "The difference between good design and great design is intelligence." Great design requires greater knowledge about the human condition and how the spaces people inhabit powers their ability to achieve success.

Had our friend's friend envisioned a different set of goals for the school project, like improved test scores, lower absenteeism, student/faculty morale, and student aspiration, the design team's investigation would have centered on a scientifically based understanding of environmental psychology: specifically, what physical and psychological qualities of an environment influence a student's ability to concentrate, promote a willingness to collaborate, and communicate a sense of collegiality. These questions would have led to a more ambitious design brief and motivated higher objectives for a successful project.

Whether the project is a home, a home office, or a large institution, the process of a user-centered project is typically more collaborative. In this scenario, the makeup of the project team varies based on the specialized information and new knowledge needed for a particular project.

Along with the designers representing the design firm, and, depending on a project's complexity, interdisciplinary experts, different user groups, and consultants may join the project to represent their specific interest, knowledge, and expertise. The project team is able to expand its role, moving beyond problem solver—addressing issues preestablished by the client—to problem identifier—participating in defining the issues with the client and identifying and applying sources of new knowledge to support and address a project-specific response.

In her book, *Place Advantage: Applied Psychology for Interior Architecture,* leading environmental psychologist Sally Augustin, PhD, clearly outlines a scientific approach to what she describes as "person-centered" places and demonstrates how person-centered goals will improve the predictability and reliability of the performance objectives of *place.*

Today, the designer's role is more complex than ever before and there is a more prominent role for social-scientific research and new knowledge to inform the design of our built environment. The financial and resource investment of space is great, and *great* designers seek out sources of new knowledge, which inform the performance aspects of their design decision making.

Understanding what physical and psychological spatial strategies can and should be employed in a specific project to alter the performance of a space is key in establishing the success criteria for a project. How daylight, view, color, and spatial organization alter a user's response and how these same issues support collaboration or promote prolonged concentration are just some of the important sources of information examined in this book.

The focus of Sally Augustin's thesis centers on the long-standing "disconnect" between research and design practices. Neither community has been very effective in bridging the gap, and both run the risk of being irrelevant without the other. At the same time, there is a wealth of knowledge in the social-scientific community that provides new sources of information for designers to assimilate and apply.

Augustin's expertise as a translator of the scientific principles behind environmental psychology and person-centered design liberates design-related research and new knowledge from the annals of the scientific journals and demonstrates its place in the design process. Through her effective translations of research semantics into design language, Augustin presents an accessible view into the field of design research and environmental psychology.

Place Advantage is a systemic demonstration of the power of new knowledge and research. Each chapter outlines the advantages to the design outcome and its impact on the quality of life, human behavior, and organizational performance of place.

The content of this book applies to the interests of students, design practitioners, and those who use, benefit from, and have the ambition to design spaces that allow the users of the spaces to successfully meet their objectives. This book is most relevant to those who are willing to recast the definition of a successful project to include successful user performance.

Neil Frankel

Neil Frankel is a cofounding partner along with Cindy Coleman in the Chicago-based design and consulting firm Frankel + Coleman. Prior to accepting the Fitz-Hugh Scott Endowed Chair for Design Excellence at the University of Wisconsin—Milwaukee School of Architecture and Urban Planning, Neil Frankel was responsible for Skidmore, Owings & Merrill's Chicago architectural interior practice. In addition to his academic commitment, he is one of five Fellows of both AIA and IIDA, and is a Senior Fellow of the Design Futures Council. In 2005, Mr. Frankel was the sole recipient of the AIAS Education Honor Award.

Cindy Coleman

Cindy Coleman is a cofounding partner along with Neil Frankel in the Chicago-based design and consulting firm Frankel + Coleman. Coleman is an assistant professor in the Department of Architecture, Interior Architecture and Designed Objects at The School of the Art Institute of Chicago, a contributing editor for Interior Design *magazine and* Chicago Architect, *and the professional advisor for the Marcus Prize, a biannual global architectural prize acknowledging architects at the trajectory of their careers.*

ACKNOWLEDGMENTS

This book would not have come to be without the thoughtful support of its editor, John Czarnecki, and his assistant, Sadie Abuhoff. Their comments have been much appreciated.

I would also like to thank all of the groups that provided images used in this book. Its pages would be a lot less interesting and useful without their contributions. Specifically, I am grateful to

Anshen + Allen

BNIM

Fielding Nair International

HOK

Journal of Interior Design

Kahler Slater

Philips Design and Philips Healthcare

I am also glad to have had the opportunity to interview Dr. Nicholas Watkins (HOK) and George Marmaropoulus (Philips Design). I learned a lot during my conversations with them and had a wonderful time. They are both great people.

Brian Scott saved this project from technical collapse many times. He is a great designer, a great "computer geek," and a great friend.

I have saved my thanks for Cindy Coleman and Neil Frankel till the end of this message because I hoped by the time I got here I'd have conjured up the words to thank them for writing the foreword to this book and for all their moral support. I still don't have the words to adequately express my appreciation. Thank you, Cindy and Neil.

OVERVIEW OF THE PSYCHOLOGICAL EXPERIENCE OF SPACE

Places matter. And we're always in one.

The design of a physical place influences the mental state of the people in that space. That shapes their attitudes and behavior. Not sure how much what we sense through our eyes, ears, nose, and skin matters? Consider these scenarios:

Susan was a poor student, and her mom could never get her to do her homework. Susan fidgeted a lot while sitting at her desk, her eyes often wandered, and she would pop from her seat frequently. Then Susan's mom changed the color of the wall behind Susan's desk from a very saturated but not very bright Kelly green to a less-saturated light green. She set up a scent diffuser that circulates a delicate lemon scent through the space where Susan studies. Susan's mom also lowered the light levels in the room in general and placed a task light on Susan's desk. Now Susan gets much more of her homework done and higher grades.

Tom's bistro was in the right part of town, and people did eat at his restaurant all the time, but they never stayed long enough to order high-margin desserts and they almost never returned to eat there a second time. Tom brought in a cooking consultant who tasted the dishes on the menu and pronounced them delicious. Then there was a plumbing leak, and the gently curving wall that ran along one side of the restaurant had to be torn out to find and repair the leak. Since money was tight, the curved wall was replaced with a straight one, although the size of the dining room remained the same. People started to order desserts and to come back for second meals at the restaurant. A waiter who had been gone during the plumbing fiasco asked Tom when he returned about how he had found the funds to expand the dining room; the space seemed more spacious now than it had in the past.

The radiation therapy treatment room at the hospital was a heavily insulated, bunker-like space. No matter what color it was painted, no one liked being there. The new director of the radiation program decided to make it more inviting by adding art: abstract images that he loved. The patients found the space even more oppressive after that. Then the new head of the hospital's art program whisked away the abstract pictures and replaced them with landscapes featuring meadows dotted with groups of trees. After that, everyone in the radiation treatment area, patients and staff, felt a little more upbeat.

Nothing ever seemed very appetizing in the light blue dining room at Celeste's. Leftovers always tasted great, however, in her yellow kitchen. When Celeste painted the walls of her dining room an orange-peach color and replaced her blue and white china with warmer-colored plates, food started to taste as good in the dining room when it was fresh cooked as it did when it was eaten as leftovers in the kitchen from plastic microwave-safe containers. Now the blue china is used during the post-holiday January diet season.

Students in Ms. Johnson's third-grade class seemed to have trouble concentrating. Then a hurricane broke the glass in all the windows around the school. The new glass installed in the windows had a transparent, nonglare coating, so the heavy blinds that had been used to cut glare were taken down. Now that the students can see the natural spaces outside, everyone in Ms. Johnson's classroom, including Ms. Johnson, has a better day.

Sean could never relax in the new bedroom space his wife designed. Sean's wife found the bedroom a cozy retreat. The bedroom walls were papered in an intricate geometric print, and Sean's wife kept lots of fragrant potpourri in bowls around the room. The bedside tables were made of shiny lacquered bronze, and the carpet was a nubby berber. The room was never noisy or flooded with sunlight too early in the morning. When Sean learned more about his personality, he found he was not as extraverted as his wife and that her decorating style was too intense for him. After painting the walls, reducing the amount of potpourri, and draping cloths over the top of the shiny bedside tables, Sean could relax in his bedroom.

Nobody ever seemed to have a good idea in conference room A. It didn't seem to be a bad place—the furniture and paint were new and heavy drapes kept daylight from creating glare on the projection screen. The chairs around the conference table were comfortable to sit in. Carl thought the space could be made better, so he stepped in and redesigned it. After Carl's efforts the room is a hotbed of creativity. The windows have been coated with a clear, nonglare film and the curtains are gone, so there is always a view to the park outside. The wide conference table has been replaced by a narrower one with a natural wood grain veneer, and the chairs around that table swivel easily so everyone at a meeting can look at anyone else. The colors are warmer now, and several intricate paintings have been hung on the walls of the room. A soundscape of classical music, with about 70 beats per minute, plays softly in the background during meetings.

These scenarios show that place design matters. They illustrate place science principles that are fundamental to the experience of physical environments. These principles can be applied in homes, schools, stores, restaurants, workplaces, healthcare facilities, and wherever else people find themselves. Everyone perceives the world around them slightly differently, but people respond to that world in consistent ways—and the exceptions to the general ways of experiencing the world can be anticipated as well.

■ PLAN OF THE BOOK

This book will introduce you to place science and make you Place Smart. After reading it, you will create spaces that enhance lives. *Place Advantage* integrates information collected through rigorous scientific research by psychologists, biologists, physicists, and other concerned professionals. This book incorporates material that anthropologists, sociologists, and designers have learned in thorough and structured investigations. Place science is a tool kit that you can use every day.

Reading this book will teach you how to create specific places that influence people in desired ways. Designing spaces is difficult because the right place is different for different people at different times doing different things. The personalities and cultures of the people who use a space influence whether place designs are successful.

Scientists have been studying how people respond psychologically to their physical environments as a separate field of research for about 40 years, although even the ancient Greeks built places like the Parthenon to create particular effects. The place scientists (also known as environmental psychologists) who have been working since the 1960s have developed a collection of theories in conjunction with their work, but not enough attention has been paid to applying the information researchers have collected—that is the focus of this book.

This book is a professional conversation with people who create places and is based on the work of many researchers. The scientific references that I think designers might be interested in reviewing are marked in the text, so interested readers can get more information. Important sources of information are listed at the end of the book. Suggested readings (marked on that list with an "S") are also good sources of additional insights. The design implications that accompany the text are a psychologist's recommendations to people designing interior spaces. They should be seen as basic ways in which the principles covered can be used, not the only ways they can be applied.

This book begins by introducing general principles of place science. These general principles are usually initially discussed in a residential context to make them immediately accessible to all readers—after all, we all live some-where. Specific chapters discuss how place science can be applied in schools, healthcare facilities, retail establishments (including restaurants), homes, and offices. Since people are people, no matter where they are, there are consistencies in the material presented in each of these chapters. Designing different sorts of places twists the application of place science in new ways, however. Retailers, restaurateurs, and the people who build schools, offices, and hospitals have learned a lot about how space influences us psychologically, and they use that info every day to encourage people to buy things, eat more, learn, work effectively, and get healthy.

■ APPLYING PLACE SCIENCE

Applying place science is challenging. People are complicated. They are a hodgepodge of rational and irrational thoughts and emotions, so their responses to places are complicated also (Vischer 2005). To create places that enhance human lives, you need to focus on a range of details and make a lot of decisions.

Some of our responses to places are inborn (Kellert 2005). Somehow, certain sorts of experiences affect people in different parts of the world in the same way, and have for generations. Colors of a certain saturation and brightness influence the moods of human beings in predictable ways, for example (Valdez and Mehrabian 1994). Personality, which is consistent throughout our life, also influences how we interact with our physical environment. Other responses are conditioned by national culture (Altman and Gauvain 1981): everyone has the same energy level while looking at a particular shade of black, but for some people that black represents author-ity and for some it denotes weakness. Culture has a big influence on the size of the buffer zone or empty space that people like to maintain around themselves in various situations, for example (Hall 1982). Germans talking to one another are situated much farther from one another than Mexicans would be in the same space, talking about the same subject. We also pick up social cues about the sorts of ways we can present the aspects of our per-sonality we want others to perceive when we personalize our surroundings. We learn and apply the associations that other members of our culture have to a pattern or smell, for example. National culture is not the only "way of doing things" designers must recognize; groups also have their own cultures and ways of communicating concepts, sometimes without words. So for members of one organization, a certain color green can be associated with an organization's award for exceptional performance, or a wily but feared competitor.

We all have associations to things around us because of groups that we're in, and we have additional associations and memories that influence our individual responses to the space around us. Place-related memories were very important for human survival in the past—we had to remember where camp was and where it was safe to sleep. Now each of our individualized sets of place memories influences the design of the spaces where we can thrive (Israel 2003). Accessing place memories is key to designing a successful space. These personal place memories mean that no two people will ever respond in exactly the same way to the same space.

Smells, colors, textures, and other sensory inputs can take on a special meaning for individuals. Even if a particular color of turquoise is the perfect color for the bathroom you are designing (according to what you have learned about place science), don't paint the bathroom that color if someone who will use that space had to take a horrible-tasting cough medicine the same shade of turquoise as a child. Peppermint is generally an energizing scent, but if your mom always chewed peppermint gum when she rubbed your back as you fell asleep at night, you will find the smell of peppermint relaxing. When you want to rev up, you'll need to smell one of the other energizing smells discussed in Chapter 5. Chapter 11 will show you how to ask questions to learn about individual sensory associations as well as a lot of other important place-related information.

Since Adler (1968), psychologists have known that for every person, there is one sense that is extra potent, that is a compelling way into his or her heart and head. It's an individual's dominant sense. When you are creating spaces that one or a few people will use, the dominant senses of those users should be recognized. Dominant senses help determine what information from the physical world makes its way into their psychological world, and what influence it has once it arrives. One of the surest ways to reach through the muddled stream of sensory signals around each of us, and into our emotional core, is through our dominant sense. In Chapter 7, you will learn how to identify one.

Human beings can take in a lot of information through their senses—but we can't consciously absorb everything going on, even in a space that doesn't seem to throw a lot of curveballs. How about this test: what does the room you're in now smell like? Unless it's unusual for some reason, you probably don't know. At any time there is so much going on around us that focusing on even half of what we're being exposed to would overwhelm us. So we all filter, and we all filter differently—we each have a set of incomplete information to use as we move forward through our world. Many of the filters we apply are woven by our cultures, which makes it easier to design spaces that will be used by more than one person, as long as all of those users have similar cultural associations. Chapter 8 discusses how national cultures should influence place design, and Chapter 7 does the same for organizational cultures.

Cultures don't just teach us what sorts of associations we should have to sensations such as colors and smells; they also teach us rules. We each have learned the place rules for our professions, families, and neighbor-hood, among others. Through the rules that it teaches us, culture organizes our place experiences. Cultural systems tell us how far to stand from other people and how we should personalize the spaces we control to nonverbally communicate desired messages. Having cultural systems in place frees us up from continually needing to devote mental energy to figuring out what's going on around us and allows us to move on to more mentally stimulating endeavors.

To apply place science successfully, you need to consider what people will be doing in any space you're designing. A space for working on a routine task should be different from a space for brainstorming, and a space for socializ-ing should be different from a space for meditating. You do something that doesn't require much concentration, and something creative and something social and something spiritual, better when you are in particular mental states. With place science, you can reliably create those states.

This book illustrates how research should influence place design, but it does not lay out a simple formula for creating great spaces. To apply place science, you have to keep all the different things we've mentioned above (personality, organizational culture, national culture, etc.) in mind. *Place Advantage* pro-vides a variety of alternatives that enhance places, but selecting from among the appropriate options for a space requires the art and skill of design. To work through an example: Saturation and brightness determine people's psychological response to a color (more on this in Chapter 5), so there are shades of red, blue, and green that all create the same emotional effect. Different cultures also have particular associations to individual colors, and people's personal experiences, personalities, and associations to colors lead them to prefer some more than others. Working these factors together with the amount of sunlight that enters a room, the colors of furniture that will not be replaced, and a myriad of other place-specific details and options and selecting colors for a space is the transformative, magic phase of the design process—and designers are responsible for that conjuring.

There are always several ways to design a psychological experience into a space. Having multiple tools to apply at any time means that your options for creating the places consistent with your programming objectives and exercising your creative freedom increase significantly beyond what you have learned through your previous design experience.

Place science is not only applicable to places you design but also to how you choose to live your life. You can create a portable environment that envelops you by wearing scents and specific colors. You can also pick spaces to meet where you know the place will help you achieve your objectives.

Our worlds are changing in superficial ways. Shepherds in Mongolia have yurts and Toyotas and cell phones. The same television advertisements, in the same languages, are shown in Holland, the Netherlands, and Holland, Michigan. Furniture shows in Milan influence the future design of apartments in Damascus and in Miami—although families in each place still use different criteria to plan their days and to determine whether they've been successful. For now. Cultural overlays on our inborn responses to place are becoming more difficult, as well as more important, to sort out.

Our place-related needs have remained much the same, even though the physical environments we find ourselves in look different than they did a few years ago. We still need to think creative thoughts sometimes, to relax at other times, and to pull dinner together. And many of us have to be really efficient about pulling that dinner together because we have many more things that we feel we need to accomplish within any 24-hour span than our grandparents did. We have the hubris to believe that our brains are evolving and that we process information in a fundamentally different way than our grandparents, but human minds and our place-related needs evolve over eons, not generations.

We're always somewhere. Make the places you design the best places for **people** to live the lives they want to lead. The physical environment alone cannot make everyone's dreams come true, but it sure can tip the scales in one direction or another.

2

FOUNDATIONS OF HUMAN INTERACTIONS WITH THEIR PHYSICAL WORLD

■ PLACE SCIENCE IN ACTION

Place science will make places you design work *for* the people who use them.

Place science is a discipline like physics or genetics. It uses structured thinking to establish how the place you're in physically influences the state you are in mentally and then determines what changes (if any) need to be made in a space to achieve personal and professional objectives. Place scientists (also known as environmental psychologists) are part psychologist, part biologist, part architect, part interior designer, and part sociologist, sometimes with a smattering of physicist, chemist, or anthropologist thrown in. Place science is not feng shui.

Place scientists have systematically gathered information about human responses to colors, smells, textures, furniture arrangements, ceiling heights, sounds, shapes, and just about anything else we find around us. They answer questions such as the following:

- How and why does ceiling height matter?
- How does personality influence the kinds of places in which people flourish?
- Are there some sorts of physical environments in which people are more creative than others?
- How should color be used in place design? How should national culture influence color selections?
- When Asians and North Americans look at a scene, what does each group see?
- What sorts of landscape views are most refreshing?
- How will (or should) places be different in the years ahead?

Scientific research by place scientists has documented patterns in how we interact with our world. After they uncover these patterns in how humans respond to spaces, place scientists can apply this information, collaborating with people designing places and products. For example, place scientists work with furniture manufacturers to determine how wide conference room tables should

FIGURE 2-1 ■ The Parthenon, an early achievement of "place scientists." The symmetrical arrangement of the columns and the scale of the elements, for example, create a serene and awe-inspiring space for religious and civic events. Copyright © iStockPhoto/Keith Binns.

be, with architects to determine how large the conference room holding that table should be, with interior designers to identify the appropriate colors for the walls of that conference room, and with homeowners who want to make their home office as productive as that conference room.

Today's place scientists are solving the same problems that people creating experiences have been grappling with since antiquity, only they are able to apply information garnered through modern science. Ancient Greek temples are perfectly balanced but large, so that the gods seem serene and all-powerful. The Greeks who built those ancient temples used many principles modern place scientists would suggest. In medieval times, fanfares and battle music triggered an emotional response—fanfares were awe-inspiring, and battle music could convince listeners to go out and kill people. Modern place scientists also think a lot about emotional responses to sound. Traditionally, royalty sits on elevated chairs so that their subjects need to look up to them, which royalty and place scientists know leads to a respectful attitude. Hitler knew just how to use music, color, and space design to inspire awe and respect—but so did the ancient Mayans. Marie Antoinette famously created a farmhouse on the grounds of Versailles so that she could live there from time to time and experience a lifestyle that was more relaxed and less complex than that of the royal court. Modern researchers studying mentally refreshing spaces would approve many of her design decisions.

■ SOUVENIRS FROM OUR LIVES ON THE SAVANNA

The long period human beings spent living on the savanna in our prehistory explains many of our responses to the information we collect through our senses (Appleton 1975; Kellert 2005; Heerwagen and Gregory 2008; Hildebrand 1999; Wilson 1984). Humans are relatively small, weak, and defenseless compared to lions and rhinos, and we seem to have developed some ingrained reactions to particular experiences to make up for our lack of physical prowess. For example, we hate sitting with our backs to an open space, such as a door, through which danger could approach, and we prefer to sleep in higher spaces in a building. Bedrooms on the second floor are less accessible than those on the ground floor.

The physical sensations we experience influence our lives in many ways that are consistent with our evolutionary past:

FIGURE 2-2 ■ Many of our current environmental responses are related to our ancestors' experiences while they scrambled to survive without the tools and technologies that we currently find so useful. Being near a tree was very desirable in the old, old days—it regulated air temperature and provided protection from at least some of the animals that preyed upon them. Copyright © iStockPhoto/Eliza Snow.

- We score higher on tests when we're in the same mood we were in when we learned the material being tested (because we're smelling the same scent, for example) or when we take them in the same room in which we learned the material—unconsciously we use clues in the physical environment, things we were looking at, etc., when we are being taught something to help us remember the material being tested or to at least put us in the same mood (which helps us remember) (Eich 1995; Wise and Hazzard 2000). On the savanna, this sort of place- or mood-specific learning would have been useful.
- Warm colors attract us, which is why the back walls of stores are often painted red or orange—they draw us in past all the merchandise, to the back of the store (Bellizzi, Crowley, and Hasty 1983). Once we get to the back of the store, we turn around and start to move through products as we return to the front of the store. This path through a store exposes us to a larger number of items for sale than we would otherwise encounter. Ancient fires cast warm light and drew us closer.
- We like sitting in places that seem like refuges, spaces in which the ceilings are lower and the light is dimmer, which are physically adjacent to an area which is brighter and has higher ceilings (Hildebrand 1999). This attraction to spaces that offer refuge and prospect makes good sense evolutionarily. It explains why we like to live in sheltered spots on the edges of parks, golf courses, and lakes. Having a connection with a brighter and more expansive surrounding area also explains why we like to be able to open the windows. Although both men and women enjoy a setting with prospect and refuge, women prefer a layout with a little more refuge than prospect and men prefer more prospect than refuge.
- We enjoy being in dappled light (Wise and Hazzard 2000). Dappled light is the kind of light we experience when sitting under a plane tree on a sunny day. Plane trees are plentiful on the savanna. In dappled light, dollops

FIGURE 2-3 ■ Humans enjoy dappled light inside and outside. The sun passing through a leafy canopy on a sunny day distributes dollops of sunlight on the ground, and our ancestors would have associated this splotchy light with good things (pleasant weather and nearby escape into the tree). Copyright © iStockPhoto/John Goldie.

of sunlight and darker areas speckle the ground immediately around us, and the lighting is brighter and more uniform beyond that area. We probably enjoy dappled light because during our ancient past when we were experiencing it, we were relaxed because the weather was good and because we had a quick means of escape (up the tree casting those irregular shadows) if we saw danger approaching.

■ We also like patterns on wallpapers and cubicle walls not to be too complicated (Rodemann 1999). Approaching trouble would have been easier to spot against backdrops such as simpler wallpapers.

■ Today, no matter where in the world you ask the question, more people will tell you that their favorite color is blue than any other color. How come? When we were living on the savanna, blue meant good things. Fresh water when seen from a distance is blue. A sky during pleasant weather is blue.

Even though our responses to many current situations are based on what was good for us during our evolutionary past, mysteries remain about why we respond to particular aspects of our surroundings in certain ways:

Why is it that if we smell jasmine after we fall asleep, we think at a higher level the next day?

Why does the color yellow so intensely please some people looking at it and so intensely displease another set of people?

Why is information recall and problem solving better under warm-hued light than cooler-hued light?

Why do our hearts start to beat in time to regularly paced sounds around us?

All of our psychological reactions can't be explained by our evolutionary past, but as you plan spaces, think of our days on the savanna whenever you're confused. This can help you decide whether you should create a beige space (no—the totally unnatural experience of being in a space with only white or beige walls, upholstery, and flooring is so alien that it sends us into a distressing, self-centered funk [Mahnke 1996]) or one with plenty of cabinets to hide possessions (yes—clutter makes us tense, as our eyes need to scan it continuously to make sure that it has not changed in a way that requires our attention—just as we would have scanned surrounding brush when we lived on the savanna) or one with daylight (yes—that helps us regulate our circadian rhythms—when they're upset, we're stressed). If an intelligent but relatively weak and defenseless animal wouldn't want to be in a space, neither would modern humans.

▪ DESIGN EXPERIENCE AND RESPONSES TO PLACES

At a fundamental level places affect how effectively we live our lives. For example, we learn best when our minds are alert but our bodies aren't. A room that is not brightly lit relaxes us; task lighting focuses us mentally on the lit material. A generally darker room with task lighting will therefore be a better place to study than a uniformly and brightly lit room. We're in the mood to eat when we're looking at warm-colored things. We're creative, as well as more cooperative and helpful, when the space around us puts us in a positive mood (Cote 1999). We can concentrate when there's nothing going on around us that shows potential of being interesting to us, but not when we're sitting in the middle of a big room surrounded by other people who may say something intriguing at any time—whether we can see them or not.

Place-design experiences or training influences our perception of desirable and effective places. Space designers experience places differently than people without all of the training that they have received (Wilson 1996). People with place design experience and training, for example, find a broader color palette acceptable than the general population. For example, designers are much more apt to find yellow-yellow-green desirable than the general population. The same yellow-yellow-green that designers relish is among the colors most disliked by the population at large. Designers need to respect the different color preferences of members of the general public and not specify that yellow-yellow-green be used in spaces that they are designing. The general public's right to dislike this color is just as valid as designers' enjoyment of the color. Designers also like to be in spaces designed in a more contemporary style, as compared to nondesigners, who like to be in spaces with more traditional styling—put people into traditional environments if that's where they'll be comfortable.

Always respect the people who will play on the sets that you create. Although personality, organizational culture, national culture, and design experience influence the specifics of how people respond to a space, all people are fundamentally the same when it comes to how they want to interact with the world around them. All people like spaces where they feel comfortable, secure, and valued. They like spaces that meet their functional needs—if they are cooking, they need a heating element; if they are doing thoughtful work, they need to be able to concentrate on that work. It is important for place designers to recognize the importance of the universal set of human needs that will be satisfied in the spaces they create and to acknowledge and value the various orientations that space users can have to a space.

Place alone does not determine who has a good day or a bad day, but places can tip the scales toward a good day or a bad day. A place with certain features can't guarantee that things will always work out there the way you intend, but it can make an experience much more likely. Changing the physical environment can guide people toward inspiration and tranquility, companionship and privacy, delight and comfort, freedom and strength.

3 BASIC HUMAN NEEDS SATISFIED THROUGH PLACE DESIGN

Why does how we process the information we get from the world around us matter? What we learn from the space we're in influences us both at an emotional and a more rational level and sparks us into one action or another. The way that information we get through our senses affects us emotionally is important because much of our behavior is emotionally based and something we actually don't think about, at least consciously. We can't override our reflexive responses—they happen so fast that they're done before we even know we'll have them. Rational responses are much easier to assess and modify.

It's hard to overstate the importance of emotion to us—our emotional state influences how we live our lives and do (or not do) things that we think are important to us. Emotions really control our life experiences—and places have an emotional influence. Places do not control emotions, but they do influence them (Russell and Snodgrass 1987).

The different sensory experiences that you are having at any one time are completely intertwined and combine to create one common mood or impression. Seeing fields of greens and blues in the daylight, smelling wildflowers, feeling the texture of grasses underfoot and the temperature of the warm spring air, and hearing birds sing together create the experience of a relaxing walk in a spring meadow—and we respond emotionally to that walk.

If a place provides psychologically contradictory sensory experiences, your feelings in that space will be determined by the relative balance of the conflicting elements, with more weight being given to sensations received through your dominant sense.

Although we're talking about physical spaces here, a place is really a lot more than that. We mirror the behavior of other people we see—which perpetuates place-based behaviors—e.g., we see other people speaking quietly in a church, so we behave in the same way. Places also have behavior rules and rituals associated with them (Aarts and Dijksterhuis 2003; Barker 1968). Place design can encourage or discourage some of these behaviors—corridors can be designed with recesses into which people who meet each other unexpectedly can duck and chat if this sort of behavior is desirable, or without such spaces if impromptu meetings are undesirable. Spaces are filled with people, each of whom has his or her own objectives and who can do a range of things that he or she personally finds desirable. In cubicles at work, people can display images that lift their spirits and wear a perfume that enhances their mood (if pictures and perfumes are allowed), but if their boss sets unreasonable objectives, the things they are seeing and smelling can only improve their day, not make it perfect.

Reiss (2004) has identified 16 basic motives that propel human beings through their lives, and all of these motives can be related to physical places, some more, some less closely. They should guide space design. Any particular space does not need to respond to every motive on Reiss's long list, but at any time, people must be able to move into one that does. For example, a particular home kitchen may not be tranquil, but a readily accessible space in the same house must be.

The 16 motives that Reiss has identified in our lives are as follows:

Power—Places provide information, either directly or indirectly, and through this information one person can influence another. European cathedrals are built to instill an awe of God, and so were Aztec temples. Those responses are not coincidental. Judges sit at tall desks on raised platforms so we need to look up at them—and when we look up at something, we feel respect for it. Power in place can be subtle: higher-ranking employees feel free to enter the personal territories of subordinates without permission, but lower-ranking employees do not reverse the tables, if they want to keep their jobs. Power can also be brutally displayed—the checkpoints spawned by global unrest are not subtle.

Curiosity—A space can help you grow and develop as a person, by providing opportunities for learning and self-enhancement. Lawrence and Nohria (2002) agree that all human beings have an inborn drive to change themselves in ways that they feel are desirable, and spaces can help us achieve those objectives. A soundproofed space makes learning a musical instrument easier on bystanders, allowing longer practice sessions. A quiet space where a person can concentrate makes it possible to learn a foreign language or uncover our own secrets, for example.

Independence—Spaces can assist us in controlling our own destiny. If they permit us to control other people's access to us or accomplish other personally (not necessarily culturally) desired objectives, places enhance independence. The option to make a space private, by closing a door, for example, is highly valued by people. When people can regulate their privacy in a space, being there usually has positive psychological ramifications. When we can customize a space so that it projects an idiosyncratic image we value, that place also expresses our independence.

Status—The design of a space itself, the objects placed in it, and how it is used communicate the relative status of its owner. Humans are pack animals and like to know who the leader of their pack is (Vischer 2005). Rank can be communicated verbally, as through a job title, or nonverbally. The placement of a group in a structure can indicate the status of the group and its leader. For example, a human resources department housed in a windowless basement suite has little status. Status is not necessarily determined by our ability to order other people around. We can rank higher (or lower) on all sorts of criteria. These criteria can relate to our areas of expertise and accomplishment. Home or workplace design can communicate status by communicating skill. Creating a highly desirable space can garner status—among tastemakers or anarchists, for example, depending on how we decide to decorate.

Social contact—Just as pack animals need to know the relative status of others in their group, they also need to interact with the other members of that group. Even the most introverted humans need regular contact with other people. When we have privacy, we can control when and how we interact with other humans. Uncontrollable social interaction is very bad for human beings; it makes us tense and panicky. We have particular place-based rules about how we want social contact with others to happen, and they are presented in Chapter 6, but as a prelude: when we're talking to another person, we like to be a particular distance from them and at a certain orientation to them (which is not necessarily face-to-face).

Vengeance—We can and do use space for evil, just as we can use it for good. Symbols of other groups can be desecrated, for example, as we seek vengeance. Even the display of championship trophies can be seen as vengeance—the winners exalting over those who have not won.

Honor—Honor means tradition here. A place readily communicates how much we value tradition. Almost all spaces show some reverence for tradition; the relative amount varies from space to space, however. Even the most avant-garde living place will include spaces to display meaningful objects, although the concept of appropriate objects can vary. A space is more traditional if larger numbers of people without design training can anticipate the elements used in it. A space that is designed very traditionally for the society in which it is found indicates stronger adherence to the prevailing value system than a less traditional space. In the United States, traditional decorating styles include colonial and cowboy/western.

Idealism—The causes we espouse are manifested in our spaces. We may eschew the use of nonregenerative resources, display a sculpture of blindfolded Justice, or hang Buddhist meditation flags to communicate our ideals to others, for example. An apparent absence of idealistic elements does not mean that they are actually absent, just that they are not obvious to the viewer. Only the owner of an object can be certain what he means to communicate through it.

Physical Exercise—Our homes provide the opportunity for us to exercise directly, if they include a gym or exercise equipment. The weekly "opportunity" to mow the lawn, and the more intermittent possibility of do-it-yourself home improvement projects also help us satisfy our desire to exercise our muscles. The way that urban planners lay out an area can encourage physical exercise.

Romance—A boudoir, or any mutually acceptable physical space, provides the opportunity for romance.

Family—Our homes help us raise our children and relate to our loved ones in the manner we desire. We can create luxurious or Spartan places for people to isolate themselves in or we can create spaces where everyone can hang out together, and we can create areas for studying—all of which communicate important information to our family. Our approach to tradition comes into play here as well. It determines what we value and how we want our families to live.

Order—We want to organize our lives; even places that are apparently disordered usually have an underlying ordering system. People differ in the way they organize their lives, and sometimes one person's ordering system is not readily apparent to other people. Cabinets and closets encourage us to systematize our belongings.

Eating—What are kitchens and dining rooms for? Even people who don't like to cook eat, and take-out food is becoming increasingly acceptable for regular "family" meals.

Acceptance—People communicate their desire for approval in spaces by following the social conventions of groups that they want to accept them. Adhering to trends in interior design signals a desire for acceptance by people who set and respect trends.

Tranquility—Place design can help people reduce stress and tension. In the best case, spaces provide restorative opportunities, which are described in Chapter 4. We can decorate our homes with objects that are meaningful to us, and being surrounded by those objects helps us to relax.

Saving—Homes and other real estate investments can be seen as a way to sock away money for the future. When we customize a space so that it represents us, we are showing the world that we own it. Places are also vast storehouses of the stuff that we value.

Place design matters for reasons that reach far beyond the basic human motives outlined by Reiss.

We all are continually assessing the information from the physical environment that filters its way down to us. We cannot stop ourselves. We think that places communicate information that is more truthful than verbal statements—so we are really motivated to figure out what is going on around us (Becker and Steele 1995). The messages sent by corporate headquarters and bedrooms are most carefully analyzed. Corporations are generally viewed as having motives to lie to potential employees and business partners in their verbal vision statements but are felt to represent their true philosophy when making real estate–related expenditures. We believe that where people intend to really relax and sleep, they need to be in a space that communicates who they really are.

Places satisfy many of the motives that Reiss identifies via nonverbal communication. Nonverbal communication is not necessarily universal communication. Members of groups using a space daily may perceive that particular messages are being presented, but visitors may not "hear" the same ones. Think about an open office workplace design. If a corporation has a history of encouraging and rewarding group work, that open office design can be seen by the people using it as a wonderful tool that helps them reach important objectives. It communicates to them that their employer respects their contribution to the firm's success. People working at a company that rewards individual work might see the same open-plan workspace as a symbol of how little their employer respects them and their contribution to the success of the firm. Visitors to either space might feel that the executives of the firms involved do no trust their employees and feel they need to continually supervise them.

We are generally very good at reading what places "say" to us (Gosling, Ko, Mannarelli, and Morris 2002). As a society we develop an unspoken dictionary that makes us all very consistent in our interpretations of places. The accuracy with which we can judge the personalities of other people and the cultures of groups based on the places that they control is stunning. You can only be completely sure, however, what places are saying to the people who use them when you rigorously investigate their meanings. In Chapter 11, we'll cover some techniques to do just that. Know that as surely as you are deciphering others, they are deciphering the places you create.

We're always in a place. The spaces that surround us help us pursue important human motives, or thwart our efforts to do so. Consciously considering the information you are conveying in a place, and how you are conveying it, will keep you centered on your "design" objectives.

UNIVERSAL FEATURES OF
WELL-DESIGNED SPACES

A well-designed space is a place where the right things happen. We fall asleep (if we want to fall asleep), we learn (if we want to acquire knowledge), or we are creative (almost anytime is a good time to be creative) in a well-designed place.

Reiss (2004) has laid out the motives that drive people throughout their lives, and physical places can help achieve all of them, as discussed in Chapter 3. A well-designed space doesn't focus equally on achieving all human objectives but digs in to make sure a few objectives are very well satisfied. Spaces are a collection of adjoining places.

A "well-designed space" can be defined in psychological terms. A well-designed place enhances life experiences—it is essential for bliss. It provides people with energy and supports their need to communicate with others and supplies inspiration and comfort that enhance lives on a continuing basis. In it people achieve their concrete and psychological goals. Being in a well-designed place leads to a desirable emotional state. Although well-designed spaces can differ in what they look like, I have found that all well-designed spaces are

- *Complying* with the activity planned, with all the right tools in place
- *Communicating* important information about the people who use them and providing opportunities for people to socialize or not. Places communicate both inside and out. What style of home was purchased? Where is the office building located? What's the store's interior design like? What sorts of pictures and objects are used in the lobby? Providing information about the person/people who use a space is the most important thing a well-designed space does. Information about ourselves and others creates the context for social interaction, and without meaningful social interaction, humans become animals. Well-designed places allow people to socialize with others, when desired, and to be alone when desired. Human beings, even the most apparently antisocial ones, need contact with other people. Socializing is key to our experience as people. People may choose to mingle through a

weekly poker game they host in their kitchen or a literary soiree in their salon, or in a sophisticated restaurant as part of a wine-tasting club, but somewhere, somehow, a well-designed place must provide people with the opportunity to socialize with others as they wish.

■ *Comforting* because they meet psychological needs for perceived control of our environment (including whether to be alone or with other people) and refreshment. Without communication humans become animals, and without comfort, humans are greatly diminished. We lose our ability to process information in a sophisticated way. We become so stressed that that tension distracts us from things we need to focus on. In a well-designed place, people can concentrate when they need to and relax as desired. They can adjust the temperature and lighting levels without any concern about what other people might think about the choices they have made. And people face a reasonable number of use-related choices—initial design decisions have structured the use of the spaces appropriately. People can also restock their mental energy in a well-designed space. Every day we use our minds over and over again to solve complicated problems. This runs down our cognitive batteries and after a while we need to recharge those batteries. Our infinitely rechargeable mental batteries can be restocked through experiences such as looking at nature flames or fish tanks or being in an absorbing place that is effortlessly interesting, such as a museum.

■ *Challenging* because they provide opportunities for the people in them to grow and develop as a person. Each of us has a different plan for the trajectory of our life, but we do each have a plan. A well-designed space helps us execute that plan. If a person's goal is to file more patents than Edison, he or she needs an appropriate lab. To become a proficient yogi requires a practice space. Learning Italian over the Internet requires Internet access.

■ *Continuing* across time, evolving and changing as appropriate. Spaces need to change as the ways people need to use them change. If a space can't change, the people or organizations using it have to relocate, which wastes human and natural resources.

A home or workplace can be a well-designed space, and so can a car, school, store, healthcare facility, or public space that people are in temporarily. The physical objectives of a well-designed place are similar in every environment— but different sorts of well-designed places take different forms. To create a well-designed place, integrate the concepts that follow with the material from Chapter 5 about sensory experience and the information, Chapter 6 about human responses to architecture and furniture, Chapter 7 about personal and cultural factors that influence place experience, Chapter 8 about national culture and place design, and Chapter 9 about the appropriate psychological state for conducting various activities. Chapter 10 will show you how to integrate all of this important information.

■ COMPLYING

One of the basic things that a well-designed place does is help people complete the task at hand. If your plans include cooking dinner, the space that you are in must provide a mechanism to prepare the food you have collected in the manner you intend. It is hard to cook a roast in a bathtub or to walk on slick floors dotted with puddles. It is difficult to write a complex report in the waiting room at a train station. It is impossible to relax when you are in a space that has so much going on visually that your eyes race from one visual element to the next. A well-designed space also puts you in the sort of mood that's appropriate for

the task at hand—a good mood when broad thinking is desired, a not-so-good mood when more straight-forward thinking would be best. (See Chapter 9 for additional information on mood and place design.)

> **DESIGN IMPLICATION**
>
> Well-designed places provide the tools that people need to accomplish what they plan to accomplish.

■ COMMUNICATING

People communicate nonverbally in places and use spoken language to socialize with others in many of the same spaces.

FIGURE 4-1 ■ Kitchens have functional zones that help us achieve concrete objectives. This space contains a stove for cooking and a sink for washing, for example.
Copyright © iStockPhoto/Emre Arican.

FIGURE 4-2 ■ This hospital room is zoned to promote healing. Patients can rest in one part of the space, bathe in a second area, and socialize with others, work, or relax on the balcony or in the nook with the couch and desk. Caregivers have workstations within the space, and patients' visitors can also use these spaces in various ways. Image courtesy of Anshen+Allen, © 2008.

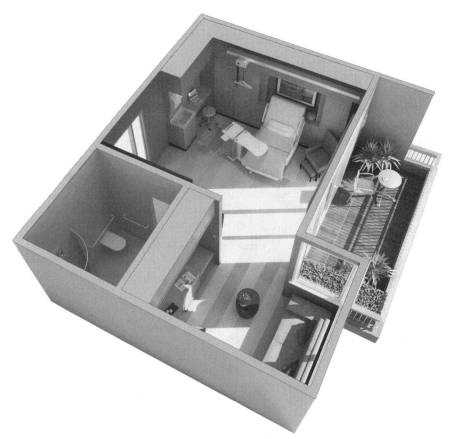

We know that we are sending signals to other people through the places we live and work, and we also know that they are signaling back, but we do not directly discuss this process very frequently (Goffman 1959). Humans are determined to learn the often unspoken language needed to unravel what other people are telling us and to send desired messages ourselves. We start to broadcast our clues once we feel comfortable that a space does belong to us. This nonverbal, and often unacknowledged, symbolic communication is why we get so concerned about selecting the appropriate sofa for *our* living room or about which pictures to post in *our* workplace. Our quest for data is one of the reasons we watch television shows that tour the homes of famous people—we feel information we can't be certain of from spoken words can be ciphered from place clues.

We trust information that we receive nonverbally and symbolically more than spoken words. Research has shown that nonverbal communication carries more weight than spoken words if there is a conflict between the two—nonverbal statements seem harder to fake (Becker and Steele 1995).

The ease with which homes communicate nonverbally is why we can walk into an empty house that we are considering purchasing and know if it is a place in which we could live happily—we are happy in places that we feel send the sort of messages we want to have associated with us.

We are remarkably good at communicating symbolically within our group culture because everyone who shares a culture speaks the same nonverbal language (Berger and Luckmann 1967). Research has shown that we can consistently and correctly infer the personality and interests of other people from the material that they present to the world (Gosling, Ko, Mannarelli, and Morris 2002). In a famous study, upper middle-class homeowners were asked to rate themselves on various personality scales and describe themselves (Sadalla and Sheets 1993). The interiors and exteriors of their homes were photographed, and people shown those photographs were able to infer the homeowners' personalities and self-images accurately.

We like to understand our relationships with other people. One of the ways that we get the information we need to do this is through spaces in use. We pick up on cues about the person who created a space (how sophisticated or well educated they appear to be, what their hobbies are, etc.) and use that info to decide how forcefully we'll argue a point or how much of our expert knowledge we need to share. Any object can have multiple meanings, and you can learn what they are (see Chapter 11).

Although some of us have more need to socialize with other people, all of us want our interactions with others to be friendly and we look for conversation topics in the stuff people place in spaces. When we see photographs of children or sailboats, we know that those are safe things to talk about. When we recognize a Lithuanian flag, we know we can discuss our common homeland. A stack of colorful but uninflated balloons indicates a mutual interest in creating balloon animals. When we're in someone else's home and office, we'll look for signals of potentially touchy topics (political or religious symbols or recent controversial books, for example) and apply this information to avoid conversational minefields. A diploma from a rival school signals it is better to discuss the weather than college sports.

We don't just communicate with the objects we choose to place around our homes or offices—we do the same thing with the architectural style of house/office we choose, the location of that home/office, the style we use to decorate it inside or landscape it outside, the colors we choose to paint the walls, and the way we arrange the furniture, for example. A current advertisement for a cleaning product drives home the point that everything in your home "talks" with its tagline, "What does your toilet say about you?" Different groups can interpret the same information in different ways based on their cultures, which is one of the reasons it is so important to talk with members of all of the groups that will use a space. A French Provincial-style waiting room can be "perfect" for some groups, "hoity-toity" to others, and "passé" to members of a third group.

If you realize that people are trying to paint a picture of themselves in their surroundings, you can make them happier in new homes and workplaces more quickly if you work with them to consciously create the desired portrait. For example, if users think that a certain color denotes membership in a group, and they want to be seen as members of that group, find a place for that color in the design—the users won't be comfortable in their new home or office until it presents the image they want to convey. People are uncomfortable in spaces that do not communicate who they are or that say the wrong thing. Children over the age of 5 or 6 and all adults living in a home need to present themselves in the place they're living.

Wanting to present different images in different spaces is both natural and appropriate. The image being presented in a workplace is often slightly different from the one conveyed at home, and there are more restrictions on how we present ourselves in the office than at home. We actually view ourselves differently in different contexts, so there is no need for consistency between home and work presentations—a person can be an ultrafeminine "lady" at home and an achievement-oriented CPA at the office. Employee well-being is higher when workers can customize their workplaces so they reflect who they are (Sundstrom 1986).

As people enter different stages of their lives, they are driven to change the spaces around themselves. The messages that the place where they lived alone before their marriage sends are different from the messages they want their home to send after their children are born. Make sure the sets for users' lives keep pace with the storyline.

Architecture and design change to reflect evolving messages that cultures want to send via the places in their lives. In the United States, women now work outside the home more frequently than they did in the past. As women started to work outside the home, the isolated kitchen at the back of the American home that previously was their sole domain became more integrated with the living areas of the home. Simultaneously, American men have become more involved with household and childrearing tasks from which they formerly excluded themselves. Women are now more nearly coequal with men in relationships, and their domain, the kitchen, is now merging into men's domain, the study, and this new type of place is evolving into a media-intense family room. In the United States, home spaces are also now increasingly isolated from the surrounding neighborhood. This increase in isolation corresponds with an increase in individualism among the general population. Other sorts of spaces also evolve to fit changing cultural conceptions. As medicine has become more closely linked in American society to well-being, U.S. healthcare facilities have become more hotel- and home-like and less institutional.

Socializing with other people is vital for our mental health. That's why solitary confinement for adults, or bedroom lockdown for children, is such a great punishment. When we're forced to be alone, we wilt. Being alone by choice is a different situation, that's a good thing, and we call it "privacy."

The physical environment itself supports or hinders our interactions with other people. To mix with other people, we need an uninterrupted view of them and often we need to see each other's eyes. If we are in a formal situation, where discussions are scripted, sitting in rows of chairs arranged like church pews is okay. That way we don't disrupt the proceedings. Sometimes, we really shouldn't interact with other people (the situation is too tense for that), for example, if we're jammed together on a subway car or an airplane and our society's personal space norms are being violated. In those instances, it's fine for us to be seated in ways that keep us from making eye contact. People who are doing work that requires individual concentration should sit so that they cannot catch each other's eyes. Children doing their homework around a kitchen table will, inevitably, talk to each other; the same children seated with their backs to the same table will not.

A well-designed space allows us to socialize or not, as we see fit. One space can accommodate several different uses if the furniture in it can be arranged several ways—a single set of furniture can be used in multiple ways or furniture for different purposes can be provided in the same space. A church discussion group can sit in a ring while talking though a section of

FIGURE 4-3 ■ Even though we are social animals, sometimes humans need to be alone. When we are alone, we can mull over recent events or concentrate to solve difficult problems. Copyright © iStockPhoto/Nikada.

FIGURE 4-4 ▪ The blinds on the windows in these offices allow people to regulate their interactions with others. All human beings need to be able to control when and how they socialize with their colleagues, family members, friends, and strangers.
Copyright © iStockPhoto/Andrey Popov.

text, for example, and meditate in the same space after moving their chairs so that they cannot make eye contact. A well-designed family room has a place for a person to sit by himself or herself, perhaps a cushioned window seat or an overstuffed chair set off by itself. That family room can also be equipped with a collection of couches and chairs where people can sit comfortably and face each other as well as a table that people can sit around and talk at closer distances to each other. When we're eating, we enjoy socializing with people that we know, which is why the big family dining table has not gone out of style. When we do eat together, the experience is so rewarding that we want to make sure that we have the capacity to repeat it.

People are reporting that they increasingly feel isolated from others, and architects have recognized this situation. Apartment buildings are being built with centralized dining areas where neighbors can and do enjoy common breakfasts. More and more single-family homes are being built with front porches where people can hang out and wait for friendly neighbors to pass by so they can begin a conversation.

DESIGN IMPLICATION

Well-designed places enable people to communicate what they want to others, however and whenever they desire to do so.

▪ COMFORTING

Spaces must provide us with a respite from the demands of our world. Being alive is, and always has been, stressful. Each age has found refuge in places that comfort it and reduce or eliminate the inevitable tension people feel.

Controlling Experience

Control over the space around us is comforting—whether that space is a family room or a workspace (Evans and Cohen 1987). Personality and culture (organizational and national; see Chapters 7 and 8) determine the general level of control desired at various times. We are all more comfortable and satisfied in spaces when the control we have matches the control we want. When we don't feel in control of what happens to us in a place, we are stressed, discouraged, and frustrated. *Feeling* in control is the key here; we don't have to actually exercise control to reap psychological benefits.

Control is the ability to change a space or the opportunity to control access to a piece of turf. Control of a particular place can result in restricted access to us personally, which is privacy. Control that establishes privacy is the most important sort of control we can have—it does the most positive things for us psychologically. We always need the option to have privacy when we need it, although we can choose not to exercise that option (Altman 1975).

Privacy really has two flavors: audio and visual. Although they are both important, audio privacy, or not being heard by and not hearing others, is most valuable to us and visual privacy, or not being seen by and not seeing others, is slightly less crucial to our well-being.

It is that ability to choose when we interact that is really the root of what privacy is all about. When we're at a rowdy family dinner, a crowd is great, but we want to be alone if we are trying to make sense of recent confusing events or if we are nursing a cold. When we are grieving or dealing with a difficult personal situation, we welcome the company of a few trusted confidants. Family homes include larger spaces where everyone can gather as well as smaller spaces for individual retreats. Within any set of spaces (workplace, hospital, restaurant, etc.), there should be several privacy zones—from places where we can have true solitude, to places for small groups or a few people to talk, to much larger spaces that are accessible to more casual acquaintances or the general public.

In both our homes and our workplaces, we need spaces where we can be alone. All of us need to be completely alone regularly so that we can mull over what's happened to us recently and integrate all of our new memories with all of our existing memories. This helps us craft a plan to move forward with our lives. We are also rejuvenated when we have privacy and often are creative in private settings as well. In many homes and offices, the only place we can be completely alone is the bathroom—which makes a relaxing bathroom design crucial. Children ages 8–12 really welcome the opportunity to be by themselves in a place, but often have a hard time doing that if they share a bedroom with others. Similarly, older individuals in group homes may share bedrooms and again have no access to a private place.

The public spaces in homes are the living rooms, and in a professional setting, they are the lobby and the largest gathering places. We present our public persona in these places; and public personas can be different from private selves. Being able to present a different "face" in different spaces gives us deeply meaningful control over our lives.

Individuals need control over their places, but so do groups—whether those groups are a dating couple or a whole work team. When people can control their experiences in a place, they feel more satisfied with their lives and more capable of facing its challenges. Similarly, when groups have a space that they can control, they become a stronger group and better able to face *their* challenges (Wineman and Serrato 1999). Groups may control a family home or a team room, for example.

Desirable control is not just about personal access; it is also about a broader ability to exercise personal judgment. When people respect our judgments about the correct lighting levels to work under or the correct temperature in our cubicle, we feel more satisfied and we perform at a higher level. All of these good feelings evaporate, however, if we believe that we will be judged on the environmental choices that we make. Facing too many choices can be demoralizing too. When we have too many choices—whether it be for room temperature or chairs to sit in—we are never really happy with the choices that we make. Too large a collection of unexplored options makes us sure that we must have missed out on an even better opportunity than the one we selected. Not every possibly changeable feature of a space should be modifiable at any one time, and among the things that are changeable, the magic number of possibilities is six. We feel confident we have made a good choice when we choose from among six options. Desirable amounts of personal control also vary person to person. People who may feel that they have been made less capable by age do not want to exercise as much control now as they did when they were younger, for example.

There are specific ways we can have control in a workspace. We feel more in control in a space when we personalize it—we can personalize a workspace by adding photos to it or decorating it or by constructing or remodeling it. We also feel more in control when we can determine the direction that we face in a cubicle or when we can adjust the lights or air circulation in that space.

When you're designing a space, think about how users could reasonably control their experiences in it, and build in opportunities for them to exercise that control. Task lighting, in addition to helping people see what they are doing, enables employees to exercise some control over their lives, for example. Furniture on wheels allows people to reconfigure an area. Sophisticated lighting systems allow people to tune in the lighting color appropriate for whatever they're doing (see Chapter 5). There are many ways to give users real and meaningful control over places.

Being Refreshed

People who spend hours every day solving mental problems, as most modern knowledge workers do, become cognitively exhausted; they deplete their stocks of mental energy. Cognitive exhaustion spreads insidiously from its root cause and degrades performance on all mental tasks, whether they involve processing information, solving a problem, or determining appropriate behavior in a particular circumstance. We become distracted, irritable, and impulsive when mentally exhausted.

Running down this stock of energy is different than being in a stressful situation. When a stressor is removed, the stressful situation is eliminated. Getting rid of a stressful noise or temperature, for example, rectifies the situation. When stocks of mental energy are depleted, they must be rebuilt.

Stephen and Rachel Kaplan, professors at the University of Michigan, have determined what sorts of places help us restock our mental energy (Kaplan 1995). The Kaplans call these sorts of places *restorative*.

The Kaplans have identified four features that characterize restorative places, with more restorative spaces having higher levels of each. The first feature is the feeling of being away. A restorative spot *seems* a long way mentally from an exhausting place. A glance away and out a window, at a painting, into a field with scattered trees, or into a fish tank can take us out of a mentally exhausting situation. An engrossing detective novel does the same thing. Second, restorative places are fascinating. That means that it is pleasurable and effortless for us to think about them. Thirdly, restorative spaces are easy for us to visit because we can anticipate what will happen in them and the things we experience in them are somehow interrelated. Fundamentally, restorative places are interesting worlds we can explore without concern. They don't need to be large. As many researchers have noted, English country gardens are restorative even when they are small because these spaces include many different plants and elements on which we can focus our attention. Finally, restorative spaces allow us to easily do whatever we are trying to do. Signs we need to navigate restorative spaces use words and symbols we understand, for example. Workers with access to restorative views perform at a higher level,

FIGURE 4-5 ■ This view is restorative. The water, open spaces, and bordering trees capture our attention, and we can effortlessly review the information presented to us through these windows—which is mentally refreshing. Copyright © iStockPhoto/ Feng Yu.

FIGURE 4-6 ■ Humans find it refreshing to look out over this sort of scene. Landscape paintings often capture similar vistas. Copyright © iStockPhoto/Nikada.

and so do people with ADHD. Restorative spaces are fast acting—they begin to affect us within three to five minutes, at the most.

Restorative spaces can take countless forms, as outlined in the last paragraph. A restorative space is always a place in which we feel safe and where we are not doing the same sorts of things that drained our stock of mental energy to begin with. They generally include positive distractions and often provide views of something green and natural. Green spaces are not the only ones that can be restorative; museums can also be restorative, for example. It is important that any scenes viewed are pleasant; the most fundamental feature of a restorative place is that people have to feel as if they can move into those spaces and have a wonderful experience—an image of a dark forest or a dense thicket of trees does not hold as much promise of pleasantness as a sunlit, savanna-like meadow with scattered trees.

You can create restorative places by designing a pleasantly distracting and easily used space. It might be a quiet space with a fish tank and a comfortable chair, a collection of potted plants in a window greenhouse, or a view out over nearby nature. The kinds of outdoor scenes that we find most restorative are not purely natural, however (Kaplan 1995). The most desirable sorts of restorative spaces to look at show clearly defined pathways through the viewed space and also some signs of human tending. We relish seeing large, gently rolling lawns, a small clump (or two) of trees in the middle of that lawn, and a rim of trees surrounding the meadow grasses. The view of those lawns can be through a window or via a video. Video images can be particularly important in spaces that can't have natural access, for example, heavily shielded X-ray areas in hospitals.

Everyone has a restoration cycle, and the cycles of people gathered together in a restorative spot can be coordinated or not, depending on when they all got to the restorative space, how depleted their energy stocks were when they arrived, and how long they take to "recharge," for example. These differences between people in the same space influence what they are able to accomplish together socially and cognitively.

Stress has little to do with restoration, but since the two are often confused, a brief digression to discuss stress seems in order. We experience stress when something happening in the space around us is diverting us from what we'd really like to be doing (Evans and Cohen 1987). This diversion from what we plan to be doing sends us into mental overload. We find ourselves compelled to think about whatever we are trying to do *and* also compelled to try to understand the stressful situation. The stressful distracter can be an unpredictable series of noises, people talking nearby in a language we understand, or light levels that are too high or low. When something is unusual, even if not uncomfortable, we focus attention on it and that attention, if it causes us to not be able to fully focus on what we are trying to do, is stressful. A warm room is stressful, if we don't expect it, for example. People being closer to us than we want is also stressful, whether it is just one person standing too close or a crowd that encircles us.

What is stressful not only varies with time but also from person to person. One person might find a particular temperature or amount of light (or shadow) stressful, while another might find that same sensory experience perfect. Individual and group differences in place-based experiences are discussed in Chapter 7 and 8.

The same things are stressful (or not) at different times. Listening to your favorite music can be a stress when you are trying to concentrate on remembering why you have thrown a particular receipt into your "save for tax deduction" box. Since we are vigilant creatures, other activity in the space we are in almost always captures a little of our attention—we focus on it because we need to know what is going on, and that need to understand introduces stress into our lives—unless we are doing something simple that doesn't require our full attention. The most stressful situations are those in which we think that if we spent just a little more time trying to understand what is going on, we could make real progress. For example, when we are doing a cognitive task, conversations in languages we speak (or almost speak because we have had at least some instruction in them) are more distracting than conversations in languages with which we have no familiarity. The same conversations would probably not distract us from a physical or visual task.

When we are stressed, our immune systems do not work as well as when we are not stressed and we do not take steps to help ourselves feel more comfortable, either. One research study found that when people are experiencing stress they are less likely to adjust ergonomic controls on their offices, for example (Evans and Johnson 2000).

Under stress, we devote some of our precious mental processing power to paying attention to whatever is generating the stress, so we have less of that energy available to accomplish our original objectives. The total amount of mental energy required to evaluate a stressor and continue on with our primary task is more than we have available unless we are doing the simplest of tasks. We blunder either complex or nonroutine tasks and are anxious when under stress. When we are stressed, we are distracted and less creative because we have less mental energy to deal with all of the different information available.

When we are stressed, we are less pleasant to the people around us; for example, we do not help them or cooperate with them as fully as we would if not under stress. When we're under stress, we really just don't have enough mental capacity left to recognize the concerns of other people.

When the stressor is removed (when we move, figure out the room is hotter than expected because it is a really sunny day and not because the building is on fire, etc.), our mental recovery begins. That recovery does not require that we spend time in restorative spaces—although being in a restorative space rarely a bad thing.

Sometimes we experience stresses that we cannot directly attribute to their cause and/or eliminate, such as the stress we experience because of the low pressure during airplane travel. In those cases, looking at something fascinating, such as a natural view, moving water, a fire (that is under control), a plant (particularly those with rounded leaves), or a fish tank can keep the stress from becoming overwhelming and can counteract our negative mood. Plants, in general, improve mood and performance in a space.

Eventually, we stop consciously perceiving low-level stressors that we continuously experience, but that does not mean that they stop being stressful for us and keeping us from working at our highest level. For example, a low hum of activity in a workplace every day continues to distract people who need to concentrate long after they have stopped consciously perceiving it. It is just as important to alleviate low-level, continuing stressors as it is to eliminate more attention-grabbing, short-term stressors. We cannot stop ourselves from channeling mental energy to resolving undesirable conditions, whether we perceive them consciously or not.

Being able to move away from a stressor is good. It is not enough, however, just to provide people with a place that they can go to escape a stressful situation. People won't use a stress refuge if they feel that there is some social taboo associated with it. If a space is seen as "where the wimps go," soon even the wimps won't go there.

If people do not have any way to eliminate, even temporarily, a stress that they are experiencing or if they try to get rid of it a few times and fail, they will stop trying to eliminate it—and devote less effort to other activities (say solving complicated mental problems) as well. In addition, unpredictable stressors (say a loud noise) are much more difficult to live with than the same sensation if it is predictable. Having control in a situation does a lot to reduce feelings of stress resulting from something physical.

If people must experience a short-term stressor (such as a loud, randomly timed noise), they are less stressed when they experience it if they have been warned in advance about it. Explaining a strange stress also reduces the stress experienced.

Stress is not objective. Stress is in the eyes of the beholder. If people feel that the experiences they are having are stressful, they are stressful to them. Social science researchers may think that a space is noisy and experience stress; online salespeople in the same space may not experience any stress—they may think it is quiet.

■ CHALLENGING

A well-designed place helps us grow and develop as people—however we individually want to define growing and developing. Lawrence and Nohria (2002) have identified the drive toward self-development as one of the fundamental motivators of human actions (along with acquiring, bonding, and defending). Development paths may change and evolve over time.

A particular sort of place can help one person become a terrific amateur cellist; another kind of place helps a person earn a doctorate, while a third sort of place can help a person become the best possible mother. The first space might be located in the midst of an active music community and have soundproofed walls so the amateur cellist can practice for long hours without disturbing the neighbors. A home with large communal spaces as well as individual retreats can help a person become the best possible mother.

■ CONTINUING

As Stewart Brand discussed in *How Buildings Learn* (1994), spaces must evolve over time. Many of the evolutions that Brand discusses are quite dramatic and expensive, but smaller-scale changes can also be difficult to implement. Simple spatial

---

DESIGN IMPLICATION

Well-designed places provide comforting psychological support.

DESIGN IMPLICATION

Well-designed places help us grow and develop as people, in the way we have planned.

FIGURE 4-7 ■ Good spaces provide the support we need to challenge ourselves in ways that we find personally meaningful. Copyright © iStockPhoto/bibi57.

FIGURE 4-8 ■ Spaces must evolve over time to reflect evolving sociological and technological situations. Copyright © iStockPhoto/jacus.

DESIGN IMPLICATION

Well-designed places evolve over time to continue to meet our needs.

reconfigurations in a workplace can cost thousands of dollars—which means often that they don't happen, no matter how good the initial reason for them. Using inappropriate spaces makes humans ineffective, and moving chews up lots of human, financial, and natural resources. Well-designed spaces are flexible and readily reconfigurable.

Any space can be well designed—whether it is a workplace, a store, a school, a home, or a healthcare facility. Well-designed places enhance lives.

5 EMOTIONAL AND COGNITIVE RESPONSES TO SENSORY INFORMATION

■ INTRODUCTION

Seeing. Hearing. Tasting. Touching. Smelling. Humans do all five continuously every waking moment of their lives. We even listen, touch, and smell while we're asleep. Each sound, taste, smell, touch, and image sends sensory information to our brain, where we process it and respond accordingly. At any moment we are having all sorts of sensory experiences, most involving more than one of our senses.

We selectively analyze the sensory information that bombards us each day; we consciously respond to only a sliver of the material that we could. The information that comes to us through our dominant sense (see Chapter 7 for more information) has the most influence on us emotionally, but all of our experiences matter and combine in an exotic goulash.

Not everyone's sense organs work the same way—some people are color-blind and others have distorted senses of smell, touch, or hearing. Since everyone's sensory net is a little different, everyone's input from a place is a little different.

Each person in a space "processes" the available information they perceive differently. How people interpret what they sense is determined by what their life has taught them is important, interesting, useful, and desirable. The smell of pine may be delightful for one person now, just as it was when she smelled it at her family's summer cottage in the Maine woods. Someone else might feel that same pine scent is awful because the scary basement of his elementary school used to smell of pine cleaning products. Sensory histories should guide how you design spaces, and whenever you are creating a space

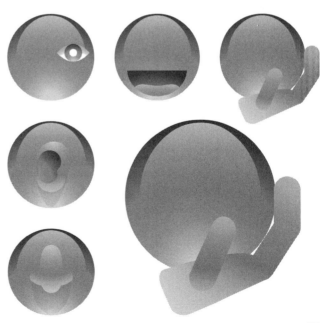

FIGURE 5-1 ■ Sensory experiences that originate in our visual, auditory, tactile, and olfactory systems influence us psychologically.
Copyright © iStockPhoto/Chin Soon Heng.

for a single person or a small group (no bigger than four people), their sensory histories should be recognized.

You can't snap your fingers and change sensory associations. If it seems that a dining room should be painted a golden hue, but the person who owns that dining room looks at the "ideal" color and thinks about the great aunt he always tried to avoid as a child, pick another color for that dining room. Multiple colors and scents and sounds and textures can be used for any purpose.

Never discount the placebo effect—or people having a certain response to a space because that is the reaction that they want to have or believe they are supposed to have. The placebo effect is real and powerful. Offices painted the most energizing colors (according to color research) may be construed as relaxing by their users—and they will be relaxing if the owners truly believe that they are. There is no way to counter a design-related placebo effect effectively.

Each of our senses makes a particular sort of contribution to our experience of a place (Morrin and Chebat 2005). Some sensory inputs have a stronger influence on how we analyze information that is being presented at the same time we have that sensory experience (our cognitive response), and other sensory inputs have a greater effect on our emotional response to a place or object. This emotional effect is unrelated to our dominant sense. Our dominant sense is the quickest way to shape our general mood; the emotional response we are talking about here relates to how we proceed with whatever we are doing when we have that sensory experience. Most of the research that has been done to differentiate the various types of influences of different sensory experiences has been done in stores because retailers have a particular interest in making sure that we are in the right frame of mind to purchase the products that they are offering.

Scents and tastes have strong emotional effects on us. Smells can help us with cognitive and evaluative tasks (is this cantaloupe ripe?), but scents we encounter while shopping, for example, primarily affect us emotionally. Specific scents can have a variety of influences on us, as outlined in this chapter—but smells also trigger associated memories, and memories have an emotional component. So we can have enhanced information-processing capabilities after inhaling a particular scent and simultaneously be in a terrible mood because a smell reminds us of the cousin we never really liked. Smells that we encounter during some sort of negative experience are quickly, and indelibly, stored in our memory banks as scents to be avoided in the future. Tastes influence us psychologically through their links to smell.

Sound has a biological influence on us—our heart beat and respiration synchronize with the rhythms around us, and those physiological responses have a direct influence on our attitudes and behaviors. When our heart beats faster, for whatever reason, we feel energized, for example. We have cultural associations to particular familiar musical forms and also find personal meaning in songs or genres of music. Music influences both the emotions and the behaviors of customers that hear it in stores, for example, and has its largest effect when people are purchasing items that they don't think about a lot or items they do not have much of an emotional attachment to; household cleaning products fall into this category.

What we feel with our skin affects how we perform particular tasks. The influences of temperature on us are basically mechanical, and texture influences us to a greater or less degree, depending on the way that we encounter a space. If we do not have the opportunity to really enter a place, its textures will not affect us at all, unless they impact our visual response to a place. What we actually touch influences us at an instinctual level. Our emotional and cognitive responses are affected by things that we feel.

Visual information primarily influences how we analyze things around us. What we see affects how we interpret the information that is presented to us about product features—but also our energy level while we do so, as well as other responses that we'll outline below. Reactions to visual information are strongly linked to the culture of the viewer. The Western world places a great deal of emphasis on visual experiences, but in other parts of the world, more equal attention is given to other types of sensory experience.

The effects of our sensory experiences are additive—that means that we need to total up the various influences of each of our individual sensations to determine our final psychological state. It is impossible to link an individual experience with a particular numeric score, but we *can* think in terms of sensations that affect us psychologically in one way or another, or that have no influence at all on us. Our ultimate mental state depends on the relative balance of the influences tugging us in different directions. When we get conflicting information from various senses, the inputs that come through our dominant sense (described in Chapter 7 and the most direct route to our emotional core) carry more weight emotionally. Environments in which the sensory experiences are consistent (nautical sorts of smells in a place decorated with nautical sorts of styles) are viewed more positively by those who experience them—and, for example, people purchase more in those sorts of places (they are particularly likely to influence impulse purchases). The purpose for which people intend to use a space should determine the mix of sensory experiences available in it.

The discussions of the psychological implications of information we receive from our five senses that follow are general. More place-specific examples and design implications are included in the special focus chapters of this book.

■ SMELLING: MAGICAL, MYSTERIOUS, AND POWERFUL

Smell is in some ways our most basic sense (Vroon 1997). It is also our most idiosyncratic—it is difficult for scientists to establish clear patterns in how people respond to smells because individual's differ in their "scent memories"(memory links between scents and particular types of experiences). However, there are some associations between smells and mental processes that have become clear.

Human beings process smells and emotions in the same part of their brains. That's why smells have such a powerful influence on our moods. Just a few molecules of air scented with emotionally laden smells can create strong emotional experiences through powerful flashbacks. One whiff of the lavender soap your grandmother used can transport you to nostalgia heaven, if you enjoyed being around your grandmother. No other sense influences us in such a basic way, so smell is a good place for us to begin our sensory explorations.

Smells can be used to put us in a good (or bad) mood, change the way that we think about our lives, and alter the way our brains work to solve problems. Many of the influences of smell on experience are difficult to understand. For example, the smell of jasmine does not influence the speed with which people smelling it fall asleep, but it does affect the quality of their sleep and their mental performance the afternoon of the day after a nighttime whiff. Another difficult-to-explain effect: men smelling grapefruit think women they are looking at are approximately six years younger than they actually are.

Sense of smell varies by ethnic group as well as by gender. In general, women have a better sense of smell than men. Korean Americans have a particularly acute sense of smell, and the Japanese have a relatively poor sense of smell. Caucasians and African Americans have intermediate senses of smell. Our sense of smell usually functions best when we're between 30 and 50 years old. Gender, culture, and age are considerations when scentscaping a place.

Some research that has been done with smells has focused on whether smells are pleasant or unpleasant, and other research has investigated more specific influences of individual scents, such as lemon or peppermint, on humans.

FIGURE 5-2 ■ Many spices have scents that powerfully affect our emotional state. The influences of rosemary, marjoram, and others are reviewed in the text.
Copyright © iStockPhoto/ sasimoto.

When we start to smell pleasant smells, such as baby powder or flowers, we get into a good mood. Our mood is so good that when we smell pleasant things, we are more interested in resolving disagreements through peaceful means than when we smell unpleasant smells. When people smell good, we link them with good things, and when the same people smell bad, they are associated with bad things. Gamblers spend more money when a casino is pleasantly scented, compared to when it is not scented at all. When we're in a good mood, we're more mentally nimble and capable.

When we smell a pleasant scent, life just seems to proceed more agreeably. We are more confident, and our evaluations of the amount of pain that we are feeling decrease. We feel that we have been in a space for a shorter period of time (think: waiting in line, for example). When we smell a pleasant scent, we are apt to linger in a space, which can be good for retailers. Men are likely to remain in a section of a store with a spicy smell, which women may not necessarily do, but both sexes prolong visits to spaces with fruity smells. A scented space will feel larger than an unscented space, and even if we do not consciously perceive a scent, a scented space seems cleaner, fresher, and brighter. When we smell pleasant things and are in a good mood, we're more apt to recall pleasant experiences that we've had, and the reverse is true when we're in a bad mood.

When we smell unpleasant scents, we are generally energized to take some sort of action to get rid of that bad smell. Getting rid of it usually has benefits beyond just making the air smell better. We'll clean up whatever is creating the odor (whether it's a kitchen or a baby) and that gets rid of germs, or we'll take other steps to eliminate the problem (we'll find and fix that gas leak). Unpleasant smells motivate us to leave spaces. The United States military is working on a "stink bomb" that it can use to clear people out of areas.

After a few minutes smelling a smell, we do not consciously perceive it any longer, but that does not eliminate the influences that particular smells have on us. We do not need to consciously perceive that a smell is present to have it affect us.

Scientific research has determined that certain smells are particularly useful for specific purposes. This scientific research has been done in carefully conducted experiments with many sorts of people. Scientists have identified the following general "scent effects":

Doing mental tasks: *Lemon* and *jasmine* improve performance on mental tasks in general. *Lavender* has been linked to improved performance on mathematical tasks. When people are working on a mentally complicated project, make their work area smell like lemons. People smelling lemon are more likely to report that they are in better health than even people smelling other pleasant smells. Cleaning a doctor's office with lemon-scented cleaning supplies can influence doctor-patient discussions.

Working at physical tasks: *Peppermint* improves performance of physical tasks. Scenting fitness areas with peppermint makes the same workouts seem easier than when you are not smelling peppermint. Peppermint makes a physical task seem less frustrating. When people smell peppermint and are doing something physical, they not only feel less tired and frustrated, but they also believe that they are performing better and with more vigor. Smelling peppermint also makes whatever a person is doing seem less rushed and like less of a hassle.

Completing tedious mental and physical tasks: Smelling peppermint encourages people to complete tedious activities. People who've got a mountain of widgets to count should break out the *peppermint*; they'll do a better job with the count.

Improving mood: *Lemon* and *cinnamon-vanilla* are particularly strongly associated with improved moods, although pleasant scents are in general linked to good moods.

Reducing tension: Smelling *lavender* or *cedar* reduces tension.

Reducing anxiety: Smelling *oranges* reduces anxiety levels. A study in a dentist's office revealed that when the space was scented with orange the patients were calmer, and this effect was particularly strong for women. *Vanilla* also reduces anxiety in the people smelling it. *Floral* scents in general (particularly *jasmine* and *hyacinth*) lessen anxiety. The smell of burning frankincense also reduces anxiety and depression. Research by Hirsch (2003) at the Sense of Smell Institute in Chicago has also shown that anxiety is reduced by the smell of *lime, marjoram, rose, lavender, bergamot,* and *cypress.* A sample application: scenting the air in rooms where people will be interviewed increases the odds that job applicants will effectively present relevant information about themselves and their experiences.

Relaxing: Many odors have been found to be relaxing. If you'd like to calm people down, you can use *lavender, rose, almond, cedar/pine, bergamot, chamomile, marjoram, heliotrope, sandalwood, vanilla, muguet, ylang-ylang,* and *spiced apple* scents, for example. Spiced apple has been shown to reduce the blood pressure of healthy volunteers by three to five points. Lavender sedates our central nervous system. Several firms now manufacture a lavender scent that can be spritzed onto bedsheets—if people have trouble falling asleep, this might be the solution. A bouquet of dried lavender

FIGURE 5-3 ▨ The scent of lavender is relaxing and has been shown to reduce tension. Copyright © iStockPhoto/Scott Waite.

will also help lull people to sleep. Hirsch (2003) has shown that *nutmeg* smells are relaxing. Some of these relaxing smells can commonly be found in gardens or outdoors, which can make a room with access to a garden breeze a particularly relaxing space at the end of a busy day.

Improving sleep: Once you've relaxed someone to sleep, if they smell *jasmine* while they sleep the odor will help them sleep more soundly and wake up in a better state to take on the world's challenges. Jasmine improves the quality, not the quantity of sleep. When people smell jasmine while they are sleeping, they wake up feeling less anxious and perform cognitive tasks better. The benefits of smelling jasmine while sleeping extend through the day—people are more alert the afternoon after smelling jasmine during a night time sleep.

Energizing: Just as many scents have been found to be relaxing, a slew of smells have also been found to be energizing, including *peppermint, lemon, jasmine, basil, cloves, neroli, patchouli, grapefruit,* and *rosemary.* These smells are all pleasant. Almost all unpleasant smells are energizing, but who wants to make a house smell like a sulfur mine to get the kids off to school on time? In general, scents that we find unusual are arousing—we try to figure out what they are and what they mean and that process is exciting. The smell of brewing coffee really is invigorating—even to rats that have no idea that drinking coffee is a morning ritual in the human world.

Increasing alertness: A whiff of *peppermint* makes people more alert, fast.

Improving creativity: Any smell that puts us in a good mood is apt to increase our innovativeness, but a *cinnamon-vanilla* smell has specifically been linked to improved creativity.

Enhancing memory: *Rosemary* improves our memory, particularly our long-term memory. Scent spaces where people consult tax accountants with rosemary. The smell will help people remember the reasons they saved some of those receipts.

Feeling healthier: When people smell *baby powder,* they have few complaints about their health.

■ HEARING: PRIMAL, DEPENDABLE, AND ENDURING

Sound regulates our emotions in consistent, powerful ways.

You can soundscape a space to create the mood that will guide the people in that space toward the successful accomplishment of their objectives— whether the space being created is a home schoolroom, a store, a workshop, or a space for leisurely dining.

DESIGN IMPLICATION

Scentscaping is a great way to create the planned psychological effect in a space. Natural, essential oils can be used in scent diffusers, but artificially created scents will also do the trick if some of the people who use a space have allergies to natural products. Scents can be diffused through small spaces, or portions of spaces, or through entire buildings. Many Japanese office buildings couple scent diffusers with heating and air conditioning systems so that invigorating smells can be pumped through a space when energy starts to ebb around three o'clock in the afternoon.

Scenting a space does not necessarily require modifications to its infrastructure. Saucers of essential oils near warm lights or air fresheners (solid or spray) with the right odor can add a desired smell to an area. A scented candle can alter the ambiance of a residential space, and so can potpourri and scent sticks. Dishes of spices and bouquets of fresh (or sometimes dried) flowers also scent a room. Opening the windows will introduce different smells into a space, particularly in a heavily scented area, such as a pine forest. The food in a person's mouth creates a private (sometimes not so private) thought-altering mechanism. By wearing perfume, cologne, or lotions, people can transport their own scent bubble from place to place and influence the situations in which they find themselves.

The scent you add to a space does not have to be so strong that users continuously notice it—smells continue to influence people even after their nose has adapted to them.

Imagine a "scent-sory" tour of a home. The scents that greet people in different areas should all be subtle and coordinated. Scent should only be used in the relatively low concentrations needed—it should never be strong enough to create a negative reaction. A space like a living room or a family room can serve different purposes at different times, so be prepared to make it smell differently on those various occasions—energizing, relaxing, a

good place to study, etc. It's great if you can open the windows or otherwise refresh the air in a room between "smells," but all is not lost if you can't. Eventually a newly introduced smell will become stronger than an existing scent and its effect will start to predominate. Changing a scent is not usually as abrupt as changing the music being played, but gradual scent shifts in a space generate more gradual mood shifts.

The smells in bedrooms should generally be relaxing, but bathrooms can be energizing or relaxing spaces. If people maintain an assortment of scenting products with a range of odors, they will be able to modify the smell in a bathroom to create the desired mood. Spraying bedsheets with a relaxing lavender mist is a really direct way to influence experience, since people are lying in bed when they are trying to fall asleep.

When people eat at home, the smells in a kitchen or dining room can be useful. Particular food smells are energizing or relaxing. Families have their own reactions to food smells that can be recognized and applied. A particular cinnamony smell, similar to spiced holiday treats, may transport family members into a festive mood. Scenting the house with that smell before a holiday party ensures everyone has a great time.

Gently use lemon or jasmine or cinnamon-vanilla, etc., in a work area, and the "scent-sory" experience in that space will be optimized for cognitive tasks. The same scents enhance performance wherever people are working, and if a home office and a corporate workplace smell the same, the scent in each place will remind people of recent thoughts they have had in the other space.

Ultimately, the best way for you to use scent in a space depends on what people want to accomplish in a space and what associations the people using that space have to the scents you plan to use. We can't control the memories and associations people have to particular smells, but we can thoughtfully apply what scientists have learned about smell to enhance spaces.

Biology and psychology come together to determine many of our emotional responses to sound (Bruner 1990). People living in all cultures find that slow, soft, complex music makes them feel sad, for example. This response makes sense because when people are sad, their voices are muffled by their relaxed vocal chords—sounds that sad people make are softened. The opposite reaction occurs when people are angry or happy—vocal cords tense in these situations and sounds are amplified. In general, the rhythm of a beat and the tone of whatever sort of object is creating that beat combine to produce a psychological effect. Responses to the basic parameters of sound, such as a beat or tone, are not culturally dependent, but responses to particular pieces of music are influenced by national culture. When we hear a specific piece of music in a memorable situation, or experience a type of music in a consistent sort of way, we develop a generalized emotional response to it.

Predictable rhythms are relaxing, while unpredictable rhythms are invigorating. Simple harmonies are also relaxing, while complex or novel harmonies are invigorating. When we can anticipate what is coming next, we are lulled toward peacefulness; when we are kept vigilant, wondering what will happen next, our energy level is higher.

In general, a slow, smooth beat is relaxing and a fast, clipped beat increases our energy level. Faster music, which increases our alertness and arousal, is great when we are doing something that requires quick thought, such as rushing through downtown traffic. Fast, loud, simple music lifts our mood, but fast, loud, complex music seems angry.

How fast is fast, how slow is slow? With sound, the relevant comparison is human heart rate (Leeds 2001). Our hearts beat 50–70 times per minute when we are at rest and relaxed. A moderately relaxing sound pulse mirrors that pace, while a deeply relaxing beat is 30–50 beats per minute. Rhythms faster than 50–70 beats per minute invigorate us. Our heart rate synchronizes with the beat of the sounds that surround us, beating at the same pace as the music we can hear or the waves from the ocean we are sitting beside. Ultimately our respiration coordinates with our heartbeat. We can't relax while we can hear an unpredictable noise because our breathing and heart cannot mimic it—they thrash around trying to capture the correct beat, and that thrashing distracts us from whatever we're trying to accomplish. Even annoying noises are more bearable if they are predictable. When they're predictable, we can develop a coping strategy. We can't concentrate if a sound is unpredictable; we're diverting mental processing power to anticipating what will happen next.

The tone of a sound influences our emotional response to it just as clearly as the rhythm of what we are hearing. Lower-pitched sounds put us in a more somber mood, while higher-pitched sounds elevate our mood and make us feel playful. High-pitched sounds, such as those made by a piccolo or a violin, energize us. The kinds of sounds made by harps and acoustic guitars are midrange sounds, and they relax us; lower pitches are very relaxing. Music played in a major key is relaxing and tends to make people feel happier while music played in a minor key is more invigorating but tends to make people feel less happy. Acoustic music and gentle, harmonious sounds are relaxing. Slow music without words can reduce stress (for example, the pressure that builds during a contentious group meeting). When music has a rising inflection, it is linked in our minds to deference, while a falling inflection is linked to dominance.

A soundscape with consistent music types and tempos is boring. To maintain alertness, the music must vary—that keeps brains alert and focusing on the world.

Music with words always piques our curiosity—we focus on the music to uncover what will be said next, and that keeps us more alert and energized than music of the same tempo and tone without words. Music with words is more distracting when people are trying to concentrate than music without words.

Less complex music, without words (or at least without words listeners can understand), is the best background for a mental task that requires concentration. It diverts a minimal amount of mental processing power from the cognitive work underway.

Music played by human beings and music played by machines both influence us emotionally. Our reactions to a piece of music are stronger, however, when it is played by a human being than when it is played by a machine—even if we are listening to a recording and don't know how the music was originally generated.

Volume plays a clear role in how sounds influence us emotionally. Lower volumes are relaxing, and louder volumes are energizing.

You can soundscape with both manmade and natural sounds. It can be hard to determine the exact number of beats per minute in a natural sound, but putting the effort into counting them is almost never worth it. Except for jungle soundscapes, which often feature howler monkeys shrieking briskly and piercingly, natural soundtracks are relaxing. Burbling brooks, rustling leaves, and similar sounds calm us quickly.

When people are trying to concentrate or be creative or make a decision, the sound around them should be quieter than 55 decibels—that's the volume of an average conversation. When they are doing a simple physical task or something that's partially mechanized, the sound level can be 70 decibels, which is as loud as a vacuum cleaner. In no case should noise levels ever be above 85 decibels, which is as loud as a lawnmower.

White noise (a fuzzy, burbling background noise that sounds like softly playing radio static) helps us do mental tasks because it creates a sound background that makes it harder to hear potentially distracting noises. White noise can be used in homes, offices, schools, hospitals, or wherever people need to concentrate. It can be created with a special white noise generator, radio static, fans, or sounds from nature. The sound of moving water is a sort of white noise, for example. To be effective, white noise should be about 45–50 decibels and should be low pitched. To be especially effective, sound engineering professionals should develop and install a white noise system.

The physical form of a space influences how sound is experienced. Sound waves bounce around in a place, and anything that makes them move in crazy, random directions will keep down the sound levels and eventually exhaust the energy in the sound waves. Sound waves are easily sent bouncing in a new direction—something as seemingly insignificant as a leaf on a plant can cause sound to change its direction of travel and dissipate its energy.

When you are fine-tuning the soundscape of a place, you are generally trying to exhaust sound waves by frequently redirecting them. Rough surfaces send sound waves off in every direction and make spaces quieter. Rooms seem quieter if they're equipped with upholstery, carpeting, suspended ceilings, curtains, and other soft surfaces that help send some sound waves toward the ceiling, floor, and other directions away from our ears. Spaces with fewer right angles seem quieter than ones with more right angles.

Sound dampeners can also be used to keep sound from bouncing from one room to another. They can ensure that sound does not travel from private spaces to public spaces, and vice versa.

DESIGN IMPLICATION

Sounds influence our psychological state in predictable, consistent ways and spaces can be soundscaped to enhance the experience of the people who use them. People who create retail spaces have been using music to control the pace of customer movements for some time. When people hear faster music, they move more quickly and vice versa, so restaurants that want people to eat up and move on play music with a quicker beat, while restaurants with white tablecloths that want their customers to invest in dessert and after dinner drinks play slower-paced music.

Playing music listeners enjoy is often a good idea. We forget less pleasant things when we hear it, such as how long we've been waiting in a line or how hard we've been working out. Scientists have found that when men are listening to music they enjoy, they work out 30 percent longer, and women work out 25 percent longer than when they're listening to music they don't like. Both men and women don't think that they have worked as hard

at the end of workouts when they have listened to music that they like. Listening to music while we're doing mental work also seems to be a good thing. When we're doing knowledge work and listening to music we enjoy, we are in a better mood, feel we are doing a better job, and work more efficiently.

The design of a space influences how sound is experienced. Starting outside, shrubs and trees planted around a building buffer the occupants of the building from exterior sound. The design of a ceiling influences how sound moves through a space. When a ceiling is insulated, just as when walls are insulated, sound waves are blocked, or at least partially blocked. Suspended ceilings can also impede sound transmission. Spaces seem less noisy if the furniture and walls include fewer right angles. The more soft surfaces in a room, the more sound waves traveling through that space will be dampened. Cloth wall hangings and curtains dampen sound, and so do carpeting, furniture with upholstery and pillows, and rough surfaces.

Greenery planted around a building acts like a sort of insulation, keeping outside noises from having much of an influence on people inside a structure. The plants deflect some sound waves back toward the street before they are heard inside.

The way that sound is experienced in a space also influences the perceived size of a room. Surfaces that absorb sound make room size less clear to us. Rooms with lots of hard surfaces and bouncing sound waves have more clearly defined physical boundaries.

■ SEEING: VITAL, FOCAL, AND INFLUENTIAL

Most people in the Western world focus more mental energy on what they see than input from any other sense. Chapter 8 discusses the sensory focus of other cultures.

When we look at something, we are bombarded with all sorts of information. As we focus on an object, the first thing we assess is its color. There is a lot more to visual experience than color—something can be shiny or have a matte finish, have simple or complicated patterns, or can be more or less transparent—and all of these physical parameters have psychological implications. We also are influenced psychologically by the source of light in a space, the forms of objects in a space, how those forms are arranged, and whether lines are curved or straight, for example. Many visual inputs influence psychological response to a space.

Color Basics

When we speak about color, we generally use words that describe its hue—we categorize something we encounter as blue or maybe bluish green or maybe even as a greener sort of bluish green—but hue is just one of the words that we can use to discuss color. Color also can be described using the terms *saturation* and *brightness*. While hue is the wavelength of a light beam, saturation is how pure a color is and brightness refers to how light or dark a color is. While brightness runs from very bright, with lots of white, through colors that are darker, saturation measures the apparent purity of a color and varies from most to least. More saturated shades are truest to the stereotyped image of that color. Less saturated versions appear muddier. Saturation and brightness can be difficult to distinguish. Fire engine red is a more saturated form of red, while maroon is a less saturated version, for example. Kelly green is a more saturated green, while military fatigues are a less saturated green. Navy blue is a darker blue, and baby blue is a lighter blue.

Scientific research has shown that saturation and brightness have a big influence on how we respond to a color emotionally (Valdez and Mehrabian 1994). Colors that are brighter and more saturated are more pleasurable; as brightness and saturation increase, so does pleasure. Brighter, more saturated colors improve our mood. The pleasure we experience being around a color is influenced more by its brightness than by its saturation. We are energized by being around more saturated colors. Being around brighter colors is not energizing, unless the colors are very bright. Energy level increases with color saturation and decreases with increases in brightness except for very bright colors, which are very energizing. Warm, saturated, not very bright colors are exciting to be around, while cool, not very saturated, brighter colors are not very exciting—so Kelly green revs us up and delicate baby blue calms us down.

Cool colors are often used in spaces where people want to be calm and warm colors where people need to have more energy, and the scientific evidence would support these color choices. Cool colors, as generally used in calming spaces, are brighter but not very saturated, and the scientific research indicates that places painted these colors are relaxing and pleasant. Warmer or darker colors, as generally used in energizing spaces, are more saturated and less bright, which leads to higher energy levels—but these spaces are less pleasant.

Red has traditionally been seen as an exciting color—and it actually is. The color we normally think of as red is saturated but not very bright. Research has shown that red puts our pituitary glands into high gear, which gives us a boost in mental and physical energy. Red (when it is saturated and not too bright) negatively influences performance on intellectual tests, so it should not be used in classrooms or other testing sites (Elliot et al. 2007). Red also seems to induce us to avoid beginning tasks at which we might not succeed. A moderate amount of red (a few chairs, part of a rug) in an auditorium can be a good idea—too much red can overcharge viewers and have negative consequences.

Pink the shade of Pepto-Bismol medicine has a tranquilizing effect on humans and also reduces anxiety—which makes sense once you know how saturation and brightness influence our responses to color. Pepto-Bismol pink is bright but not very saturated.

These rules do change when we think about the strongest, brightest, saturated colors—these shades are just shy of white hot. These colors are so exciting to look at that they can prevent us from focusing on or noticing other visual elements in the same space.

Women are more susceptible to the effects of saturation and brightness than men. Most spaces are used by both sexes, so the different responses of each sex are generally not relevant—but keep them in mind when designing places that will tend to be visited more by members of one sex than the other.

Our responses to saturation and brightness are instinctive and universal, but they are not the only influence on how we respond to a color. We also learn associations to colors as we grow up in a culture. These associations are just as important to consider when selecting colors as our physiological reactions, and we will talk about them in detail in Chapter 8 when we are discussing the meanings that different colors have for various national cultures. Since there are so many colors available to accomplish any psychological objective, it makes sense to select colors that not only have the appropriate saturation and brightness, but that also have desirable cultural associations.

The final influence on response to a color is personal experience. If a person has an aversion to a color because of some past event, that aversion can't be overcome with logic. It simply exists. There are many colors that can be chosen in any situation; there is never a reason to select one to which people have negative associations.

Colors in Combination

When a space is decorated with subtle variations of the same color, the effect is relaxing, except if the color being subtly varied is white or beige. When upholstery, walls, ceilings, and other elements in the room are all fundamentally white or beige, we get tense (Mahnke 1996). In beige or white environments, we are understimulated, which can be just as unpleasant as being overstimulated. In both cases we can become restless and have trouble concentrating. Being over- or understimulated also makes us extremely emotional.

Colors are usually used in combination, and the contrast between those colors influences us psychologically. Figure C-3 shows a color wheel. When colors that are directly across the color wheel from each other are used in a single room, the space seems exciting. When a color is paired with the two colors on either side of the color opposite it, a space seems comfortable. Large differences in saturation and brightness between the colors used in a space enhance this energizing effect. When several cool colors that are about equally bright are used together, they are particularly calming, and when several warm colors are used together, particularly if they are at several different levels of brightness, they are particularly energizing. When colors that are near each other on the color wheel are used together, the effect is not as lively, and relatively calming.

When several colors are used in combination, the pairing is more pleasant the larger the contrast in brightness between the colors. We also prefer to see colors together if they have roughly the same saturation.

Our experience of any color is determined by the amount of space in a place painted that color—we are more influenced the larger the size of the space colored. A fire engine red vase has a different level of psychological influence than a fire engine red carpet or accent wall.

Not only are colors not used alone, but generally, they are also not perceived alone—the way that a color is seen is influenced by the colors used in the areas immediately around it. As a color is viewed, the way that it is seen starts to shift toward the color that is opposite the neighboring colors on the color wheel. For example, a reddish tile in a bathroom will appear redder if the neighboring tiles are painted a greenish color, but not if they are painted a more bluish shade. Red and green are opposite each other on the color wheel.

Patterns

Colors are not just used in adjoining blocks; they are also used intertwined into patterns. The patterns we see also influence us psychologically. Seeing a complicated or novel pattern is exciting, and the more patterns (of any level of complexity or novelty) in a space, the more excited we become. Generally, we prefer simpler patterns around us, in wallpapers and upholstery, for example. This makes sense from an evolutionary perspective—it would be easier to see trouble approaching in a simpler landscape pattern than a more complicated one. Smaller-scale patterns are generally preferred to larger-scale ones, probably for the same reason—it is easier to see something approaching in a smaller-scale landscape pattern than in a larger one. Smaller patterns also make small spaces seem larger.

We find it soothing to look at certain patterns that are mathematically similar to ones that occur in nature. These patterns are called natural fractals, and they are present in a field of grass that is being gently rippled by the wind, clouds moving across the sky, or a winding stream. Natural fractal patterns are also found in views out over natural scenes, in the patterns made by flames, and in fish tank ripples. Coincidentally, these patterns are found in the patterns that dappled light (described earlier) form on the ground. The calm mental state induced by these sorts of patterns has been found to spur creative, high-quality mental activity. The regularity in natural fractal patterns (although that regularity may not be immediately apparent to the untrained eye) makes it easy to spot upcoming trouble. Natural fractal patterns can be hard to identify, but designers indicate when these patterns have been used. Jhane Barnes, for example, has marketed a line of textiles based on natural fractal dimensions.

Color Preferences

Humans are consistently influenced by the saturation and brightness of colors, and any desired psychological effect can be created by colors from various hue families with appropriate saturation and brightness levels. In any context, the hue choices that we make reflect our hue preferences. Within cultures and ethnic groups, there are patterns in preferred hues.

Around the world, blue is generally the most preferred hue. For citizens of the United States, there is detailed information available about the most preferred shades of blue. A study by *American Demographics* reveals that 21 percent of Americans select Palace Blue as their favorite color and that 23 percent of U.S. citizens have painted their bedrooms blue. Yellow is generally the least preferred hue overall. Yellow is the only hue that the population likes less than orange.

Within the United States, Generation Y (born after 1978) has indicated a preference for particular hues, as reported by *American Demographics*. This generation generally prefers bolder hues in the orange, pink, and green families. Hues preferred by younger Americans are sophisticated, particularly when compared to other generations' choices at their age. Sophisticated hues are created by mixing multiple colors together. Abstract patterns are preferred by Generation Y, if patterns are used, but generally members of Generation Y would prefer to decorate with solid colors.

Hue preferences also vary by ethnic groups within the United States. In the United States, various ethnic groups named different hues as their favorite when queried by *American Demographics* (Paul 2002):

- When white Americans were asked what their favorite color was, 43 percent said blue, 15 percent green, 13 percent purple, 10 percent red, and 7 percent black.
- Asian Americans picked blue (40 percent) as their favorite, followed by purple and black (each 11 percent) and yellow and green (each 9 percent).
- Among African Americans, 38 percent selected blue, 16 percent purple, and 12 percent green, black, or red as their favorite color.
- Hispanics were most likely to select blue as their favorite color (35 percent), followed by purple (18 percent), red (15 percent), and green or black (each 11 percent).

Each group also had least favorite colors:

- White Americans reported their least favorite color was pink (23 percent), followed by orange (21 percent), brown (17 percent), yellow (9 percent), and gray (8 percent).
- Asian Americans reported orange or pink (each 17 percent) as their least favorite color, followed by brown (14 percent) and green or gray (11 percent).
- African Americans identified their least favorite colors as pink (40 percent), orange (16 percent), brown (10 percent), and purple or white (6 percent).

- Hispanics generally identified orange as their least favorite color (22 percent), followed by brown (18 percent), pink (17 percent), and yellow (12 percent).

American Demographics reports that African Americans favor saturated reds, yellows, and browns, in general, while Hispanics tend to prefer warm, bright colors.

Other researchers have investigated combinations of colors that are favored by different cultures around the world for interior color palettes. These preferences are important because the use of preferred colors improves people's moods. National differences in preferences are reported in Chapter 8.

Symbolic Meanings of Colors

Hue preferences are tied to individual associations and personal factors, but each national culture also links symbolic meanings to colors. These meanings are often just as powerful as personal associations, and they are also universal across a cultural group. Since so many hues can produce the same psychological effect, there are always many color options that can be used in any situation, so cultural associations to particular hues should play a key role in developing any color scheme. Symbolic associations to hues by particular national cultures are reported in Chapter 8.

Color and Activity

The way color is used in a space directly influences how we move through it. Retailers have known for a long time that we are drawn toward warm colors—that's why the back wall of a store, or the area with the merchandise with the highest profit margins, is often painted a warm shade. Consumers can concentrate and make purchase decisions when surrounded by cool colors but don't process information as well in spaces designed with warm colors—so warm colors are best for areas where impulse purchase products, for example, are displayed. If you want to draw people toward the end of a hallway, paint it a warm color.

Activity level in a space can be readily predicted from how energizing the colors in a space are. Colors can be used to encourage a desired activity or to provide an anecdote for that activity. For example, imagine a playroom space where children will be active—it can be painted an energizing color to encourage play or a relaxing color to help manage the play-generated excitement of the children. The designer (and the parents of those children) must identify and encourage the desired behavior.

Color and Perception of Room Sizes/Orientations

Colors not only move us toward or away from particular places, but they also change our perceptions of room shape. Practitioners have known for some time that walls that are painted warmer or darker colors seem closer to us than they actually are, while walls painted cooler or lighter colors (or neutral shades) seem farther away than they really are. These effects have been used to change perceptions of uncomfortably shaped rooms. Scientific research has confirmed that colors' space distorting effects are reliable and valid. Ceilings that are too low can be made to seem farther away if they are painted a light color, and any surface that is too close is mentally pushed back if it is painted a cool, light, unsaturated color. Alternatively, walls can be moved in if they are painted more intense colors that are warm and saturated. Painting different walls in a room different colors, two warmer and two cooler colors, for example, can dramatically change the physical sensation of being in a space.

Contrasts between colors used on objects and walls in a space also have a big influence on how large a space feels. When a piece of furniture's color is in dramatic contrast to the background (generally wall) color, that contrast makes the furniture seem closer and bigger—so the color of furniture and other objects in a room can also be used to create a particular perception of the space's shape.

Size-distortion effects are influenced by the texture of the walls in a space. More textured walls have crevices on their surfaces that cast shadows and make any color on them seem darker. That makes the space seem smaller than the same room with the same paint color applied to smooth walls. Shinier surfaces make a space appear larger when they make the walls seem to be a lighter color.

We expect certain types of colors in certain sorts of places. Darker colors are found on the floor or ground, medium-level colors on the walls, and light colors on the ceiling (Durao 2007). People designing the interiors of spaceships make sure that one interior surface is a dark color, so that weightless astronauts can orient to it, as they would to the ground on Earth. When we don't find darker colors on the floor, medium-dark colors on the walls, and light colors on the ceiling, we become stressed. Light-colored carpets not only get dirty quickly, but they also make us confused. Light colors are also an energy-efficient choice for ceilings; ceilings painted light colors reflect more light than ceilings painted darker colors.

Colors and Eating

Restaurateurs know that warm colors make us hungry—they use plenty of reds, yellows, and oranges in spaces where they want to encourage us to eat. These colors (when of appropriate saturation and brightness) make us feel energized, and from that energy comes hunger. Warm tones in a dining room will make diners more boisterous and also increase their caloric intake during meals. Too many highly saturated and moderately bright colors in a space can make us too energized to eat, or do anything else. No room can be decorated entirely in energizing colors! Blue plates and lights have been found to curb appetites.

Colors and Temperature

Color influences the perceived temperature of a space. Places that are painted warmer colors seem significantly hotter to people in them than places of the same actual temperature that are painted cooler colors. This effect is strong enough that thermostats can actually be changed about five degrees when the color painted on the walls changes.

Symbolic Influences of Color Brightness

Just as certain sounds inherently seem good or bad, certain colors convey "goodness" and others "badness." Adults and children interpret brighter objects as better than darker-colored objects.

Colors and Perception of Weight

Darker- and warmer-colored objects seem heavier and smaller than lighter- and cooler-colored objects of the same size. This influences apparent visual balance in a space (more later in this chapter).

Responses to Individual Colors

Scientific research has shown that men and women prefer different red tones, yellow based and blue based, respectively. They also prefer different blue tones, with women preferring redder blues and men preferring greener blues.

Pepto-Bismol pink is calming for adults—it can soothe an agitated prisoner faster than some sedatives. Pink has a somewhat different influence on children. Kids under six were stronger and in a better mood while in a room painted pink (specifically painted DuLux Vanity Fair DCC#3K) than in a room painted blue (DuLux Bluebird DCC#33F).

Geographic-Specific Responses to Colors

The color and intensity of light outside is slightly different in various parts of the world; these differences alter the way that colors are perceived and those differences in the way colors are actually seen lead to different psychological effects. A particular shade of red does not look the same on a wall at the equator and on a wall in Boston. If a building is not located on the equator, where a room is in a building influences the intensity of the natural light it receives and how colors in that space are experienced. In extreme northern latitudes, colors can look very different when painted on walls in rooms on different sides of the same building, for example. In the Northern Hemisphere, the same color looks cooler in a room with a northern exposure than it does in a room with a southern exposure, where it seems warmer and brighter.

These differences in how colors are perceived influence apparent saturation and brightness levels. To determine their psychological effects, colors must be assessed on-site in the location where they will be used.

Seeing Textures

We also see finishes, and they also influence us psychologically. When viewed, a shiny surface is invigorating while a matte finish is relaxing. Our response to texture becomes more complex when we feel the textures as well as see them—more on that later.

Visual Proportions

The golden ratio of visual proportions influences us psychologically and triggers particular, pleasurable brain waves. We like things that show this ratio.

The golden ratio has been repeatedly found to result in pleasing compositions—whether they are audio or visual. The ratio is 1:1.6 or, if A and B are dimensions of an object, $(B/A) = [A/(A+B)]$. Rectangles whose side lengths (A and B) are in the golden ratio are preferred. The ancient Greeks used the golden ratio when they designed the Parthenon (see Figure 2-1). Interestingly, listeners think major sixths in music sound great, and in a major sixth, the ratio of the frequencies being experienced is the golden ratio.

Form and Line

Form and line have an important influence on the psychological experience of being in a space. They have an effect on the pleasantness and energy level of a place.

A form is a three-dimensional solid. More angular, rectilinear forms are described as masculine and more curved forms as feminine. Our psychological responses to forms are consistent with the related stereotypes. Rectilinear forms generate an impression of action and efficiency, while curved forms create more of a relaxed feel in a space. People generally prefer rounded forms to more angular ones. Symmetrical forms are more relaxing than asymmetrical ones. Variations in form, like variations in color, need to be used with care, with a moderate number of forms in a space being optimal—a moderate number means that a space is neither boring nor exhausting.

Lines are two-dimensional images. They create effects that are similar to those seen with these shapes. Whether lines we see are straight or curved, the direction in which they are oriented and the number of lines in place influence us psychologically through their symbolic connotations. A straight horizontal line is calming. This horizontal line can be created by the top edges of pieces of furniture, for example, or it can literally be painted on a wall. Multiple horizontal lines around a room are bad, however. They make us feel tense—they seem like multiple horizon lines and that is an effect that just isn't naturally occurring on our planet. Just as straight horizontal lines are relaxing, straight vertical lines indicate stability. Straight vertical lines can be created in the folds of drapes. Straight diagonal lines produce a different effect than either horizontal or vertical lines. They indicate activity, with lines at steeper angles to the floors being more energizing. Gently curved lines are relaxing. V shapes draw our attention faster than other shapes and hold that attention, as they signify threat or anger. More curved shapes, such as those found in the happy face's smile, have happy connotations.

In general, objects and patterns with curved features are preferred to those with pointed features and sharp angles. Research has shown that we associate circles with softness, happiness, goodness, love, life, brightness, lightness, warmth, quickness, and quietness. We link squares with hardness, sadness, evil, hate, death, darkness, heaviness, cold, slowness, and loudness.

Visual Quality

Enhancing the visual quality of a space makes it more likely that anyone entering it will find it a desirable place to be. Jack Nasar and other researchers have identified features that create visual quality in a space. Generally, we like a space that is interesting but not confusing. This happy medium between interest and confusion can't be quantified, and the way it is created varies from project to project. A space is interesting, for example, if all of its intriguing points are not obvious at once, but revealed as people move through it. Walking along curved circulation routes lined with art that changes periodically is interesting, but too much or too little complexity can be unpleasant. Including those curved pathways in an otherwise predictable building shape brings the overall space into a comfortable range, for example.

Nasar is able to make some generalizations about the sorts of spaces that produce various psychological effects (Nasar 1994). Spaces that are ordered, moderately complex, and a more typical style are pleasant; whereas more complex, less ordered spaces with an atypical style are more exciting.

The things we see in a space can vary in many ways. They can differ, for example, in color, shape, height, and the material they are made out of. All of these sorts of differences increase our interest in a space as they increase visual complexity. A space is more complex when there is more variety in the individual elements within it, and those elements are arranged in less of a pattern. Things that are more complex are more interesting to us. Too much variety in a space creates excessive visual complexity. Curvilinear natural forms and the smooth sorts of transitions between spaces found in nature enhance the visual quality of a space as do plants and water, even though they can make it more complex. Designing a space along a diagonal axis, instead of one parallel to a set of walls, can also add a level of comfortable complexity to a room.

Nasar feels that order is desirable in these moderately complex spaces with high visual quality; it further reduces the possibility of chaos—and chaos makes us tense. Clutter in a space increases disorder to an unpleasant level.

An area is coherent when there is a rhythm or pattern in what people who move through the space experience. Rhythm can be created by repeating forms and colors, for example. Order cannot come at the expense of novelty—if it does, a space will be too boring. Something unanticipated is novel, and novelty piques our curiosity and draws our attention (Nasar 2000).

Nasar has written a multipart survey that can be used to develope visually effective environments (Nasar 2008). First, people who will use a space

FIGURE 5-4 ■ A very ordered space—it is carefully organized and the overall effect is calming, inviting reflection.
Copyright © iStockPhoto/Nikada.

select adjectives that identify the desired character of the space being developed. The adjectives provided include *soothing, adventurous,* and *familiar,* for example. Next, Nasar presents people who will use a space with images varying on an assortment of important design attributes such as orderliness, coherence, and variety. Depending on the stage of the design process, these images can be of places that are either similar in function to the space under development (later, more concrete, design phase) or different (earlier, more conceptual, design phase) from the space being developed. Office workers might thus look at pictures of office workspaces or hotel lobbies, for example. People rank the images presented in terms of how appropriate their character is for the space under development and briefly discuss the spaces that they feel are most consistent and least consistent with the desired "personality" of the space being designed. The survey enables designers to identify space designs that are too boring, those that are too "interesting," and those that are just right—the ones with high visual quality.

Designed Patterns for Spaces

The elements of a space can be arranged so that they take on particular patterns—the rhythm, symmetry, balance, and harmony of these elements can be described. Rhythm, symmetry, balance, and harmony contribute to the visual quality of a space by creating "interesting order." All are judged in reference to a focal point. Rhythm and its colleagues can be found in systems of colors as well as shapes and forms because colors lead to impressions of size and weight (light colors appear to weigh less, for example, and darker colors appear to weigh more).

A rhythm leads people through a space visually and adds to its order. Rhythm relates to the way elements (colors, shapes, light beams, textures, etc.) repeat throughout a space or gradually change through a space. It can be more or less obvious, but spaces need some sort of rhythm or design pattern to be cohesive. A space is unified when all of its components relate to a single concept—but a space becomes boring if there is too much consistency. Some variety in use of shapes, colors, and textures, for example, comfortably increases the stimulation we receive from an environment.

FIGURE 5-5 ■ Rhythm leads users through a space that also provides prospect and refuge to visitors.
Copyright © 2007 Farshid Assassi, courtesy of BNIM.

FIGURE 5-6 ▪ The rhythm in the arches at this airport is calming, and the sunshine that pours through the windows reduces stress.
Copyright © iStockPhoto/byllwill.

Symmetry and balance can be used with any design elements: colors, shapes, textures, or three-dimensional masses. The discussion that follows will use the term *object* to simplify the discussion. A symmetrical arrangement is less energizing than an asymmetric one because the symmetric arrangement is predictable and the asymmetric one is not. Perfect symmetry in a space is not usually good—it makes an area seem very static and lifeless. Spaces in which all objects are predictably placed are too symmetrical and are also not very stimulating. Ornamentation, for example carvings on buildings, is continuously stimulating to us because we see new things in it each time that we look at it. Clutter lacks any sort of symmetry and is extremely stimulating—clutter can even make us agitated. Piles of stuff (papers, books, or whatever) should be kept neatly concealed in drawers and cabinets to reduce visual distractions.

Balance is frequently used in interior design. Balance is described in terms of a focal or central point, which adds a certain stability to a space. In situations with formal balance, identical objects are arranged in a consistent pattern around the central focal point. When informal or asymmetrical balance is used the objects arrayed are not necessarily identical, and their arrangement creates equilibrium in spite of these differences. Objects that are perceived as heavier will be closer to the focal point to balance objects that appear to be lighter and are farther from the focal point of the arrangement, for example. Things that are unusual for some reason—due to their color, shape, amount or type of ornamentation, or texture, for example—carry more visual weight and must be counterbalanced by other items of equal apparent weight or by multiple objects whose visual weight counterbalances theirs. Things that are lighter colors are perceived to weigh less than otherwise identical darker-colored objects. Informal balance makes people feel more relaxed in a space, while a more formal balance makes people feel, well, more formal, better able to predict future events, and that a space is orderly.

A space that lacks harmony sets us on edge—and that's unpleasant. A harmonious space is inherently pleasant. Things in a space are in harmony when they have something in common. This common factor can be any sort of design element: a color, a three-dimensional form, a texture, or a type of surface. Repeating this feature makes a space seem unified. A space cannot contain only harmonious items—if it does it will be boring. So a few green elements in a generally blue-toned space are a good idea.

Light

Light levels and colors influence how we think and behave in a space.

When light intensity levels are low, we find a space relaxing, while invigorating spaces are more brightly lit. In general, higher levels of light are psychologically and physically stimulating. Light levels of 700 lux wake us up. We feel less tired when the lights are at 300 lux than we do in spaces lit to 100 lux. For comparison, a full moon is less than 1 lux, twilight is 11 lux, and full sunlight is 10,000 lux. When light levels are lower we tend to have more intimate conversations and speak more quietly. We also may take more risks when it is darker (280 lux) than when it is slightly brighter (770 lux). More dimly lit spaces seem more private, particularly if more brightly lit spaces can be seen in the distance.

FIGURE 5-7 ▪ The timbers in this old wooden roof are in a complex but symmetrical arrangement that captures our attention and invites visual exploration.
Copyright © iStockPhoto/resonants.

Some of the ways that light levels influence us are intriguing. Our evaluations of other people are higher if we rate them while we're sitting in a darker room (lit to the level of 150 lux) than in more brightly lit spaces (1,500 lux). In those more brightly lit circumstances, we also think more broadly than at the lower light levels, and we can be more creative when we think broadly. More brightly lit rooms seem more cheerful, which in turn makes us more cheerful.

Lighting can be direct or indirect. Under direct light, the light from the bulb shines directly on the surface that needs to be lit. Indirect light is bounced off another surface before it reaches the place where it's needed. Indirect lighting makes a space seem larger. Direct light increases our energy level. When more of the lighting in a room is indirect than direct, brightly lit rooms seem more cheerful. Both indirect and direct lighting need to be used in a space for it to be well lit; direct light fills a place with intense light, but it can be harsh on the eyes. Indirect light is not as intense as direct light, so it may not be bright enough for reading and similar activities. It is best for lighting shadowy spaces. Eliminating those shadowy spaces makes the light levels in a room more uniform overall, which is less stressful for our eyes.

FIGURE 5-8 ▪ Informal balance captures our attention and interjects energy into spaces where it is used.
Copyright © iStockPhoto/ FreezeFrame.

Spotlight-like lighting draws more attention to people and objects and the additional information learned about people and objects because of that light is energizing. Concentrated lighting also subdivides and organizes spaces—it is regularly used in restaurants to create a "territory" around dining tables. The way that light falls in a space can influence who is socially active by including or excluding individuals who are lit or not lit by its glow in an interacting group.

Lighting a room with a more general, consistent, moderate intensity of light is relaxing.

The sort of lighting that we find most desirable and soothing is related to our evolutionary, and sunlit, pasts. We prefer the sort of dappled light that is experienced while sitting under a tree on a sunny day. The random dollops of light that fall on the ground around us then, combined with the brightly lit area surrounding that tree, create our ideal lighting condition. A similar effect is created when indirect light is used to create asymmetric lighting patterns on a floor.

Light can be different colors. A difference in the color of light that we don't consciously perceive can dramatically influence how we feel psychologically. The color of a lightbulb is readily determined. Lightbulb packages are usually labeled as a certain number of degrees Kelvin, and numbers of degrees Kelvin correspond to lights of certain colors. Counterintuitively, numbers of degrees Kelvin that are lower represent warmer light. Regular incandescent lightbulbs, which produce warm light, are generally 2,500–3,000 K, while warm white fluorescents register at around 4,000 K. Sunlight at noon is around 5,000 K, which is also the color of a cool white fluorescent bulb.

Under warmer lights we are more relaxed, and under cooler lights we are more alert.

Under warm white light we

- take more risks,
- perform better on tests of our short-term memory and problem-solving skills than when in cool white light or in artificial daylight,
- prefer to resolve disputes with other people by collaborating with them and are less interested in avoiding these socially difficult situations, and
- are more likely to get into a better mood (if we're female).

Under cool white light we

- do not recall novel material that we have stored in our long-term memory as well as under warmer light,
- experience more stress than when we are in full-spectrum artificial light, and

▪ are more likely to get into a better mood (if we're male).

Light and color work together to influence our behavior. When we are in a place with warm colors and lots of light, we focus on the space we are in and are more active physically. When we are in a space with cooler colors and lower light levels, we focus on our thoughts and reduce our level of physical activity, so we concentrate better on a mental task.

Lighting levels and the color of light work together to influence our mental state. When we're under warmer light at a relatively low level (150 lux), we are calmer and more awake than if we experience the same warm colored light at 1,500 lux. People stay in a good mood longer when they are in a relatively dark (300 lux) and cool-colored light or at a higher lighting level (1,500 lux) and warmer-colored light. Cool lights at lower intensity levels are more restful than the same lights at higher intensity levels.

Daylight is different from artificial light in several ways—it has more colors in it than artificial light. In addition, sunlight changes color and intensity in the course of the day, ranging from more warm at sunrise (around 2,000 K), to more white around noon (around 5,000 K), to a warmer light again around sunset. It's important to spend some time in daylight every day, and the bigger the windows in the rooms we use and the closer they are to the ceiling, the more likely we are to be able to do so while inside. Daylight's light cycles help us regulate our circadian rhythms and that keeps us in a good mood and improves how comfortable we feel, mentally and physically. In office environments, daylight has been shown to have these effects while also improving job performance, job satisfaction, and intention to remain employed at the same place. People in hospital rooms with more daylight need less pain medicine after surgery than patients in rooms without as much daylight. The full-spectrum fluorescent lightbulbs currently sold do not provide the benefits that daylight does. When compared to standard fluorescent bulbs, full-spectrum bulbs do not enhance our psychological or physical comfort.

The color of light influences the way colors used on walls and furnishings affect us emotionally. Warmer light intensifies warm colors. It has the opposite effect on cool colors. Cooler light has just the reverse effect on cool and warm colors. Halogen lighting distorts colors in a space less than other lighting sources.

FIGURE 5-9 ▪ People walk near lights and lighted surfaces. Placing lights along walls in a hallway organizes travel in that space and ensures that people can efficiently move through it. Copyright © iStockPhoto/xyno.

■ TOUCHING: SUBTLE, SENSUAL, AND UNDENIABLE

FIGURE 5-10 ■ The light from this warm incandescent bulb is relaxing and invites people to linger in this comfortable space. Copyright © iStockPhoto/Rick Rhay.

Our ears evolved from patches of skin, and our psychological responses to things we feel are similar to our responses to things we hear.

When humans are massaged with short, abrupt, rapid strokes, we are energized, just as we are when we hear fast-paced music. When we are massaged with long, continuous, slow strokes, we relax, just as we relax when we hear slow music. Consciously or unconsciously, we often adjust massaging showerheads to meet our momentary needs to be relaxed or energized.

Touching smoother surfaces (such as hardwood floors or cotton)—whether they are on floors, walls, upholstery, or anywhere else—is not as interesting and therefore not as exciting as touching rougher surfaces (such as pebbled pathways or textured paper). Many North Americans are particularly soothed by surfaces that feel like cotton flannel, apparently because we have peaceful associations to flannel from our childhoods.

People walking barefoot on large smooth stones, like cobblestones, feel tranquil and energized at the same time; they experience a sort of peaceful burst of adrenalin. This peacefully excited state is coupled with lower blood pressure readings than when people are walking on smoother surfaces. In this sort of mental state, we think more broadly.

While feeling rounded surfaces has relaxing beneficial effects, touching (or seeing) jagged or angular edges makes us tense.

A space with fewer variations in textures is more soothing, while a space with more variation in textures is more energizing. Too many textures make a space seem chaotic, however.

Temperature influences our mood and behaviors in a space. We are more cognizant of downward changes in temperature than upward changes. Our hands and feet are more sensitive to cold, and our heads are more sensitive to heat. Radiant floor heating and slightly higher air-conditioning ducts reduce stress by helping us feel comfortable in a space. Women and men do respond differently to the same temperature, and men are more comfortable at high and low temperature extremes than women. Generally, slightly hotter temperatures are more relaxing, and slightly cooler temperatures are more invigorating.

DESIGN IMPLICATION

Textures have a big influence on the experience of being in a place. The rougher the texture, the darker the colors applied to it seem, and the darker the colors on the walls, the closer the walls appear to people in a space. Shiny, smooth-textured walls seem farther away from people in the room. When spaces have shiny walls, which reflect more light, they seem to be a lighter color and the space seems larger (and therefore less crowded, etc.).

To make spaces energizing, use shiny surfaces on the walls—whether they be glossy or metallic paints or wallpapers or mirrors. To make a space seem more relaxing, switch to matte finishes.

Touching smoother textures is more relaxing, feeling rougher textures is more energizing, and "felt experiences" should be designed with these effects in mind.

Only a few different textures should be used in a space. More textures make a space more interesting, but they can also ultimately make a space more confusing.

▦ TASTING

Since this book focuses on designing spaces, research about how tastes influence our lives is not addressed here. It is important to know, however, that relaxing tastes reinforce relaxing smells and are familiar, while invigorating tastes reinforce invigorating smells or are novel.

▦ FUTURE SENSATIONS

People are beginning to focus more intently on their sensory experiences. An increasing number of sensation-rich products are becoming available.

We can now purchase lightbulbs in a range of colors and light fixtures that change colors continually, for example. Major manufacturers have created scent-dispensing products, such as Scentstories from Procter & Gamble, which plays a scent record cycling random (from a scientific perspective) smells within a space. The Red Sky shower from Dornbracht coordinates showerhead flow rates with particular smells. Even run-of-the-mill products have started to incorporate scents. A scented suit is available in Asia (increasing the market for scented fabrics in general), and an alarm clock from Hammacher Schlemmer wakes people up with the scent of coffee. A British firm is marketing a sofa that releases a pleasant smell when its pillows are plumped. These products do not reflect scientific research, but package and sell folk traditions.

There is also a growing interest in the commercial uses of smell, not just to sell products and experiences but also to sell homes.

There is an explosion of interest in color. More color options for appliances and other objects are reaching the market, and the colors selected for objects and environmental elements are being more thoughtfully considered than in the past when fewer culturally appropriate hues were available. One of the reasons for this is that people currently in their twenties and early thirties were exposed to more saturated colors when they were children than previous generations, so they have grown used to the frequent use of dense color. In addition, color selections are increasingly seen as way to express individuality.

Visual customization is spreading beyond color now to texture, luminance, and iridescence.

▦ CONCLUSION

When you are designing a place, the most general use for that space should drive its design and be the focus of your efforts. For example, when you are working on a bedroom space, the color of the ceiling and the general soundscape of the room will have a more significant influence on how relaxed people in that bedroom feel than the texture of the rug. The color of the walls seen while lying in bed will have more of an influence on the experience of this space than the imagery in the painting hanging above the bed headboard.

Flexibility can be incorporated into spaces that you design. Scents are easy to change, and changes in scent are followed by changes in mood. The "landscape" is different from different sections of the same room. Looking toward the middle of the room from one corner, the view might be of an energizing array of colors and lines, but in a window seat in the same space, you might be able to create a curtained sanctuary with a restorative view out over the yard. Changing the color of the light in a space also quickly changes the moods and behaviors of people in it.

The many sensory inputs we experience when we're in a space influence our psychological response to it. Each of those sights, smells, sounds, and tactile sensations is an opportunity to create a space in which people will thrive.

6

HUMAN REACTIONS TO
STATIC ELEMENTS

The basic architecture of a place and the furniture that fills it have as much of a psychological effect on us as the colors we choose for those spaces and the ways that we soundscape them. Columns, windows, and ceilings, for example, all have a big influence on what we think and do. It is difficult to change architectural elements of a space, so it is important to be clear about the psychological implications of various ceiling heights, window sizes, and other "built-in" features in a structure before a commitment is made to live or work in it. Furniture can be expensive, so working with existing furniture and using it to full advantage, or purchasing the most appropriate new furniture, can be nearly as important a consideration as using the basic structure of a space to its best advantage.

Designers can coincidentally create architecture that is advantageous psychologically, without having any training in place science. The ancient Greeks and Romans recognized that architectural forms exert powerful forces. They designed many civic buildings so that the relative proportion between the sizes of the elements (column heights, portico widths, etc.) pleased the people in those spaces. The Netherlands is gloomy during the winter, but there are many large windows in the homes in Dutch cities. Those windows catch every ray of sun available, which brightens the mood of people in those homes. The ceiling heights in some kitchen breakfast nooks are lower than in the rest of the room and that is appropriate psychologically—we interact differently in a space with a lowered ceiling. People with training in place science can develop spaces that are strong psychologically by plan and not by coincidence.

Do not despair, however, if you must work with a space that is architecturally less than optimal for the activities to take place there. Often you can take steps to counteract an inappropriate feature. For example, small spaces can make some people tense all of the time and other people tense part of the time. Large spaces can make some people tense all of the time and other people tense part of the time. Unusually shaped spaces can have the same effect. Color and texture can be used to change the apparent size and shape of spaces, however, as discussed in Chapter 5.

People have definite preferences for certain architectural features, and when they find them in a space, they are more comfortable and relaxed. However, architecture and design alone can never completely determine the experience we have in a place. For example, people generally prefer ceilings that are flat or that rise or fall 4 feet for every 12 feet along the flat plane of the floor. People also prefer that the walls of the spaces they are in meet at angles that have 90 or more degrees. Walls that meet at smaller angles are undesirable. We'd rather be in a room with windows than a room with no windows. We also prefer square rooms to rectangular ones. If we have a square office with windows and walls that meet at right angles but a tyrannical boss, however, we will be negative about our job.

We like places we're in to be similar to places we are familiar with, but we never want them to be so predictable that they're boring. We get bored if a place has no unexpected elements. In a public setting, this means that we like to wonder what might be beyond a gentle turn in an aisle we are following, being fairly certain that there's no possibility of anything really awful, such as a saber-toothed tiger, lurking there. We enjoy being tempted to move forward because something wonderful may happen. We hate to get lost in that public space, and landmarks help prevent that from happening. We like a space in which we can have a variety of experiences and we can be intrigued (and reassured) by sights, smells, sounds, and textures.

We are willing to put some effort into determining what's going on in a space, and we do like to be able to understand what is happening around us, but each of us has our own individual "effort limits." What we're doing influences how challenged we want to be by the place we're in. We like a place-based challenge, but we don't like being overwhelmed. There is one exception—if we're trying to get something done, whether we're cooking dinner at home or in the kitchenette in a motel, we prefer a completely typical design for the space. However, if we're up to something more emotional, such as enjoying time with our friends, an atypical space design seems like a better choice.

■ ENTRYWAYS

Entryways signal transition from one space into another (Alexander et al. 1977). Those transitions can be made memorable or uneventful.

With their wider field of vision, it is not surprising that men respond differently than women to transitional zones that lead from one space to the next. Men generally find an entryway that is more clearly sheltered more desirable than women do. Men tend to feel more exposed when entering an open space than women, although both genders would experience a more contained entryway as a cozy introduction to a space.

First impressions are powerful and enduring. What anyone sees from the entryway of a space is very significant. Our first view of a space determines how information about that space will be organized in long-term memory, and that influences how easy it is to remember information about that place later. For example, if our view from the main entrance of a home is of an unusual sofa, we will use the memory of that couch to organize information in our brain, and we may not remember accurately the design of tabletop lamps or the size of the room.

■ CEILINGS

Interior spaces have true ceilings, and when we're outdoors, less substantial structures and vegetation hover above our heads. The distance between the top of our head and the bottom of some other surface is important. Ceiling height has a big influence on us psychologically, and we have very different experiences in places with lower ceilings than we do in places with higher ceilings. Alexander, an architect and architectural theorist associated with the University of California, Berkeley, studied the meanings of varying ceiling heights in interior spaces and the influences that each of those heights can have psychologically.

Alexander and his colleagues (1977) found that lower ceiling heights create a more intimate place where we can relax. Higher ceilings put us in a different mood. They make a situation feel more formal and make people very attuned to behaving in the ways that others expect them to behave. Varying ceiling heights within a single space is desirable because we are able to find an area within that larger space with the ceiling height that is appropriate for the mood we desire. Alexander's work indicates that for larger, more public situations a ceiling height of 10 to 12 feet is appropriate. When the gathering is more social and less formal, lower ceiling heights are desirable, and Alexander suggests that they come down to between seven and nine feet. Other research has shown that ceiling heights of 10 feet are generally preferred in this situation. When two people are having a more intimate conversation, Alexander recommends that the ceilings be six to seven feet high, which is approximately the height of the canopy of a double bed. Six to seven feet is, however, fairly low for two people who are standing up. These suggested ceiling heights can be adjusted to be slightly higher in warm weather climates—so the heat can rise above the heads of space-users.

Alexander builds from his research and hypothesizes about how the ceiling heights he suggests came to feel appropriate to us. His most compelling explanations relate to interpersonal spacing and the way that sound bouncing off of a ceiling influences our apparent placement in a space. If we are having a conversation in a place with a high ceiling, the sound waves bouncing off of the ceiling make the people we are talking to sound as if they are farther away from us than they actually are. Since they sound that way, and we pay a lot of attention to audio feedback when determining relative position, we think of them as farther from us than they really are and treat them accordingly. When people speak to us from a distance, the situation is formal—people delivering prepared talks stand farther from us than old friends we've just run into in front of the drugstore. Conversely, sound waves bouncing off of a lower surface make the speaker seem closer, and when people are closer to us we are often having a more intimate or less formal conversation with them. Because of the sound wave bounce trick, we feel more of a personal bond with people speaking with us in a lower-ceilinged place. Consider a conversation between two friends—first in a formal ballroom and then in a booth at a restaurant where the ceiling has been lowered over the booth—they will have quite different conversations in each space.

> **DESIGN IMPLICATION**
>
> Ceiling heights must be appropriate for the activity planned in a space.

■ SEAT PLACEMENT

People prefer to sit with their back against something really solid, such as a wall or a sturdy room divider. Research has shown that seats like this in coffee shops are always the first ones chosen by customers (Waxman 2006). In public situations where we want to relax, for example while eating, we like to have our backs protected. The tables or booths in restaurants in which

FIGURE 6-1 ■ Diners will feel comfortable in these booths because nothing can sneak up behind them and turn *them* into lunch. The most prized spaces in restaurants are booths or chairs against walls that shield patrons' backs.
Copyright © iStockPhoto/Ivo Gretener.

patrons' backs are covered seat the happiest diners, and many cultures arrange seats around the exterior wall of a room. This is particularly likely to be the case when bulkier furniture is being used and it is a little more complex to shift in place to continually reassess what is going on just out of view. This desire to protect our backs makes sense. When we had less technology and were living on the open plains, there were plenty of hungry creatures ready to sneak up behind us and turn us into their lunch.

People talk to other people most readily when they can see each other's eyes—we are gregarious creatures and find it hard to pass up a convenient opportunity to socialize. It is hard for people to talk to others with whom they cannot make eye contact. To encourage discussion, seat people so that they can see each other's eyes, and if you wish to curtail interaction, do the reverse. You might want people to interact at a dinner party or at an informal meeting, so seats arranged in a circle or around a table would be appropriate. At a more formal meeting or any session where audience participation is not desirable, line seats up in rows of chairs that all face in one direction.

FIGURE 6-2 ■ Few people will be comfortable sitting in this bank lobby. The backs of people in these chairs are against a wall, but it is made of visually permeable glass.
Courtesy of Sally Augustin.

In many waiting rooms, it's best to have some seats where people can sit in family/friend groups and some places for people to sit alone. If someone is alone in a service setting, he often doesn't want to talk to other people there. If that person alone accidentally catches someone's eye because his seat faces her seat, he either has to make conversation, which he doesn't want to do, or ignore the other person, which is rude and creates tension. It's best if that person who is alone is not placed in an undesirable situation. In doctor's offices and in airports, people are often under a lot of stress, so "solo" seats are particularly important in those situations.

Particular "rules of engagement" apply when people sit around a table. Cross-corner seating that allows people to talk or not and make eye contact or not, as they want, is very desirable. Sitting across the corner from another person is great for a casual conversation or a situation in which people must work individually. It is also a good orientation for a discussion that may be stressful and during which people may want to occasionally break eye contact. Having nearby artwork or a window to which people can politely divert their eyes if they need a brief "interaction break" is a way for one person to break eye contact without seeming to evade or avoid another person.

FIGURE 6-3 ■ Seats can be arranged to encourage people not to talk by keeping them all facing the same direction. In certain situations, conversation among people in a space is counterproductive. Copyright © iStockPhoto/ Andrew Horwitz.

FIGURE 6-4 ■ The members of the Dutch parliament, who use this space, can easily engage each other in conversation. This sort of interaction between legislators is desirable. Copyright © iStockPhoto/Jan Kranendonk.

When we can't ignore the presence of other people, we are more interested in cooperating with them. People tell researchers that if they were competing with other people, they would sit across a table from them and that they would sit side by side with someone they wanted to cooperate with, but it turns out that it is much harder to compete with someone when you are looking him or her in the eye. People sitting across the table from each other are likely to end up working together to solve a problem, no matter what their initial intentions—it seems that when we look directly into someone else's eyes, our desire to get along overcomes our desire to conquer. The opposite situation occurs when people sit side by side or can't see each other clearly. Although people chose side-by-side seats because they intended to work together, it is easier to break eye contact (and thereby loosen that cooperative bond) when sitting side by side. As a result, often people sitting side by side become involved in more heated discussions than they intended.

We are also more likely to cooperate or work toward a common goal with someone who is closer to us as opposed to someone who is farther away from us. We're apt to compete with that person who is a little farther away. That competition can lead to higher productivity. In any context, appropriate interaction distances are culturally determined (see Chapter 8 for additional information). Chairs should be positioned (or "positionable") accordingly.

At a rectangular table, one of the seats at the short ends of the table is usually occupied by the group leader. This is known implicitly to everyone seated

FIGURE 6-5 ▨ Cross-corner seating can be useful in many situations, particularly during conversations that may cover difficult topics—participants can gracefully break eye contact. Copyright © iStockPhoto/ bubbalove.

FIGURE 6-6 This bench provides passersby with many seating and orientation options. They can sit so that it is easy for them to make eye contact with other people or on parts of the bench where comfortable seating postures preclude direct visual contact—all of which leads to different levels of intimacy, cooperation, etc.
Courtesy of Sally Augustin.

DESIGN IMPLICATION

Different seating configurations are best under different conditions. Provide a range of seating arrangements, or flexible seating, to accommodate these differences.

around the table, so no one but the leader does sit in the "leader spot." The leader will also sit so that he can see the door; monitoring who is entering and leaving is a way to control the session. During a meeting, attendees focus their attention on the leader. It is important that meeting rooms gracefully accommodate these unspoken rules about the way the space will be used. For example, if there is a window behind the seat the leader will use and bright sunlight comes through that window during the course of the day, it will be difficult for attendees to look at the leader, and that will distort the session.

At a round table, it is difficult not to be looking into everyone else's eyes and there is no leadership position at the table, so a round table is perfect for leaderless discussions or negotiations. A square table is almost as effective as a round table in these contexts.

Dining or conference tables that are wider than 5½ feet frustrate conversation, so they should not be used in situations in which true conversation is desired. When tables are wider than 5½ feet, the heads of even the people sitting directly across from each other are so far apart that people interact in a formal way (see the next section for more details and Chapter 8 for how these distances may vary by culture). If social conventions require that the pretense of an open conversation be maintained, but it is not actually desired, a conference table more than 5½ feet across may be the perfect gathering spot.

In general, when there is a physical barrier between us and the person we are talking to, there is more psychological separation between us as well—the situation is a little more formal, a little less collegial. A desk or an expanse of tabletop forms a physical barrier, for example. The situation is reversed when the "barrier furniture" disappears—for example, if we are sitting close to each other at a round conference table or in nearby armchairs. Sometimes more formal conversations are desired and other times more informal discussions are best, and several nearby furniture configurations make a space suitable for several types of conversations.

■ PERSONAL SPACE

Our personal space is a three-dimensional bubble that surrounds us and moves with us (Aiello 1987). This bubble can only be entered with permission, and its size is determined by our culture and the situation. When our personal space is violated, we experience stress. We don't do a very good job of judging how far we are from another person—and often our judgments are in the direction most likely to cause trouble, at least if we're North Americans. We think we're farther from other people than we actually are and think other people are closer to us than they actually are.

Our personal space bubble is really not just one sphere; it is really a series of concentric spheres, each of which denotes a zone that is appropriate for different situations. We could also call these interpersonal spacing zones. Hall (1982), decades ago, identified these zones as the intimate zone, which extends out to 18 inches from our bodies, a personal zone that is from 18 inches to 4 feet from our bodies (into which we invite personal and professional contacts whom we know well), a social zone that extends from 4 to 12 feet (that can be frequented by those we know less well and that is used in formal situations), and a zone that extends farther than 12 feet from us, which is used in formal group settings. Our personal space bubbles extend a little farther behind us than in front of us—which is one of the reasons that we like to sit with our backs to a wall. All national cultures have personal space zones. The distances presented above are accurate for North Americans; Chapter 8 provides information about the relative sizes of personal space zones for other cultures.

A number of factors need to be integrated to determine preferred personal spaces.

■ People police different-sized personal space zones around themselves based on their relationships with the other people nearby and their status relative to those other people in the area. The greater the difference in status between two people, the larger the distance they will remain from each other. When we are with our boss, our personal space bubble is larger than when we're with someone we've been dating for a while. We stand closer to old friends than recent acquaintances. Human beings have a fundamental, inalienable interest in the status of the person they are interacting with—whether they want to acknowledge

FIGURE 6-7 ▥ The executive assigned to this desk can choose to sit across the desk from guests or beside them at the conference table, as appropriate. Each of these seating configurations is useful in particular social situations.
Copyright © iStockPhoto/Don Bayley.

this or not. People of higher status should make sure that their chair is slightly farther from their subordinates than the distances that the subordinates maintain from each other.

- Gender also determines how far we stand from each other—male-male pairs in European cultures maintain the largest interpersonal distances, with female pairs interacting at closer distances. The spacing maintained by mixed-sex pairs depends on their relationship. If the relationship is not romantic, the distance maintained will be about midway between that maintained by the male-male pairs and the female-female pairs.

- Men generally have larger personal spaces than women in the same situation.

- Men are more concerned when their personal space is invaded from the front than women are. Women are more concerned about invasions from the side. Therefore, women respond more positively to unknown people who sit in front of them, while men have the same response to people who sit by their side.

- In general, men respond more negatively to personal space invasions than women. Women become just as stressed when they are too far from other people as men are when they are too close to other people.

- People who are taller have larger spaces than people who are shorter, and adults have larger personal space zones than children. So all else being equal, chairs should be placed farther apart in areas where people are generally taller than they are in areas where the population is, on average, shorter.

- Personal factors influence personal space. Anxious people maintain larger personal space zones than others—which has repercussions for the design of various sorts of waiting rooms, restaurants, and other public spaces. People who are introverted or worried about how they will be judged maintain larger personal distances. So do people who feel rushed, competitive, and anxious. Personal space zones increase with infirmity, which often is directly related to age.

- Culture comes into play to determine preferred personal space zones. Some cultures, primarily those from northern climates, prefer larger personal space zones than people from more southerly climates. Germans have larger personal space bubbles than Mexicans. More information about these sorts of cultural differences is reported in Chapter 8.

- Physical conditions affect the amount of personal space we want around us. At higher temperatures we are more likely to feel crowded than we are at lower temperatures. When it is darker, we also like to maintain larger distances than when there is more light.

- When about 60 percent of the seats in a space are occupied, people perceive it as full and will sit somewhere else, if possible. This will happen with students in cafeterias and people attending a church service, for example. People will look for other places to eat the first time that they find a section of a cafeteria 60 percent full, but people will not find another church until the one that they have been attending is consistently more than 60 percent full. Seating capacity should be provided to either keep people in a space or drive them from it. In some cases, more seats may be provided than would technically ever be needed to ensure that the 60 percent full threshold is not met.

Our personal space bubbles are three-dimensional and slightly pliable. If our personal space in one direction is restricted, the other dimensions in which it extends move out—the bubble deforms but it doesn't break. If we must stand or sit closer to other people than is desirable, it is better if the ceilings in that space are higher. Waiting in line to buy tickets in a low-ceilinged space is very unpleasant.

It seems that when the ease of escape diminishes, we want more space between us and other people. When ceilings are lower or we are farther from a door or window, we want more personal space to encircle us. We have larger personal space needs when we are in a corner than when we are in the center of a room and when we are indoors as opposed to outdoors. Dimmer light leads to larger personal spaces between people who are not romantically involved. Our personal spaces are generally a little larger when we are sitting side by side than in any other configuration and when a room is generally narrower.

Breaking eye contact; looking down, away, or to the side of a person who is too close; and changing body orientation are the universal responses to invasions of personal space. When we are forced to be too close to each other because of limited "real estate"—say in an elevator or on a crowded subway train—we make sure to avoid catching the eye of people who are intruding on our personal space. Sometimes the related gyrations are quite impressive. Providing things to look at, which we can at least pretend interest us, makes these situations less awkward.

Being too close to other people is a problem, but so is being too far away from them. Women are more sensitive to the social awkwardness of being farther from other people than the situation justifies than men are. All of the correction mechanisms in play when people are too close to each other are also used to reduce the real or apparent distance we are from other people, just in reverse.

DESIGN IMPLICATION

The spaces that you are creating must recognize the personal space needs of their most frequent users.

Spaces can be designed to make people feel comfortable, regardless of the users' personal space sizes. A place must accommodate all personal space bubble variations. Chairs and other furnishings should be mobile to allow the appropriate distances to be maintained. Furniture on wheels helps, but if furniture is lightweight, the wheels are not necessary. Moveable furniture isn't useful if the design of a space doesn't provide areas to move it into. Columns, pillars, half walls, and similar features can prevent chairs from being positioned comfortably and people from sitting/standing at desired distances from each other. Architecture can also help people maintain comfortable distances from each other. Using several floor levels in a space reduces personal space invasions—those different floor levels require that people maintain greater distances from others.

It's not possible to estimate how many people will willingly share a table or a sofa until the relationships between those people and the conditions that bring them together are known.

Providing people with some sort of visual image that they can focus on instead of each other creates a graceful way for people to cope with tight spaces they are experiencing. When there is some sort of focal point in a space—a painting, a fish tank, a burning fire, or an antique, for example—people have a ready topic for discussion as well. This makes it much easier for them to socialize with each other, if necessary or desirable. The television monitors in use in elevators are popular during rush hours! It is useful if these conversation starters/activity generators are in a central location and visually accessible from the entire space.

▨ SEEN OR NOT SEEN

When we're doing something that is easy for us, often because we've done it lots of times before, we actually perform better if there are people watching us—which means even when we don't have any visual privacy (Aiello and Doulhitt 2001). When we are doing something that is more difficult for us, for example, something we haven't practiced frequently, having other people watch us is a problem and harms our performance. That is why we write or perform other thoughtful tasks better while isolated but spur ourselves to increased speeds when we ride our bicycles together.

DESIGN IMPLICATION

Think about the relationship between task difficulty and the number of onlookers when planning a space.

▨ CROWDING

When we feel crowded, we feel stressed, and we don't do whatever we're supposed to be doing too well and we don't win any citizenship awards either (Baum and Paulus 1987; see Chapter 4 for details on what happens to humans when they are stressed).

Whether we feel crowded or not depends on the number of people in a place and whether we feel our personal space has been invaded, which is determined by how close people are to us. When we are crowded, people will be too close to us, but when people are too close, we are not necessarily crowded. If the only other person in a large space stands uncomfortably close, our personal space is invaded but we are not crowded. If we are in a large sea of cubicles, and everyone is at the closest limits of our personal space, say 18 inches, we will probably feel crowded, even though our personal space may not technically be invaded. Crowding is an individual interpretation of a situation.

In the same conditions, men are more likely to feel crowded than women, and they experience more stress when they feel crowded than women do. These gender differences start to become obvious by the time boys and girls are nine years old. Since men have better peripheral vision than women, spaces can seem more spacious to them, depending on the placement of other people in a space, which may be one of the reasons that they are more apt to spread out and recline on pieces of furniture than women.

The physical design of the space we are in influences how crowded we feel there. Rooms on higher floors are perceived as lighter and less crowded than identical rooms on lower floors. People who live in high-rise buildings feel more crowded than people who do not live in such buildings, but feelings of crowding are reduced for people who live on the upper stories of these tall buildings—possibly because they have views that residents of lower floors do not. Whenever rooms/apartments are arranged along long corridors and people are therefore more aware of how many other people share their floor, residents feel more crowded than if rooms/apartments are arranged along shorter corridor sections.

Lighter, brighter spaces are, in general, perceived as less crowded, whether those higher illumination levels are produced by artificial lighting, daylighting, or the use of light colors or patterns on the walls. Places where people may be crowded together, on occasion, should be painted lighter colors. Lighting design can also be used to influence room size—when only the walls of a room are lit, the space seems larger than if the walls are darker because only the middle of the room is lit. Even light levels throughout a space make it seem larger. Smaller rooms need proportionately larger windows than larger rooms to be comfortable. Spaces seem less crowded if they are mirrored.

Even if the number of square feet in the rooms being compared is identical, we feel less crowded when we're in a room with higher ceilings and when we're in a space with straight, as opposed to curved, walls—although we do prefer curved shapes in furniture and other objects. The same space can thus be comfortably used by more people if the walls in it are straight instead of curved. Rooms with bookcases with nothing on them also seem larger; this is true even when the walls of the rooms being compared are actually the same distance apart and the bookshelves are encroaching on otherwise usable floor space.

If we're forced to live in a high-density situation, the more zones (from public to private) in our home, the less psychological distress and social withdrawal we experience.

Escape options and distractions decrease perceptions of crowding. Not surprisingly, places seem less crowded if they seem to provide clear escapes through doors and windows. If there are desirable distractions, such as plants or furniture, at the edges of rooms, spaces seem less crowded than rooms without those distractions. At least when we know the other people in a space, we feel less crowded when we are facing toward each other than when we are facing away from each other, which has repercussions for the way furniture should be arranged in a smaller space.

A rectangular room seems larger than a square room, even if both are actually the same number of square feet—although we generally prefer square rooms to rectangular ones.

Even how long we have been in a space influences how large it seems to us. The longer we've been somewhere, the smaller it seems. People who have been in a room for as little as half an hour find it smaller than those who have just arrived. It's also true that after we've been using a place for a while, it starts to bore us.

Neat spaces seem less crowded than messy ones. This is true even if the two spaces in question are actually the same size and contain the same stuff. An ordered space is easier for our eyes to review and our brain to understand and seems larger than a disordered jumble. Similarly, putting more furniture in a room makes the space seem smaller than it did before all of the furniture arrived.

Paths seem longer when they turn more, when they intersect with other paths, or when the carpeting on them changes. So the apparent size of a sea of cubicles, for example, can appear larger when the circulation through it is more organic. Making a sea of cubicles seem larger is generally a good thing because firms often seat as many employees into a space as possible to save on rent. Paths seem longer when traveling along them is boring, so changing artwork and other details along a circulation space regularly can make walking along them seem quicker—which can be useful in spaces like workplaces where not every needed facility can be located nearby. When we are walking toward something that we find desirable, we pay less attention to the area we are walking through, which has design repercussions. Often objects that put us in a good mood, such as desserts in a buffet line, are visible in the distance, and any changes in floor levels, for example, on the way to those desserts can be particularly hazardous. Distance can be good in some cases—when unconventional art is placed farther away, people respond to it more positively than if the art is closer to them.

We can add physical barriers in a space to reduce crowding in Western societies (see Chapter 8 for information about how national culture influences whether people feel crowded). Those barriers can be made out of furniture of various sorts, plants, or decorative elements such as artwork and pillars. Chairs with arms provide neat space boundaries that chairs without arms and coaches lack. Adding windows also can reduce feelings of crowding.

When people are warned that they will be crowded (or encounter any other stress, for that matter), the psychological ramifications of being in that situation are reduced considerably. So when all else fails, at least warn people about upcoming tight quarters.

> **DESIGN IMPLICATION**
>
> More people are not always better—but too few can also be a problem. Apply room size-distorting techniques to influence how big a space seems to be so that it feels less crowded or more populated, as necessary.

■ TERRITORIES

Humans have personal territories (Brown 1987). A territory is a controlled area of any size; a territory can be a single seat or a multi-acre estate. They help us maintain the level of privacy we desire and preserve our sense of who we are as people. We tell ourselves and others who we are through the way that we personalize our territory. Territories teach us about other people through the ways their owners customize them, so we know more about how we should relate to others when we encounter them. Clear territories help us know who controls a space and who is in charge there. People feel more powerful in their own territory. Men maintain larger territories than women do.

It is harder to maintain a territory when there are lots of doors in a space. Physical features that clearly mark territorial boundaries (such as cubicle walls) smooth the whole process of maintaining a territory, as does ready visual access to these boundaries. Boundaries can be walls, but they can also be rugs, changes in paint color, or variations in ceiling height.

Groups need territories just as individuals do. Families are groups, and it is important that there be spaces in any home that they see as their own group space. This group space, which is often a family room or living room, is just as important for the psychological health and well-being of this *group* as individual areas are to family member's *individual* well-being—and if we are members of better functioning groups, we are happier. We are also part of employee groups at work. Group rooms at work are just as important to our lives as family gathering spots are at home. Group territories can have the same sorts of physical boundaries as individual territories.

> **DESIGN IMPLICATION**
>
> Recognize that people will maintain territories in the spaces you are creating, and design so those territories do not distort your plan for the space.

■ DESIGNING WITH NATURE

Human beings are most comfortable in spaces that capture the essence of our primordial homes (Kellert 2005). We can relax in them and restock our mental energy there. The places where we lived before we'd developed too

FIGURE 6-8 ■ Calm water has a soothing psychological influence on people, which may be useful where this pool is located, directly outside a hospital. Community Hospital of the Monterey Peninsula, Monterey, CA. Photo by Lawrence Anderson/ Courtesy of HOK.

FIGURE 6-9 ■ This hospital lobby incorporates many natural materials, which is a biophilic design strategy. Biophilic design recognizes the important relationship between human beings and their natural environment. Curt Knoke Photography, Shawano Medical Center, Copyright 2007, courtesy of Kahler Slater.

many conveniences (or to be truthful, any real conveniences) had certain distinct features. Even though we're many generations removed from our prehistoric past, those distinctive aspects of our first homes continue to please us immensely, make us feel more satisfied with a space, and put us in good moods.

The biophilic design movement focuses on recreating desirable aspects of our early homes in current spaces (Kellert 2005). Biophilic design is a holistic approach that influences both architectural and interior design decisions. It acknowledges the importance of environmental responsibility, but moves far beyond being "green." Biophilic design recognizes the psychological satisfaction inherent in living in spaces that use natural design themes (colors, forms, patterns of movement, etc.). When we incorporate elements from nature's stylebook into current places, we mimic nature, either overtly or subtly.

Stephen Kellert (2005) and Judith Heerwagen (with Gregory 2008) have written extensively about designing with nature in mind. At a fundamental level, biophilic design can be thought of as including natural materials and plants in a space as well as forms that are found in nature, such as archways that look like branches meeting overhead, circular staircases that swirl like seashells, columns that look like tree trunks, and carved floral ornamentation.

More sophisticated biophilic design moves beyond direct to more symbolic representations of nature, and also incorporates abstract aspects of the experience of being in nature as described carefully by Heerwagen and Gregory (2008). In nature, there is often, for example, a sense of smooth movement (a breeze blows and a tree sways, a brook moves along, the sun shifts and so do shadows, etc.) that may be missing in current interior environments. A fountain or a mobile can add movement to a space. Design also becomes more satisfying to humans when abstractions from natural forms are used in a space. Humans enjoy being in spaces where they feel protected but from which they can look out over the world around them (see the description of prospect and refuge in Chapter 2). That effect can be mimicked in interior spaces using balconies that survey atria, inglenooks, and combinations of lighting levels and ceiling heights.

In nature, sensory experiences are rich and evolve over time (Heerwagen and Gregory 2008). Natural spaces are said to be "sensory rich" because they

FIGURE 6-10 ■ The natural forms in this church form a stark contrast to the lines of the modern office tower behind it. Use of shapes and other design elements that are reminiscent of the natural world is a principle of biophilic design.
Copyright © iStockPhoto/Daniel Stein.

FIGURE 6-11 ■ This mobile adds a moving element to its indoor environment, which is consistent with biophilic design. Copyright © iStockPhoto/Paul Giamou.

appeal to more than one sense; this complete sensory package is often missing in modern interiors. Compare the experience of walking across a modern lobby with that of strolling across a forest clearing as Heerwagen and Gregory (2008) have done. Walking across that lobby you see a range of different things (the surfaces on the walls, floors, and ceilings; signage; and the security desk, for example). The texture beneath your feet never changes, however, and all smells have probably been engineered out the area. Music is sometimes broadcast in lobbies and the footsteps of other visitors may also be heard. In the forest clearing there can be dramatic differences in light levels and a large range of plants and animals to catch your eye. The sounds of your footsteps will blend into the natural sounds, such as the wind and the calls of birds. Textures will change under your feet and fingertips, and a mixture of smells (some good, some not so good) will keep your nose occupied. All interior spaces can, with care, be designed to provide the same full sensory experience as the meadow—for example, a carved frieze will look different at each viewing, as it is lit in different ways. In a natural environment, this variability in sensory experiences is compounded through regular, cyclical changes (e.g., daylight varies in color over the course of a day). Cyclical changes can also be incorporated into interior spaces.

Not only are natural places filled with a variety of satisfying experiences, but they are also filled with information (Heerwagen and Gregory 2008). That information is available at different levels. The overall plan of a space can communicate something, but focusing on specific elements in the space presents even more information.

Many features of good biophilic design were recognized long before the phrase was adopted. These include using daylight to illuminate an interior, creating spaces such as inglenooks off of larger rooms, and making humans feel comfortable in a space by making it neither too complicated nor too dull. Since antiquity, good designers have incorporated rhythm, harmony, and balance into structures, as biophilic design experts such as Judith Heerwagen would suggest.

Biophilic design is unusual in recognizing that a built space must be rooted in its site (Kellert 2008). That connection can be created by using local materials and responding to the ecology of the region, as well as the history and culture of those living nearby, for example.

DESIGN IMPLICATION

Incorporate direct and symbolic natural elements and experiences into the design of spaces you are creating.

Windows design influences how effectively we connect with the natural world. Bloomer (2008) feels that when people look out over nature through large picture windows, they feel no connection to what they are seeing, that they are as distanced from it as humans are from animals at a zoo. He recommends detailing window reveals and mullions with patterns reminiscent of nature or with a rhythm (created through size, for example). These sorts of window reveals and mullions invite touch. Adding "touch" or haptic appeal to the visual power of the scene seen through the window increases the positive effects of the window and links viewers to outside nature.

Natural materials age and develop (leather upholstery changes through use), and that may be one of the reasons that we find them so desirable.

The architecture and furniture design of a place has a significant psychological influence on us. Careful consideration of these aspects of a space forestalls costly reconfigurations—a space is psychologically strong and viable at first use.

FIGURE 6-12 ■ These windows have the sort of detailing suggested by Bloomer (2008). That detailing links people inside the spaces with the world they are surveying.
Courtesy of Sally Augustin.

7 PLACE DESIGN THAT REFLECTS INDIVIDUAL PERSONALITY AND ORGANIZATIONAL CULTURE

People have personalities and groups have cultures. Personality and culture are both worldviews. They are systems for understanding and action that influence the physical environments in which people are successful.

This chapter discusses organizational culture, which is the code of thought and behavior that a defined group of people follows. National cultures, in contrast, characterize citizens of a particular country (a more complete definition of national culture is provided in Chapter 8). We can identify the same sorts of organizational cultures in every national society. The ways that each of those organizational cultures is expressed does vary from country to country, however. In Chapter 8, we will discuss how national culture tweaks the way that our organizational culture should be recognized in our physical environment.

In a world where parts inventories are not a concern, each space assigned to a specific person would be consistent with his or her personality, as described in the first section of this chapter, and each group space would be completely consistent with the culture of that group. Since we do not live in a perfect world, it is best to let organizational culture drive space design for groups of people, with individual spaces customized for personality, if possible.

■ PERSONALITY AND PLACE

When a space will be used by a single person or a group of people with similar personalities, user(s)' personal factors should guide design. When place design is consistent with the personalities of the people who will use that space, the place created addresses users' psychological needs. Matching place to personality on a larger scale (more than three or four people) or when the personalities of the people who will use a space are not similar, evolves into coordinating organizational culture and place. People doing similar jobs often have similar personalities, which can streamline the workplace design process. If you are creating space for a group of workers, test their personalities using the questions included in this chapter to verify they are indeed similar.

Personality affects how we interact with our world and what aspects of those interactions we enjoy (Little 1987). Personality is a long-term characteristic of who a person is—it is very different from mood. Moods vary from minute to minute, but personality changes very slowly, if at all, over the course of a lifetime. In addition to personality, we each have a consistent sensory hierarchy and a dominant sense. Our particular dominant sense is the most immediate pathway to our emotional core. Everyone relates to the spaces around them in a unique way even though there are consistencies among personality types. People's personality, their place history, and their personal sensory hierarchy determine the best spaces for them.

Personality has many facets. For example, people draw energy from within themselves or from the world around them. They also feel more or less in control of their destiny, and those personality factors, among others, influence the spaces in which individuals flourish.

An individual's personality determines whether he should furnish his living room with more sofas or chairs, and whether those sofas should have generally straighter lines or generally curvier lines, for example. Personality determines whether nubby or smooth upholstery is best. Personal factors govern how to arrange the chairs on the patio and what to do with the inherited antiques. Personality affects whether the idea of wrapping the walls of their living room with shiny silks makes people feel exhilarated or exhausted. It influences whether they relish the idea of creating unique spaces within their house, or if they are happier when the interior design of their home is just slightly different from their neighbor's. It determines whether they are clutter-enablers or clutter-busters.

You should use the knowledge that you will obtain about user personality in this chapter when you apply the information from Chapter 5 about how people respond psychologically to their sensory experiences. In Chapter 5 you learned about certain colors that are energizing, for example. If you find that the person who will use a space you are developing is introverted and visually dominant, you can use this new information to make sure that colors are used with appropriate care in her home.

Different facets of personality provide different details about the environments in which people will be happiest (Little 1987). Questions I have written to uncover place-related aspects of personality and ways of interacting with the external world lead off the subsections in this chapter. The questions provided should be answered by the people who will use the spaces you are designing. Each set of questions is followed by a discussion of how to interpret answers to them. Personality factors are discussed in declining order of importance (based on my experience) for place design.

Personality data are prone to misuse. It is easy for people without much background in the area to decide that some personality profiles are more desirable or more appropriate than others. It's a good idea not to share one person's profile with others and to view the personality information you collect as extremely confidential.

Factor 1—Gathering Energy

Which word or phrase in each of the pairs below describes you better? Even if neither of the options describes you exactly, one will come closer than the other.

A	B
1. public	private
2. enjoy dinner with a few friends	enjoy large parties
3. select homes with fewer interior walls	select homes with more interior walls
4. need lots of time alone	don't need time alone
5. lively	quiet

Give yourself one point for extraversion for each of the following that you have selected: 1A, 2B, 3A, 4B, and 5A. Give yourself one point for introversion for each of the following that you have selected: 1B, 2A, 3B, 4A, and 5B.

Extraversion points:

Introversion points: (Each set of responses can also be tallied by the researcher.)

Some people draw energy from the people and things around them, and other people are drained by being around other people. Carl Jung, an early psychologist interested in personality, focused on understanding how humans differ on this continuum (Myers et al. 2003). He called people who draw energy from the world around them extraverts. People who are drained by the world around them and who draw energy from within themselves are introverts. Introverts do a better job of detecting incoming information than extraverts. That is why they are so often overwhelmed by it. People who are more extraverted relish being in sensory rich spaces with multiple vibrant colors, louder and faster music, more extreme textures, curving paths, and dramatic incense. Introverts definitely do not. Extraverts like spaces that change; introverts are not keen on spaces that differ over time. Extraverts are more interested in displaying objects that tell other people things about themselves that they find important—after all, that might spark conversation!

Introverts and extraverts have different conversation norms. Extraverts like to be close to other people and to establish and maintain eye contact with them. When they are furnishing their homes, extraverts prefer to use more couches in their living rooms than introverts. Extraverts favor more open seating arrangements—that means there aren't pieces of furniture between people who are carrying on a conversation. An extravert would not be pleased to find a tall sturdy table between himself and a conversation partner—but an introvert would. Movable seats are popular with introverts—that way they can back away from an extravert who has strayed into their personal no-go zone, which is smaller than that of the extravert. Introverts like other people; they're not social pariahs. They simply want to be able to interact with others as they choose to do so. Introverts prefer to sit in some sort of furniture arrangement that allows them to gracefully look away if they want to break eye contact. A window or painting in view provides just such an opportunity. So does a semicircular arrangement of chairs, as opposed to a more circular arrangement. An introvert prefers an oblong table to a round one; round tables encourage interpersonal interaction and they make extraverts very happy, but all that forced togetherness can make an introvert tense. Introverts prefer wider walkways than extraverts—they make it easier to look away from approaching people, if necessary. They are also more interested in blocking sound from other people than extraverts are.

Extraverts choose more open home floor plans, where one space blends into the next. Introverts prefer homes with more clearly defined, separate spaces for particular activities and people. In general, extraverts prefer homes with fewer walls where people can move easily throughout all areas, public and more private. Introverts prefer to have a private space in their home.

Extraverts engaged in independent, heads-down work won't keep on task for long if they have the opportunity to make casual contact with someone and start up a conversation. When extraverts make eye contact with someone,

FIGURE 7-1 ■ This home has an open floor plan of the sort that would appeal to an extravert. Copyright © iStockPhoto/Jorge Salcedo.

it's hard for them to resist talking with them. Extraverts who need to concentrate must sit so that they can't see other people or overhear conversations that they might feel compelled to participate in. These isolated spaces need the high level of stimulation that extraverts crave, however. Putting an extravert in a beige box will motivate him to find additional environmental stimulation, probably by getting up and walking around. Trying to sit still and concentrate just doesn't work for an extravert. Sitting still without adequate input from the environment makes him distracted and tense—and unable to concentrate. Radio programs that would be distracting to introverts, for example, help extraverts stay focused. A less stimulating environment is great for an introvert—they do a fine job of entertaining themselves.

Factor 2—Processing Information

Which word or phrase in each of the pairs below describes you or your attitudes better? Even if neither of the options describes you exactly, one will come closer than the other.

A	B
1. uncomfortable with ambiguity	comfortable with ambiguity
2. don't notice subtle details	notice subtle details
3. intuitive	straightforward
4. note trends	ignore trends
5. bad at repairing things	good at repairing things

Give yourself one "explicit processor" point for each of the following that you have selected: 1A, 2B, 3B, 4B, and 5B. Give yourself one "implicit operator" point for each of the following that you have selected: 1B, 2A, 3A, 4A, and 5A.

Explicit processor points:

Implicit operator points:

People absorb information from their surroundings in different ways (Myers et al. 2003). Some are more likely to take in information in a straightforward way, and others are more likely to put their own spin on the situation. The first set of people are "explicit processors" and the second set are "implicit operators."

Explicit processors (*explicits* from here on out) prefer symmetrical floor plans, at least in their homes, while implicit operators (*implicits*) enjoy being in spaces that are more unconventional. Explicits enjoy more classic styles in furniture, while implicits are more adventurous in their decorating tastes. Explicits are more apt to choose to live in colonial farmhouse-style interiors, for example, while implicits are more likely to select contemporary or modern interiors.

Explicits are more aware of their immediate surroundings than implicits, who are likely to be distracted from their immediate sensory experiences by mental associations with their surroundings. While an explicit is deciding whether something is hard or soft, an implicit will be deciding whether it is like the one in his grandma's house (Tieger and Barron 2007).

When implicits add something to their environment, their mental associations with it must be appropriately relaxing, or inspirational, or welcoming, or whatever the space they are designing requires. Explicits are more concerned with how useful an item is, and implicits are more concerned with the aesthetics of an object. Implicits are more likely to think about a space holistically, while explicits focus on individual components of a place.

Factor 3—Managing Life

Which word or phrase in each of the pairs below describes you better? Even if neither of the options describes you exactly, one will come closer than the other.

A	**B**
1. more organized	less organized
2. conscientious	adaptable
3. may make decisions without some information	well informed when making decisions
4. more casual	more formal
5. spontaneous	premeditated

Give yourself one "planner" point for each of the following that you have selected: 1A, 2A, 3B, 4B, and 5B. Give yourself one "improviser" point for each of the following that you have selected: 1B, 2B, 3A, 4A, and 5A.

Planner points:

Improviser points:

Myers and Briggs, the authors of the popular personality test, describe some people as more concerned about living organized lives; these people are "judgers" in their system but "planners" here. People who prefer to live more spontaneously are "perceivers" in the Myers-Briggs system but "improvisers" here (Meyers et al. 2003). Planners need spaces that allow them to organize their things and be efficient; improvisers prefer spaces that are more casual and also more original and lighthearted than the sorts of spaces desired by planners.

Improvisers aren't that organized, although they may try to be (Tieger and Barron 2007). Improvisers keep their lives in order with physical reminders of various sorts, so they need space to arrange or display these reminders. This may mean that they need bulletin board space to pin up bills to be paid and counter space for piles, for example. Since improvisers are less organized, they tend to be more frantic as deadlines approach, so their workspaces cannot be too stimulating. Improvisers are also more likely to lose focus than planners, so their environments must have the capacity to shield them from distracting elements.

Improvisers tend to gather more physical material before making a decision than planners (Tieger and Barron 2007), so they need space to lay out all that stuff while making a decision. They also need a place to store all the collected items once the decision is made.

Improvisers keep a lot of things that "might be useful in the future" (Tieger and Barron 2007), so they need more space than planners for clothes, household objects, and "stuff" in general.

Factor 4—Reacting to Events

Which phrase in each of the pairs below describes you better? Even if neither of the options describes you exactly, one will come closer than the other.

A	B
1. startle easily	do not startle easily
2. prefer quieter background music	prefer louder background music
3. prefer silence when concentrating	silence not necessary when concentrating
4. sensitive to strong scents	not sensitive to strong scents
5. can sleep through "anything"	easily woken by noises and lights

Give yourself one point for more environmental sensitivity for each of the following that you have selected: 1A, 2A, 3A, 4A, and 5B. Give yourself one point for less environmental sensitivity for each of the following that you have selected: 1B, 2B, 3B, 4B, and 5A.

More environmental sensitivity points:

Less environmental sensitivity points:

People who are more sensitive to sensory input need environments that reduce or blunt the stimulation they experience. For example, more sensitive people should make sure that their bedrooms have heavy drapes that can be closed at night so morning sunlight and singing birds do not wake them up too early. They also benefit from the use of sound-absorbing materials in their homes and offices—they should carpet floors, for example, and purchase upholstered furniture. Background white noise, either official white noise or quietly played music they enjoy, should be available in their bedrooms. It will mask noises that may hinder falling asleep. This same soundtrack is useful in spaces where they need to concentrate, such as in their office.

People who are more sensitive to environmental stimuli prefer to study or do thoughtful work in an isolated or screened spot. In this way they are like introverts. Sights and sounds not related to their project at hand are more distracting to these people than to people not as sensitive. Simply plugging in an iPod and looking into a corner will not necessarily provide a thought-conducive environment, however. The music can be distracting, and the corner view is cognitively stiffling.

Restorative experiences are particularly important to people who are sensitive to environmental stimuli. Views of nature, fish tanks, and flames replenish stocks of mental energy. More information about restorative experiences is included in Chapter 4.

Introversion is distinct from environmental sensitivity. Introverts *want* to be in less sensorially rich environments, while people who are environmentally sensitive *need* to shield themselves from sensations they find undesirable. Introversion is a broader concept than environmental sensitivity.

Factor 5—Directing Life

Which word or phrase in each of the pairs below describes you or your attitudes better? Even if neither of the options describes you exactly, one will come closer than the other.

	A	B
1.	life success is determined by chance	life success is not determined by chance
2.	fate determines happiness	happiness is not determined by fate
3.	superstitious	not superstitious
4.	long-range planning is useful	long-range planning is pointless
5.	my life is controlled by others	I control my own life

Give yourself one "control own fate" point for each of the following that you have selected: 1B, 2B, 3B, 4A, and 5B. Give yourself one "controlled by fate" point for each of the following that you have selected: 1A, 2A, 3A, 4B, and 5A.

"Control own fate" points:

"Controlled by fate" points:

Individuals can feel more or less in control of their own destiny. People who fall more heavily into the "control own fate" category require more flexibility in their environments than people "controlled by fate." People who feel they control their own destiny prefer to modify their places to meet their current needs. They select furniture they can move and use several different ways. They enjoy owning a table that can be set at several different heights and that can function as a coffee table, a buffet table, and a craft area, for example. They prefer the same sorts of open seating arrangements (in office environments) that extraverts do.

People who feel that they control their fate prefer environments with more linear elements, while people who feel controlled by fate prefer spaces that are more curvilinear, according to a classic study by Juhasz and Paxson (1978). No organic, marshmallow-soft sofas for people who feel they control their fate; save those for the people who feel controlled by fate. Similarly, people who feel that they control their own fate prefer curtains with vertical pleats that fall to the floor to looping curtains pulled to one side with tiebacks.

People who feel controlled by fate are more likely to create a particular space and then to continue to use it once it becomes familiar. They are also likely to have a number of personal mementos of various sorts that they want to display, so ample areas to display these items should be included in spaces that belong to them.

Individuals who feel more in control of their fate are more concerned with preserving the natural environment than those who are not. This has repercussions for material selections and incorporation of environmentally responsible design principles in place plans.

FIGURE 7-2 ■ This sort of rectilinear environment would appeal to people who feel that they control their own fate. HCA Stone Oak Hospital, San Antonio, TX. Courtesy of HOK.

Factor 6—Monitoring Others

Which phrase in each of the pairs below describes you better? Even if neither of the options describes you exactly, one will come closer than the other.

A	B
1. liven up a party	don't liven up a party
2. can befriend anyone	find it difficult to start friendships
3. comfortable in public	more comfortable in private situations
4. modify behavior for different situations	don't modify behavior for different situations
5. sometimes my thoughts don't match my actions	my thoughts and actions coincide

FIGURE 7-3 ■ This space, with its many curved elements, would appeal to people who feel that their lives are controlled by fate. Copyright © iStockPhoto/laughingmango.

Give yourself one point for higher external monitoring for each of the following that you have selected: 1A, 2A, 3A, 4A, and 5A. Give yourself one point for lower external monitoring for each of the following that you have selected: 1B, 2B, 3B, 4B, and 5B.

Higher external monitoring points:

Lower external monitoring points:

Higher external monitors regulate their behavior based on information they receive from their social environments, while lower external monitors find similar sorts of guidance within themselves. The symbolic messages that objects send are of paramount important to higher external monitors. Higher external monitors may be very attuned to what is currently fashionable, and they, in general, are quick to copy behaviors of others that they find pleasant or useful. They are very motivated to make a good impression and act in a way that others feel is appropriate. Lower external monitors are less concerned about other people's opinions.

Factor 7—Seeking Exhilaration

Which phrase in each of the pairs below describes you or your attitudes better? Even if neither of the options describes you exactly, one will come closer than the other.

A	**B**
1. more variety in life is desirable	less variety in life is desirable
2. dangerous places are exhilarating	dangerous places are scary
3. visiting new places is exciting	visiting new places is unpleasant
4. like riding on roller coasters	dislike riding on roller coasters
5. driving faster is more fun	driving faster is not more fun

Give yourself one point for higher sensation seeking for each of the following that you have selected: 1A, 2A, 3A, 4A, and 5A. Give yourself one point for lower sensation seeking for each of the following that you have selected: 1B, 2B, 3B, 4B, and 5B.

Higher sensation seeking points:

Lower sensation seeking points:

Some people are more exhilarated by strong sensory inputs than others. People who get more positive charge from exciting activities are sensation seekers. These people enjoy being on roller coasters or visiting new places.

People who have a stronger desire for sensations they find exhilarating enjoy being in more sensorially intense places, with louder levels of background noise, stronger scents, brighter colors, and stronger lighting, for example. They also categorize messy rooms more positively than neat rooms, while people who are less interested in sensation seeking do the reverse. In the less neat conditions, a larger amount of information is conveyed visually; there is a more varied range of objects visible. Messier spaces are also more visually complex—ideal conditions for the high sensation seeker. Low sensation seekers prefer more orderly types of environments, containing less varied assortments of items. Low sensation seekers tend to feel that spaces are larger than high sensation seekers do because they focus less on the objects within the spaces and more on the room volumes themselves.

People higher on sensation seeking are more likely to multitask than people who score lower on this dimension.

High sensation seekers have a bias toward looking at the right side of anything or any space, while the general population is biased toward the left side of a space (i.e., they see the middle as more toward the left than it actually is). This means that high sensation seekers are more apt to favor items toward the right and to place favored items toward the right.

Although sensation-seeking may seem to overlap significantly with extraversion-introversion and environmental sensitivity, research has shown that it is a separate psychological construct.

People living in cities develop a higher set point for environmental stimulation than people who don't live in cities. As a result, their environments generally should be more colorful, more fragrant, and louder than those of country dwellers. Residents of either area can have different preferences for exhilarating experiences. The repercussions of differences in accustomed stimulation levels are particularly apparent when both city and country dwellers move to the suburbs—people from the city find their new homes unpleasantly quiet, while people who are used to living in the country find them unpleasantly loud.

Additional Personal Factors to Consider

Some people are more interested than others in showing where the space that belongs to them begins and ends. We can call them more border conscious and other people less border conscious. When people or groups are more border conscious, it should be easier to determine the edge of the spaces they control—with changes in carpets, different paint colors, or walls, for example. Using a tool that Kaya and Burgess (2007) have developed, you can tell if an individual or a group (average the individual results across the entire group) is more or less concerned about having spaces they control clearly delineated. The Kaya and Burgess test requires individuals to circle their preferred seats on a floor plan of a classroom. The classroom plan should show a focal wall, such as one with a whiteboard, and parallel rows of tables with individual chairs facing that wall. People who choose seats at the ends of those tables are more concerned about their territory being clearly marked than people who choose chairs in the middle of the rows.

Individuals vary in their need for uniqueness, i.e., the importance to them of being different from other people, for example. People who want to distinguish themselves from others are particularly interested in doing so via actions that society feels are very expressive of who we *really* are. Our clothes and the places that we use (e.g., homes, cubicles, cars) are generally felt to represent our true selves. Therefore, people who want to be unique will want to distinguish themselves through place design. This quest for "differentness" can be identified by visiting places currently in use by the people who will "own" the space in development.

People can differ on other aspects of personality that relate to place design, but there are only so many personal factors that you can consider when designing a space.

The average personality in the United States' population is changing. People are becoming more extraverted, on average. Since extraverts flourish in different environments than introverts, namely one with more intense and faster-changing sensory inputs, as discussed above, this means that more complex environments are becoming popular, and more places to socialize will evolve. Increasing people's ability to socialize may not be desirable in all situations, however. In workplaces, for example, increased visual shielding between workers will be necessary to help those increasing number of extraverts concentrate on their work. Young people now are more narcissistic than previous generations, and this means that individualized and distinctive home and workplace design are becoming increasingly important.

Dominant Sense

Dominant sense is determined using the following questions that I have written:

Answer each of the questions that follow by selecting one of the responses provided. Choose the answer that *best* describes *you*.

1. During the winter, if you're thinking about spring, which do you anticipate most eagerly?
   a. Change in the appearance of the area around your home
   b. Sound of the wind rustling through the new leaves
   c. Smell of the new grass and flowers
   d. Feel of the spring breezes on your skin

2. If you were consulting with a company designing showerheads, would you be most eager to work with the designers to enhance the way the water leaving the showerhead
   a. Looks as it moves toward your body
   b. Sounds as it hits surfaces such as your skin, the walls of the shower enclosure, or the floor
   c. Tastes or smells
   d. Feels as it hits your body

3. After attending a dinner party at a friend's house, which feature of the experience are you most likely to be able to describe in detail to another friend the next day?
   a. Appearance of the dining room
   b. Music being played while you ate
   c. Tastes of the food
   d. Texture of the food you ate

4. On a long plane trip, which of the following would you be most likely to find annoying?
   a. An ugly pattern in the upholstery of the seat in front of you
   b. Loud engine noise
   c. The smell of burnt food
   d. Cabin being too hot or too cold

5. Are you most interested in the way a new pair of dress shoes
   a. Looks on your feet
   b. Sounds as you walk on different surfaces
   c. Is ventilated to reduce "foot smell"
   d. Feels as you walk

6. When selecting a new fan to ventilate your kitchen, which are you most likely to be influenced by while making your purchase?
   a. Way the new fan looks
   b. Sounds that the fan makes as it works
   c. Smells the fan will remove from the air
   d. Feel of the current of air created by the fan

7. Which of the following would you most enjoy doing?
   a. Looking at art you enjoy
   b. Listening to music you enjoy
   c. Tasting foods you enjoy
   d. Floating in water that is the perfect temperature

8. When you are visiting a home that you are considering purchasing, which is the first modification from the list below that comes to mind?
   a. Changing the color of some of the walls
   b. Installing your sound system

    c. Placing potpourri throughout the house

    d. Changing the floor coverings so they are comfortable to walk on

9. If you were going on a vacation to a new place, which of the following would you most eagerly anticipate learning something about?

    a. Colors and textile patterns that are the favorites of the people living in the place you will be visiting

    b. Sounds and music popular in the place you will be visiting

    c. Special scents in the new place

    d. Feel of the air: the temperature, humidity, and prevailing winds in the place you will visit

10. When you meet a person for the first time, which are you most apt to notice?

    a. Pattern in his shirt

    b. Tone of his voice

    c. How he smells

    d. Feel of his skin as you shake hands

11. When you remember your favorite place, what kind of memories pop into your head first?

    a. Visual images

    b. Sounds

    c. Smells

    d. Textures against your skin

12. If you were buying presents for yourself, which would you buy?

    a. Things you like to look at

    b. Things you like to listen to

    c. Things you like to eat

    d. Things that feel good to touch

13. When selecting a new puppy, which feature would be most likely to influence your selection of a particular dog?

    a. Its markings

    b. Sound of its bark

    c. Its smell

    d. Feel of its fur

14. What would distress you most about a new toaster you received as a gift?

    a. It looks bad.

    b. It makes a bad sound while toasting.

    c. The bread smells bad while toasting.

    d. The texture of its cover feels unpleasant.

15. During a walk on a lovely summer evening, what are you most apt to notice?

    a. Patterns of light and dark made by shadows

    b. Sounds made by nocturnal birds

    c. Smell of the night-blooming flowers

    d. Temperature of the air

16. Relaxing at the beach, what would you focus on?

    a. Patterns in the sand or the clouds

    b. Sound of the waves

    c. Smell of sunblock and the sea

    d. Feel of the sand and water

17. When you are picking out a new car, which are you most interested in?

    a. Color of the upholstery

    b. Sound that the engine makes

    c. Smell of the interior and the air filtration system

    d. Vibrations (not the sounds from the engine) as you drive the car

18. Which of the following would you most enjoy about being in a warm summer rain?

    a. Appearance of the raindrops

    b. Sounds of the rainstorm

    c. Taste of the raindrops

    d. Feel of the raindrops hitting your skin

19. Which would be the best enhancement that engineers could make to personal computers?

    a. Making the images that appear on-screen more vivid

    b. Creating better sound systems

    c. Adding a capacity to smell items shown on the screen

    d. Enhancing the way the keyboard buttons feel under your fingertips

20. What are friends most likely to ask your opinion about?

    a. Wallpaper patterns

    b. Sound systems

    c. Potpourri scents

    d. Massaging showerheads

Determine your dominant sense by awarding yourself one vision point for each "A" selected, a hearing point for each "B" selected, a smell/taste point for each "C" selected, and a touch point for each "D" selected.

Vision points:

Hearing points:

Smell/Taste points:

Touch points: (Again, scores can be tallied by the researcher.)

We vary in our dominant sense (Adler 1968; Schifferstein and Spence 2008). Our dominant sense is the most direct route to our emotional, psychological core. Whether we perceive a sensation or not has nothing to do with our dominant sense. A sensation can be influencing us through our dominant sense channel even if we are not aware of it. For example, all of us with normal, functional olfactory systems will experience the same smell, but it will have more of an emotional influence on smell/taste-dominant people. The reason that one sense is dominant in one individual, and another is dominant in another person, is not known at this time.

This express route to people's mental state through their dominant sense should be used with discretion. Don't overload this sensory system. You should keep a person's dominant sense in mind when you use the information from Chapter 5 about influencing life experiences through the senses. Gradually add sensory inputs through the dominant channel to any space you are creating. Check continuously with users of the space to assess their emotional reactions to new sensations. When the desired effect has been achieved, stop augmenting the space. If the space users are hearing dominant and you have equipped a place where they want to relax with a sound system to play relaxing music and a fountain so that they hear the relaxing sound of moving water, and they feel that the space is relaxing, its soundscaping is complete. Do not add the sculptural wind chimes that make deep, relaxing sounds outside the window of the room. You can always return and add the wind chimes later if the users are not as relaxed in a particular space as they would like to be.

There is no best dominant sense—if you are a visual person, you are a visual person. Being visually dominant is no better or worse than being a person who is more emotionally influenced by sound, smell/taste, or touch. It is simply different.

People's personality and dominant sense influence their unique experiences with the places around them. Learning about these personal factors enables you to effectively adapt and apply the general information we have presented about human relationships with physical environments to create spaces that enhance specific users' lives.

■ ORGANIZATIONAL CULTURE AND PLACE

People individually have personality, but groups of people also establish ways of getting things done that give them something like a personality—an organizational culture. A culture reflects what is valued by a group of people, how they like to get things done, and what gets done at all. An organization's culture has space implications, just as a person's personality does. You can identify an organization's culture, just as you can determine a person's personality.

Edgar Schein (1992) has said that groups use both visible and invisible symbols to keep track of their own culture and to show it off to others. Individuals use the same sorts of tools. At the individual and group levels, rituals, behaviors, values, rules, and objects are used to share information.

Places can support or thwart cultures. When place design is consistent with organizational culture, people are more certain about what is truly important to their organization and feel more comfortable that they know what behaviors are appropriate. An organization's spaces need to make a consistent nonverbal statement overall, although spaces specifically for individual groups can vary in tone.

Before you can design to support a culture, you need to identify it. You can determine the culture of an organization using the techniques I have developed that follow.

If you do not have much time or many resources to determine an organization's culture, ask yourself who the organization would be if it were a person—that person's personality is the human embodiment of the organization's culture. Gerald Zaltman (2003) has shown that we often compare one thing to another in our minds to understand it. As soon as you start designing an organization's space, you start comparing (consciously or unconsciously) the organization to other people or groups that you know better, particularly if you have been unable to thoroughly explore the space users' culture. The comparisons Zaltman describes save a lot of mental effort—once you learn enough about something to be confident what it is like that you already know, you can proceed without making an effort to learn more about it. If people we are talking to using comparisons are from the same national culture that we are, they immediately form a mental image similar to ours when the comparison is mentioned. For example, if we (as people from North America) see parallels between a medical group we are working with and a relentless Wall Street stockbroker, we know that the group we are working with will sacrifice comfort to be more competitive, likes the status rewards that come from success, and doesn't pay much attention to traditional ways of doing things. People who have grown up in our national culture will share our preconceived notions about stockbrokers.

Based on whatever exposure you have had to a group, you might personify it as a social recluse who is into the latest technological gadgets. If so, make sure the space you design can accommodate today's and tomorrow's technology. Don't build a lot of spaces for people to hang out casually, but do create the needed number of conference rooms. Spaces where people can sit in a semicircle and look at a screen would be great for this kind of group—the technology is there and the people gathered around the table can make eye contact with each other when they want to, but they can also gracefully break eye contact whenever they want—which is great for an introverted tech geek. Higher cubicle walls (or real walls) around workspaces would be appropriate for a group with this personality because technology tinkerers want to be able to concentrate. Make sure that there are in-house amenities like cafeterias at this organization. Occasional serendipitous over-hearing of conversations and casual interactions can be useful, and a cafeteria provides a natural space for this. Including a cafeteria illustrates how designers sometimes create a space at a site that may seem inconsistent with an organizational culture—if it will help an organization satisfy needs that it might not naturally acknowledge.

If you are designing a store or a museum or a workplace for a group that you see as a social maven, design plenty of space to socialize—but also include places that meet people's various physical and psychological needs and where they can retreat to do their jobs if their work requires concentration. Recognize the specific requirements of various individuals and groups when creating a space for this group. Responding to those needs acknowledges the importance of each group member.

If an organization seems as if it would be an East Coast preppy, make sure the space you are creating has a traditional feel to it. Use colors and finishes that you might find in a classic setting from decades past. This sort of organization doesn't want to be avant-garde in the way that it looks or acts, so don't try to force it into that mien. Make sure that it has access to all of the technology it needs to do its job, however. The members of this group value traditions and rules—recognize that fact when designing spaces for their use.

Each of the three examples above is cursory, at best. In the design of any space, there are hundreds more design decisions that need to be made than the few profiled here, but if you use the "who would they be" technique, you will find that decision after decision follows naturally from your initial personification. It is easier to keep track of who your client group is if you gather objects, images, etc., that they would hypothetically feel comfortable with and keep them together in a box or mounted on a wall. In moments of indecision, you can take a look at the things you have collected and make the needed decision.

The problem with identifying the sort of person an organization would be in this way is that you might not have enough information to do it correctly. Also, to properly design a space for an organization, you need to recognize that all the parts of that organization are not the same and each can have a different culture. A comprehensive design plan needs to represent the composite culture in spaces shared by the organization, but group culture in group-specific spaces. Knowing each group in an organization well enough to figure out what sort of person they would be is a daunting task.

Groups determine cultures, not individuals. Although individuals can be surveyed to determine the organizational cultures of the groups that they are part of, written surveys do not provide the useful, nuanced information that can make a place design successful. Group discussions are the most effective way for designers to learn about organizational culture because during a discussion individuals who share a culture can interact to more accurately describe their group's modus operandi. To learn about an organization's or a group's culture, I have found it useful to ask groups the following sorts of questions:

- If this organization/group were a person, what sort of person would he or she be? What would his or her hobbies be? Where would he or she go out to eat? Who would his or her friends be? What sorts of clothes would he or she wear? For each question, the precise answer doesn't matter so much as the reason that the answer was given—what was the underlying message the speaker was trying to express?
- How do things get done around here?
- What's it like here during [name a relevant sort of professional crisis]?
- What is important at this organization/group? What is rewarded? Who gets promoted?
- What is the most important thing for new employees to learn about working here?

Scholars (Cameron and Quinn 1999; Schein 1992) have assessed the patterns that they see in organizational cultures in different ways, but for space design, my experience indicates there are three organizational cultures that should be recognized. These cultures are roughly similar to the three people described in the last few paragraphs. One culture is driven by being successful, in its chosen field (the tech geek). The second is driven by concern about people—either those in the organization or in a client group that it serves. This sort of culture corresponds to the social maven. The third and final type of culture is like the preppy, focused on processes and traditions. None of these cultural types is a complete and exact match for the true culture of an organization, but each provides a broad template that can be used to understand the group.

An organization that is driven by success will, quite naturally, do anything (mostly legal, but not necessarily so) to be successful. Most of the groups driven by success are committed to achieving some sort of financial objective, but the group could be striving for something else—perhaps the most thrilling movie special effects or finding a cure for cancer. The success-focused group will go to the limit of its financial resources to create the spaces needed for people to work toward the group's objective. Often, these spaces are crammed full of technology, whose operation the building envelope must facilitate.

If task complexity is high and a workplace is being designed, people working in a success-focused group may have traditional cellular offices. Conference rooms are designed for effective meetings. Conference rooms and other sorts of team spaces are very important to people in success-focused organizations because often multidisciplinary groups of individuals must work together to achieve group success. People matter to this organization as a means to a successful end, so cafeterias and other amenities on-site will enhance worker effectiveness. People working in this culture will personalize their workspaces with whatever is necessary for them to be effective, which might be a six-foot African mask or a flock of parakeets—and their workplace must somehow accommodate either. Employees in a success-oriented group will change their workplace in whatever way they feel is appropriate to meet their goals—so furniture that might lose a leg if it is slid from one place to another is not a good idea in spaces for these groups. People who perform better will have spaces that reflect their status and accomplishment, but so will people who have the potential to perform well in the future.

An organization driven by concern about people ideally creates a humane space. Firms can be people-driven groups. Although no firm survives without earning income, for a people-driven firm, providing a desirable place to work is almost as important as that income. This sort of organization incorporates refreshing elements into workspaces so that employees will not only work well but also find it more pleasant to be at work. This kind of group makes sure that as many employees as possible have restorative views (see Chapter 4 for more details), and work in places with curving circulation because this promotes refreshment in a space. Artwork will change from time to time for the same reason. People in this sort of organization want their coworkers to clearly understand who they are, so they need to be able to personalize their cubicles with mementos of family and friends. They also want to show others their hobbies and what they value. Spaces that can't be personalized gracefully are personalized anyway. Group areas are developed to meet the needs of each particular group, so each is different. There is a cafeteria and fitness center on-site, if at all possible, so that employees can be healthier. Different people in the organization have different levels of status, but no one has so little status that he can't be comfortable doing his job.

This group optimally lives in an environmentally responsible way because it really cares about the environment, not because it is a way to save money or look good to civic groups. People matter to groups with this culture—they are much more than just cogs in a production machine. Thinking about how much a group of this type values its members should provide a nudge in the right direction when you are making design decisions.

An organization focused on processes (often derived from traditions) can be the most complex to design for—until you've been around it for a while, it's hard to know all of its rules. In efficient organizations of this type, processes are rules and rules are king. To be fair, often having rules and structures in place has been key to the success of this firm. In this sort of organization, making status differences clear via workplace design is important. Ideally, design typicals are painstakingly developed, and deviations will be rare; for example, handicapped employees may be the only one able to obtain exceptions. For example, managers of a certain level will have a conference table and a pair of side chairs in their offices, no matter how likely they are to have meetings there. Managers at a lower level do not have that conference table and those chairs, even if they need to have many crucial meetings in their offices. If there is food service in this sort of organization, there are likely to be two cafeterias—one for executives and the other for the rest of the employees. That's also true for whatever other amenities this firm may supply to its workers.

Many of the process-focused group's rules lead to efficiency (efficiency is just as important here as effectiveness is to success-focused groups and human comfort is to people-focused cultures), and efficiency ideally is reflected in space design. With straight walkways more people fit into an area, and that is more important to the decision makers than the psychological advantages of walking down a winding path instead of a straight one, for example.

In optimal process-focused workplaces, group spaces are efficiently distributed throughout the space and outfitted with rectangular tables, so it is always clear who is boss. Almost all conference rooms are outfitted with the lowest common denominator technology. If a group needs to hold a videoconference, it can reserve a videoconference room on the soonest available date. The number of videoconference rooms on-site is based on a time utilization study completed sometime before, which has become nearly legendary because of the sway it holds over firm operations.

For a process-driven group, the general design standards for its industry are very important. For example, imagine that you are designing offices for a law firm. If the design standard at this time is for every beginning lawyer to have a cellular office, each beginning lawyer at the firm you are working with must have a cellular office. If eventually industry standards change, so that beginning lawyers sit at large, open studio tables, then the beginning lawyers at the firms you are working with will need to sit at large, open studio tables.

Any one of these cultures could happily find themselves in a range of design aesthetics. The important design differences between places for each culture are tied to the key adjective that could be applied to each of their environments:

Success Focused—Effective

People Focused—Comfortable

Process Focused—Efficient

Many of the specifics for the design of each organization type should be based on the activities of the group. Both an insurance company, with its thousands of employees, and a legal firm, with its hundreds of employees, can be a process-oriented group, but the task complexity and design norms for each group can be quite different. Those differences in primary activity should drive space design with open work areas for a low task complexity group at the insurance company and private, acoustically shielded offices for lawyers doing very complex tasks, for example.

Many organizations now think that it is important to represent their brand in their offices. Different organizations use different definitions of *brand,* but ideally the sort of message that they are trying to send about their brand would be consistent with the message that they're sending to themselves and others about their organizational culture. So brand is reflected in a space when organizational culture is recognized there—except for the window dressing to make sure the firm's logo colors appear somewhere in the reception area.

Individual personality and organizational culture influence the sorts of physical places where individuals and groups can achieve their objectives. Using the tools provided in this chapter, you can make sure that personalities/cultures and places are coordinated.

8 NATIONAL CULTURE AND PLACE EXPERIENCE

Where you were born influences what you focus on when you look at a picture (Nisbett 2003). A lot.

If you were raised in a Western culture (the United States, Europe, Australia, etc.), you focus on the central element in an image. If you were raised in an Eastern culture (Japan, Korea, China, etc.), you more equally review everything in an image presented to you.

If the culture of the place where we grew up influences what we see in a picture, what other effects does it have on how we experience the world around us? As it turns out, our national culture is a key influence on how we live in our physical world. Our national culture, the culture we were raised in, has a very important effect on the sorts of spaces in which we thrive as well as how we perceive what surrounds us.

National culture organizes our place experiences by giving them a context. Having cultural systems in place frees us up from devoting mental energy to figuring out everything that's going on around us and allows us to move on to more mentally stimulating endeavors. Physical environments that are consistent with culture help us understand what is important and socially acceptable in a place. Since we can't absorb all of the sights, sounds, and scents that surround us and might be important, culture helps us focus on the same information that others around us will focus on—because we can choose to flout a national culture, but we can never ignore it.

Cultural systems tell us how far to stand from other people and how we should personalize the spaces we control to nonverbally communicate desired messages. Culture provides the dictionary we need to correctly interpret nonverbal communication and the swirl of activity around us. Communicating through the symbolism of facial expressions, gestures, objects (chosen and rejected) and place design, we can make statements that would be difficult, awkward, or impossible to present through words.

Culture defines values. As Amos Rapoport (2007) has discussed, a person's values find expression in her lifestyle and her expectations regarding the physical locations in which she will live that lifestyle. A culture that believes that men and women should be separated in the course of their daily lives would expect that there would be separate areas for men and women to interact in their homes. A culture such as Russia's, which values people having the opportunity to socialize while dining around a large table, requires that there be a space in the home for such a large table. Cultures that value sharing food among family members must have a space in the home where all that food can be safely and pleasantly prepared and consumed.

A national culture is the code of behaviors and values followed by people from one particular country. Although there are regional differences in cultures in larger countries, we won't focus on them here because generally people living within one nation are similar enough to each other, and different enough from people living in other countries, for our place-based discussion of culture. Since country borders sometimes do not correspond to ethnic boundaries, there can be an inconsistency between the geographic area occupied by a particular group and the nation that gives them their name. For the discussion in this chapter, that happens rarely enough that we can ignore it.

Professions, religions, hobbyists, and businesses, among others, also have cultures—they are organizational cultures. These social systems spring into existence

A

FIGURES 8-1 A TO D ▪ People from very different national cultures will be comfortable in each of these rooms. Each space uses structural elements and sensory stimuli (such as colors) in ways that are consistent with the national cultures of their primary users. Without that consistency, people are tense and distracted; they cannot thrive.
Copyright © iStockPhoto/Alain Couillaud, Andrey Rodionov, atbaei, and Imre Cikajlo, respectively.

B

within and across particular national cultures, but there are consistent types of groups found in all national cultures. While national cultures may lay out certain society-wide values, group or organizational cultures outline more specific rules for how a narrower set of behaviors should be completed. Organizational cultures and how they should influence design are discussed in Chapter 7.

Some differences in the architectural *styles*, or building forms, used by different cultures result from the climates and landforms that builders find themselves in. Tight-fitting doors can prevent heat from escaping from a home in the winter. People who live in hotter climates value higher ceilings because hot air can accumulate in them. Across generations, people living in locations with high ceilings come to expect high ceilings in the places where they live. Even if they move to cooler climates, these people will find higher ceilings appropriate because they are linked psychologically to "good places to live." Over time, these connections may fade, or they may not, depending on how motivated individuals are to assimilate into the architectural

C

D

culture of their new neighbors by social, economic, or political considerations. In this chapter, we lay out how national culture should influence place design, but we do not discuss specific details of particular nations' architectural traditions. How the ornamentation on turrets in country A differs from the ornamentation of turrets in country B has been left to other authors.

The appropriateness of architectural forms for the physical climates in which people find themselves in their homeland and their symbolic communication of social value from one generation to the next, along with building codes and zoning requirements, helps preserve the diversity of architecture in different parts of the world. Changing architecture to change how people live their lives is not successful whether it is done on the macro scale of a city or on the micro scale of a workplace. People adapt the new sorts of places in which they find themselves to their existing social systems and not the reverse.

This chapter focuses on how differences in national cultures should influence place design; it gives practical form to theoretical concepts. The material presented is relevant to the design of homes, schools, workplaces, healthcare facilities, and retail spaces. The other chapters in this book focus on place-related similarities across national cultures. The material in this chapter can be used to fine-tune spaces being developed in particular places. The chapter begins with a discussion of the ways national culture influences how we perceive the world and goes on to describe the ways it affects how we use the spaces around us.

Places that thoughtfully recognize the cultural system(s) in which they are embedded are places where people are physically and psychologically comfortable and can thrive. The most important design implication to draw from this chapter is that people from different parts of the world can respond to the same physical environment in very different ways. These differences must be acknowledged and reflected in place design.

DESIGN IMPLICATION

People from different national cultures thrive in places that reflect how their specific national culture perceives and uses its physical environment.

▩ DIFFERENT WAYS TO PERCEIVE THE WORLD

None of us are video cameras capturing all of the images and sounds (not to mention textures, smells, and tastes) that surround us—if we consciously registered the entire environment around us, we'd be too busy to actually respond to any of it. So our cultural filter restricts what we allow into our brains for processing and then determines how we respond to what we do take in.

National cultures vary in the attention they pay to information they receive through different sensory channels, although all able-bodied people can physically sense the same stimuli. The senses that people use most frequently to gather information are not necessarily the same as their dominant sense, described in Chapter 7. A dominant sense is the most direct route to affecting someone emotionally, and varies from person to person, while the primary senses that people use to collect information from their world are culturally conditioned.

The sensory worlds of some cultures are more diverse than others. People in the Americas and most other Western countries are very attuned to their visual worlds, while other cultures consciously collect more and different types of information from the spaces that surround them. Particularly during social interactions, for example, Arabs are much more attuned to scent and touch than Americans. In northern Europe and the United States, much of the richness of smell in our environment has been removed. In the United States and northern Europe, smelling body scents is not viewed positively and a great deal of effort is focused on eliminating them. There is also a movement in the United States to forbid the wearing of scents or the use of scented cleaning products in public spaces because some citizens are sensitive to them. People often use scents to broadcast details of their personal identity, so forbidding their public use could literally be depersonalizing.

Some businesses have begun to recognize the emotional links that Americans, as all humans, inevitably form to smells (see Chapter 5 for more details). These companies are attempting to brand places with scents. Westin Hotels and Singapore Airlines are at the forefront of this movement. Although the smells selected by these firms do not appear to be scientifically developed using the criteria outlined in Chapter 5, they are intriguing attempts to communicate through the sense of smell. In North America, smells are also being used therapeutically in gardens for people with dementia—use of familiar plant scents helps these people retain contact with their world.

The Japanese create multisensory, place-based experiences; their spaces are thus much richer in a wider range of sensory details than those in the West. Nuances of experience such as changes in humidity, temperature, and shadow fall are often carefully considered during the design of Japanese spaces. In Japan, spaces can be distinguished by what the experience of actually moving through them is like, and places are designed so that their perception is not complete unless people integrate information they have collected in different parts of the space and use their imaginations. The experience of moving across different surfaces is psychologically important to the Japanese. Tactile experiences are largely lacking in American interiors. The French are also very concerned with a range of sensory experiences. As a culture, they have developed a refined palette for food and art, for example.

People from West African cultures are much more attuned to audio and proprioceptal (body placement) information than people of European ancestry. Some researchers believe that the tradition of communicating through dance in these regions leads to these differences.

Even when people from different national cultures are actually using the same sensory channel, they may not be gathering the same information with it. Consider sound. In Asian cultures, such as in China and Japan, people learn not to notice more personal sounds that other people make in the course of their daily lives, but do learn to focus on neighborhood sounds that help them manage their daily lives. Since they often live in tight quarters with insubstantial barriers between them and their neighbors, Asians learn behavioral and perceptual rules that help one family separate itself acoustically from its neighbors. North Americans would process both the noises from neighbors and from the neighborhood.

> **DESIGN IMPLICATION**
>
> If people from multiple national cultures will use a space, provide several consistent sensory inputs, as outlined in Chapter 5, to ensure that all of the people in a space have the desired psychological experience. If only one national culture will use a space, be sure to provide culture-appropriate sensory inputs.

When exposed to the same image, people from an Eastern culture, such as Japanese, will perceive more of the entire scene. People from Western cultures, such as Americans, will focus on the foreground objects and remember them in great detail, but will have a much less detailed memory of the background elements of the images than people from an Eastern culture. Asian interior and garden design tends to be complex, and therefore require intense analysis. Ways of looking at scenes may thus be reinforced by what is being looked at, and vice versa.

The Western focus on the foreground objects and the Eastern attention to the entire image is consistent with Asian attention to the spaces between objects (Hall 1982). The space between objects is generally ignored in the West because it is "empty." Westerners see little reason to focus on spaces that are empty and many reasons to focus on spaces that are occupied. In the East, people focus on spaces between objects as intently as the objects themselves and thoughtfully consider the features of those spaces, such as their shape.

The sounds and smells that we find pleasant, as well as relaxing, are determined by experiences that we have within our cultural context. Smells of meat cooking often have very different associations from culture to culture— my delicacy and link to fond memories is not necessarily a delicacy for you or linked to any of your fond memories—to you it may just be vile. Memory associations to sensory input are shortcuts to emotional experiences, and those emotional experiences are tightly linked to our attitudes and behaviors, as discussed in Chapter 5. Different cultures also find different musical intervals acceptable.

Our life experiences make us prone to different sorts of perceptual tricks. People who are used to living in places where the interior walls meet at right angles in the corners perceive the world differently from people who grow up in spaces where they do not. People who have grown up in places where there are right angles in the corners think lines with outward-facing arrows at their ends are longer than lines with inward-facing arrows, which are actually the same length. People who live in places where the walls do not meet at right angles in the corners (for example, in a round structure) do not make the same mistake. Modern engineering can make faux finishes very convincing, and the apparent roughness of a surface that is actually smooth leads to unusual sensations while walking, and this inconsistency between what we expect and what we encounter can be unsettling.

The language that we speak is largely determined by our national culture, and it has a basic influence on how we experience some aspects of the world. The way our language names colors affects how we perceive them, for example. In Russian there are different terms to describe light blue and dark blue, and Russian speakers are much quicker at distinguishing between different shades of blue than English speakers, whose language names blues differently. The separate terms for different shades of blue seem to make the task of identifying these differences easier and the distinctions between them clearer. Not all cultures even distinguish the same hues as separately named colors. Many languages do not have distinct words for blue and green, for example. The Japanese did not traditionally differentiate these colors and relatively recently added a word for "blue" to Japanese. When tested in labs, people speaking languages that do not have different words for blue and green can indeed differentiate these colors.

> **DESIGN IMPLICATION**
>
> The language that we use to talk about places influences how we perceive them. Native speakers of the language that will be spoken most frequently by the users of a space should be asked for their opinions on design concepts using that same language. Tools to collect this design-related information are provided in Chapter 11.

Personal space, as we discussed in Chapter 6, is the distance that people are comfortable maintaining between themselves in different situations. These distances vary by national culture, as we'll talk about soon. In general, people from Latin America stand closer to each other when talking than Japanese people, while Americans stand and talk at a distance between those favored by the Japanese and Latin Americans. All of these relative distances are clearly observed when people are speaking their native languages. When Japanese people speak English and Latin Americans speak English, however, the personal spaces between them get closer to the distances maintained by Americans speaking English. When the words of languages are learned, it seems that some of the cultural rules associated with those languages are also learned, and those rules are followed when the languages are spoken.

Methods of perceiving the world can be symbolic. Kluckhohn (1953), an anthropologist, believes that societies can feel that they have one of the following three orientations to nature: subservient to it, dominating and exploiting it, or in a harmonic balance with it. The relationship that people feel they have with nature has repercussions for the materials used in a structure and the visual connection between inside and outside spaces.

In cultures where man is dominated by nature, fewer connections between interior and exterior spaces are desirable, although interior spaces should always have some connection with exterior spaces so that people are refreshed by outside views. When people live in places where natural disasters are more frequent, they are more likely to feel subservient to nature, and thus also want to be sure that the structures they use are resistant to natural assaults.

Societies that feel that they dominate nature are amenable to more extensive nature views and use of renewable and nonrenewable natural materials in the interior design of a space. Americans have traditionally held this orientation to the world.

Homebuilders in the United States are more likely to ignore the climate and terrain where they are building than builders in other parts of the world. This is consistent with the American focus on dominating nature and the financial resources that are regularly available to U.S. homeowners. For example, in warm parts of the Caribbean, rooms may be built with high ceilings to capture heat. In warm parts of the United States, air-conditioning may be installed and ceilings may not be any higher than in colder areas of the country.

Cultures that feel they live in harmony with nature, such as many Native American societies, relish extensive views of nature, but are judicious about the use of nonrenewable resources in their environment. This view of humans' relationship with their natural environment is becoming more prevalent as concern about the health of the planet spreads. As the worldwide push toward environmentally responsible living takes hold, there will be a greater demand for spaces that acknowledge that man lives in harmony with nature and that nurturing the natural environment is also good for our psychological health.

■ DIFFERENT WAYS TO USE SPACE

People process the particular bits of information that they pull from the world around them. This processing is influenced by their national culture. Designing spaces without considering national culture thus greatly decreases the odds of satisfying person-place interactions. All national cultures create some similar types of spaces. Each culture develops places to sleep, eat, play, work, and worship, for example, but these spaces do not necessarily look or feel the same.

Regardless of national culture, all desirable spaces meet the criteria discussed in Chapter 4, providing opportunities for the following:

- Comforting
- Communicating
- Challenging
- Complying

Comforting

Spaces are comforting when they allow us to control our experiences in them, reflect our concern for quality of life and roles we play, and indicate our orientation to the future and distinguishing relative status. Control of our environment is crucial to our physical and mental well-being, as detailed in Chapter 4. When we are in control, we feel much less stress, and we make changes to our surroundings to keep them mentally and physically comfortable. People without control often give up—and they don't just abandon efforts to influence the environment. Someone who is always too hot or too cold at work will stop trying to solve a difficult problem before others, for example.

We can control our environment by regulating our personal space, developing territories that belong to us, and preventing people from intruding on our privacy.

PERSONAL SPACE AND PRIVACY

The sizes of personal space zones vary by culture, as does the way that privacy is established.

DESIGN IMPLICATION

The sizes of personal space zones vary among cultures. Rooms, circulation spaces, and furniture arrangements must be designed with these differences in mind, or people using these spaces will experience stress. Stress has negative repercussions, as discussed in Chapter 4. When several cultures will use the same space, the space must be designed to allow people to vary the distances at which they interact—chairs and other furnishings should be mobile to allow the appropriate distances to be maintained. And spaces have to permit furniture to be moved—pillars, half walls, and similar features can prevent chairs from being positioned comfortably and people from standing at desired distances from each other. Interpersonal spacing has repercussions for design decisions ranging from how many chairs can be placed around a table to how wide a walkway should be. It's not possible to estimate how many people will willingly share a table or a sofa until the relationships between those people are known and their culture is identified.

Members of different cultures have different mechanisms for ensuring that they have the privacy they require. Privacy is a fundamental human need, so place design must permit people to regulate access to themselves in the ways they have been taught by their national culture.

Personal space, as discussed in Chapter 6, is the distance that people keep between themselves in various situations. The size of this distance varies from situation to situation as well as from culture to culture, and it is used to communicate important relationship information. Across all cultures, people with closer relationships are physically closer when conversing, for example.

Adult members of each national culture know the appropriate distance to stand or sit from other people in their culture—although they may not be able to verbally describe those distances. All coherent adults know when their space rules are being violated. When members of "close" cultures find themselves in the same places as members of "far" cultures, the air grows tense. It seems to the "far" culture people that people from the "close" cultures are rude and "in their face." People from the "close" cultures feel that those in the "far" cultures are rude and standoffish. Teaching adult members of each culture about how another culture likes to operate can be useful, but interpersonal distancing is so clearly imprinted on us as children that it takes a lot of patience and understanding to overcome our inherent concern when people are at the *wrong* distance.

Hall (1982) and subsequent researchers split the planet's cultures into those whose members like to be close to each other and those that prefer to maintain a greater distance between themselves. People who tend to stand relatively close to each other include southern Europeans and Latin Americans, while northern Europeans and Japanese people are among the national cultures that maintain larger distances from each other, for example. Experiments have shown that southern Italians and Greeks stand closer to talk than people from Sweden and Scotland, with people from the United States talking at an intermediate distance. Also in Europe, Dutch interpersonal zones are larger than those of the French. The French maintain closer distances between themselves than northern Europeans, the British, and Americans, but interact at distances that are farther apart than the true Mediterranean cultures. Within Latin America, Costa Ricans chose tighter interpersonal distances than Panamanians or Colombians. Other research has shown that people from the United States, the United Kingdom, and Anglo-Canada have larger personal space zones than Asians (Chinese and Thai), who have larger zones than central and eastern Europeans (Austria, France, and the Netherlands) and French Canadians, and that Latinos (Brazilians and Italians) have smaller zones than the Europeans and French Canadians (Beaulieu 2004).

No matter what their national culture, people need privacy from time to time. More information about privacy is provided in Chapter 4. Some cultures value privacy more than others; for example, North Americans value privacy more than Turkish people, but people from Ireland, Senegal, Borneo, and the United States seem to have similar privacy needs. All cultures have developed tools that ensure that their members can have desired levels of privacy.

When people from Western societies such as Europe, North America, and South America want privacy, they look for physical barriers to provide it although sometimes sunglasses or chair arms are the only privacy-creating tools at hand. People from Eastern cultures, such as China and Japan, have developed ways to act that give them privacy without walls. People from these cultures will just not look at others or just not seem to hear what is going on nearby—even if the others they are trying to shield themselves from are just across a desktop from them.

Within a workplace, in particular, a need for privacy must be distinguished from a need to concentrate. Places that Western workers find private are also often places where they can concentrate. Places that workers from the Far East find private are not necessarily places where they can concentrate. Far Eastern workers may need to devote some mental energy to ignoring what is going on around them even though they are in a place they would categorize as private. That diverted mental energy reduces cognitive focus on the task at hand.

Hall (1982) works his way from one world culture to the next and discusses how each uses space. His conclusions and those of other researchers are quite consistent and reported together here. Germans, like other northern European groups, maintain larger personal spaces than Americans would in the same situations. Germans value true, substantial walls and doors around their spaces as well as solid furniture (the heavier it is, the harder it is to move too close for comfort).

English people interact with the spaces around them in a slightly different way than the Germans. They use both behavioral and physical means to preserve their own privacy. The British, for example, can simply just not talk with one another if they want some privacy and a lack of walls and doors prevents them from achieving privacy through physical means. The British value control over their own environment, but see giving environmental control to some and not others as a way to distinguish status, which is also very important to the British.

How do people from countries rimming the Mediterranean Sea use personal space and privacy? People living in these parts of the world interact at much closer distances than Americans, the British, and Germans. Latinos transplanted from Europe to other parts of the world continue to interact at close distances. Arabs, in general, maintain closer personal distances than Americans. Even though Arabs are closer together during conversations

FIGURE 8-2 ▨ Physical barriers are associated with privacy in Western societies; behaviors can play a similar role in Eastern societies.
Copyright © iStockPhoto/Gill Henshall.

than Americans, they speak more loudly. Arabs generally face each other more directly (face-to-face as opposed to side by side) during conversations than Americans. Like the British, Arabs can isolate themselves from other people simply by not interacting with them. To Arabs, privacy between family members is not as important as separation from people outside the family.

On to Asia. Japan and China are very intensely settled. These cultures compensate for the intense crush of humanity surrounding them by being polite, reserved, and carefully filtering things happening around them, as described earlier. Even when the Japanese subways are not crowded, travelers feign sleep to psychologically separate themselves from their neighbors. The Japanese build the same sort of sustentative walls around their family homes that Arabs do and also couple them with less significant walls within each family home. Indians also value interactions between family members, but seek to separate their families from the world outside their homes.

Since many of its cultural norms are British, it is not surprising that people from Australia tend to interact at the same distances as people from the United Kingdom. People from Indonesia, however, talk more to strangers than people from Australia, and sit closer to them in public spaces than Australians do.

Some African groups also distance themselves mentally from nearby people to achieve needed privacy.

CROWDING

Different national cultures define crowding differently, but research has shown that all people suffer when crowded (Evans, Lepore, and Allen 2000). It is not true that Asians are less adversely affected psychologically in higher-density situations than others. However, Asians do seem more tolerant of crowding than southern Europeans, who are more tolerant than people from the United Kingdom, for example. Among the Chinese, crowding is more acceptable when among family members than when surrounded by strangers. For all cultures, when people feel they have more control over the situations in which they find themselves, they are less psychologically damaged by crowding. They may feel more in control if they believe they can leave a crowd whenever they want, for example.

Spaces can be designed to minimize the negative consequences of high-density living, and different national cultures do this in different ways. For example, multiple uses can be made of the same space. Traditional Japanese structures often use the same place for several purposes—eating, sleeping, socializing, etc. The Japanese are meticulous about the design of the small spaces that are available to them, and also pay attention to the full range of sensory experiences that they can have in a particular place, as discussed earlier in this chapter.

CONCERN FOR WELL-BEING

Hofstede and Hofstede (2005) have determined that in some countries people are more attuned to quality of life and interpersonal relationships than recognition and challenging work, and in others citizens' priorities are reversed. Countries whose citizens that have relatively less concern for quality of life include Japan, the Philippines, Australia, China, Austria, Germany, Great Britain, Italy, Ireland, Venezuela, Mexico, Colombia, and the United States. Countries where people are more attuned to quality of life include South Korea, Thailand, Russia, Portugal, Finland, Denmark, the Netherlands, Norway, Sweden, Spain, France, Chile, and Costa Rica. People living in cultures that are more concerned about quality of life take more behavioral cues from the physical environments in which they find themselves than others and take more steps to sustain the natural environment.

IMPORTANCE OF RULES

In some countries, Hofstede and Hofstede (2005) have found that people are more comfortable with ambiguous situations and see less need for rules, while people living in other countries are more concerned about ambiguous situations and have more rules.

Countries that are apt to have relatively more rules are in Latin America, in Latin Europe, or around the Mediterranean. Other countries that have many rules are Japan, South Korea, Russia, Poland, Belgium, and Turkey. Countries whose citizens are relatively less apt to be concerned about rules are in Asia (except for Japan and South Korea) and Africa. Additional countries fitting this description are the Netherlands, Denmark, Sweden, Ireland, Great Britain, India, the Philippines, the United States, Canada, New Zealand, and Norway.

In countries with fewer rules, novel situations are valued. People living in these countries are relatively more interested in opportunities to relax than people living in cultures with more rules. In countries with more rules, there is more concern with cleanliness than in less rule-focused countries, which has implications for material choice.

APPROACH TO THE FUTURE

Hofstede and Hofstede (2005) have identified cultures that differ in their focus on the future, as opposed to immediate rewards. People from cultures with a future focus are interested in using resources, including money and time, effectively and efficiently to reach important goals while people with a more immediate orientation have a greater respect for following tradition and immediate gratification. People from cultures with a more immediate orientation are also, however, more interested in following trends than people with a longer focus. People with a future focus are generally more open to new ideas, but not trends.

Countries whose citizens are relatively more oriented to the future include China, Hong Kong, Japan, South Korea, Brazil, India, and Hungary. Those with citizens with a relatively more present orientation include Great Britain, New Zealand, Canada, the United States, Portugal, Spain, the Philippines, Nigeria, and Pakistan.

DISTINGUISHING STATUS

Work by Hofstede and Hofstede (2005) has also shown that people from some countries are more interested in communicating differences in relative status or power than others. These citizens are more accepting of relative difference in status and power. Differences in status can be shown in individual homes or workspaces or in amenities, such as nearby public parks or cafeterias provided for workers.

The Hofstedes' research has shown that countries whose residents are relatively more accepting of differences in power include most Asian countries (such as Malaysia, the Philippines, China, India, and Indonesia), eastern European countries such as Russia, Latin countries (in Europe and South America), Arab countries, and African countries.

People that are relatively less accepting of differences in power include those from German-speaking countries, Israel, Nordic countries (Denmark, Finland, Norway, and Sweden), the Netherlands, the United States, Great Britain, New Zealand, Ireland, Australia, Canada, and Costa Rica.

Communicating

People need to communicate with other people—but on their own terms. Territories are a communication tool. Territories, as described in Chapter 6, are spaces to which the owner controls access. They are places where individuals and groups feel that they can manage their own lives, socialize with others on their own terms, and symbolically communicate their images of themselves.

TERRITORIES IN GENERAL

All national cultures value territories, but they can define them differently. While the French see public spaces as freely accessible to all, for example, Germans see spaces such as beaches as places that can become the "property" of particular groups who claim them for defined periods. German groups also claim larger spaces than groups from other countries. Groups can define even home territories differently. Americans, for example, think of the sidewalk and curb in front of their home as their territory while Greeks do not, and each group's concern with property maintenance stopped at the edge of their perceived territory.

An oriental harem and an American family room may seem very different, but they are actually quite similar. Both are spaces where family members can relax and form or preserve familial bonds, within the bounds set by the values of their cultures. Across all national cultures, home spaces are sacred places of refuge from the pressures of the world at large. Every home has a central meeting space, but the form that space takes can vary from culture to culture. Americans tend to gather in a family room or den, while Russians will sit on chairs pulled up to a table, and that table could be in several different rooms in their home. Home spaces remain the purest physical manifestations of national culture, as workplaces and retail spaces are more significantly influenced by pressures from other national cultures.

In Western societies, the rooms within a home have more distinct functions than in the Far East, the Middle East, and Africa. Even in modest homes in the West, a kitchen is generally differentiated from bedrooms and living rooms, for example. In Japan, rituals accompany the transformation of a space from one function to another during the course of a day. In the West, as the trend of more people living alone escalates (as discussed in Chapter 12), this differentiation of spaces within the home may diminish. Within multiperson homes, when rooms are used for several purposes, residents usually have learned to mentally isolate themselves from other people living in the same home or to spend less time in the home. When rooms are used for a single purpose, residents are more likely to use walls, doors, and other physical barriers to achieve desired levels of privacy.

DESIGN IMPLICATION

Spaces consistent with the culture of the people living in them provide users with the support they need to be the sort of people that their culture has taught them to respect.

SPACES AS TERRITORIES

Hofstede and Hofstede (2005) have determined that cultures can differ on how much members of the culture value their independence or their interdependence with others. Whether a national culture values individual independence and self-sufficiency or intragroup interdependence and responsibility has implications for a territory's exterior and interior design. Places whose residents the Hofstedes have identified as valuing independence relatively more include the United States, Australia, Great Britain, Canada, New Zealand, Germany, the Netherlands, Belgium, Denmark, France, Sweden, and Italy. Places that value interdependence relatively more include Venezuela, Peru, Chile, Mexico, Pakistan, the Philippines, South Korea, Hong Kong, Indonesia, Singapore, Malaysia, Taiwan, China, and Portugal, as well as East Africa and West Africa.

Independence-minded cultures value representing a person's individuality in the spaces that he or she uses, while cultures that value interdependence relish representing group membership and behave differently. When residents of a country value interdependence with group mates, they are more likely to create homes, for example, that conform to rules established for their social group. They indicate they are part of a group by respecting the home design rules established for that group. Members of cultures that value independence want their home to be significantly different from the home of the people who live next door. Neighborhood rules and building design that allow for easier expression of individuality in independence-prizing areas prevent considerable neighborhood strife, particularly since cultures that value individual independence are more likely to engage in do-it-yourself activities and, in general, to modify spaces to meet their psychological needs.

Members of some cultures are more apt to accept their environments as they are and to change their personal objectives based on the capabilities provided by their environments, and members of other cultures are more apt to change the places they encounter to meet their needs. Some social scientists say people from cultures that value independence feel that their environment should conform to their needs and are more apt to change it so that it does so, while people from more interdependent cultures feel that they should accommodate themselves to the social and physical situations in which they find themselves.

In cultures that value independence, homes are more likely to be seen as status symbols than they are in cultures that value interdependence.

Whether a national culture more highly values individual independence or intragroup interdependence also has repercussions for very specific design features used in homes. People from cultures that value interdependence are more likely to draw energy from within themselves instead of from their environments, as described in the discussion of personality factor 1 in Chapter 7. This has a significant influence on the preferred forms of sensory input, also discussed in Chapter 7.

In more independence-minded cultures, people generally value privacy more highly. People in more interdependent cultures are more receptive to sharing resources than people in independence-oriented cultures and also more apt to think in terms of group ownership of a space than more individualistic cultures.

Research has also shown that people from cultures whose members view themselves as interdependent with others interact at closer distances than people who feel that they have more freedom to act independently of those around them.

Whether people are from countries that value independence or interdependence also influences the kinds of shapes they prefer. People from countries that prize interdependence prefer rounded shapes and people from independence-oriented countries prefer more angular shapes. This is consistent with the preferred mental states of people from Western (energized) and Eastern countries (calm). In the East, people prize spaces that are calm; many Eastern countries

> **DESIGN IMPLICATION**
>
> Consider whether a space will be used by people from a culture that values individual independence or intragroup interdependence more highly and design accordingly.

value interdependence, and rounded shapes are associated with harmony. In the West, where independence is king, energizing spaces are more desirable and angular shapes are associated with energy.

The social dynamic and design of a home are dramatically influenced by the number of generations that live in the structure. This varies by culture. In cultures that value individualism, older members of the family try to remain independent as long as possible and often move from their own homes to group living facilities so that they are "not a burden" to other family members. In these societies, young people establish separate households as soon as it is feasible to do so. This creates a market for single-family homes at a range of price points, from starter to established levels. In societies that value interdependent links more than individualism, particularly in Africa or Asia, more generations live together.

COLOR PREFERENCES

Furnishings, artworks displayed, and even the architectural style of a building all signal information to people who visit a space, as well as the people who use it every day. One of the ways that national cultures communicate desired messages is through their use of particular colors.

Although color saturation and brightness have the same psychological effects on everyone (as discussed in Chapter 5), specific national cultures have preferences for particular shades and associations to particular hues.

Park and Guerin (2002) have investigated combinations of colors that are favored by different cultures around the world for interior color palettes. These preferences are important because the use of preferred colors improves people's moods. The collection of colors selected as most desirable by each culture studied by Park and Guerin (2002) was seen as "more comfortable, inviting, coordinated, and sophisticated" by that group. The favored palettes are combinations of colors of various hues, with varying levels of saturation and brightness. Of those tested, five were particularly desirable to various groups of people.

Palette A (C-8), characterized as being "simple and cool in appearance," uses neutral colors that are not very bright or saturated, with large brightness and low saturation contrasts between colors placed next to each other. It was the color palette most preferred by people from Eastern cultures and least preferred by Western cultures. It was the combination of colors most preferred by the Japanese, and the second most preferred by Koreans, but the least preferred by the English. These results are consistent with the fact that the preferred psychological state of Asians is relaxed while North Americans prefer to be energized.

The collection of colors that Western cultures found most desirable in an interior environment (and the third most preferred by Eastern cultures) is colorful, using reds, blues, greens, and yellows, albeit subtly (Palette C [C-9]). It utilizes warm hues, with moderate levels of brightness and saturation, and low brightness contrasts and medium saturation contrasts between adjacent blocks of colors. This collection was the set of colors selected as most desirable by American citizens. It was the second most desirable to the English and Japanese, and the least desirable set of colors to Koreans.

Koreans found most desirable a collection of neutral hues with a fairly even split between warm and cool colors (some obviously red and blue), midrange brightness and low saturation overall (with comparable numbers of colors with strong and moderate levels of saturation), and high contrasts in saturation between adjacent colors and middle levels of brightness contrasts (Palette E [C-10]). The Japanese also found this collection of colors highly desirable for interior environments.

The British found most desirable, and Americans second most desirable, a collection of warm colors of moderate brightness and saturation, with moderate brightness contrasts and low saturation contrasts between adjacent colors (Palette F [C-11]). These moderate levels of contrasts result in a low level of stimulation to viewers overall.

The palette least preferred by all of the cultures tested had bright but unsaturated neutral colors, with high brightness and medium saturation contrasts between adjacent colors (Palette D [C-12]).

Different cultures not only have different preferences for various colors, but they also have learned associations to particular hues.

Colors have traditionally been used to link people to political causes, and it is important to consider current associations when designing a space. During the Second World War, Mussolini's Fascists wore black shirts, and Hitler's Nazis wore brown shirts. Nowadays, red is linked with communism throughout the world, while orange is used by reform-minded Ukrainians, and yellow is the color of pro-democracy groups in Kyrgyzstan. Many Moslems link green with their religion, and for some of these people green has therefore taken on political associations.

American Demographics (Paul 2002) has identified specific color associations, through experts who were primarily Americans. Among the associations they report are:

DESIGN IMPLICATION

Since so many hues share saturation and brightness levels that can produce the same psychological effect, there are always several color options that can be used in any situation. Cultural associations to particular hues should play a key role in developing any color scheme.

Red	competition, emotion, optimism, violence
Orange	extraversion, adventure, celebration
Yellow	creativity, imagination, optimism, newness
Green	nature, balance, fertility
Blue	dependability, protection, purity, peace, trust, loyalty, patience, hope, perseverance
Purple/Violet	spirituality, creativity, wit, sensitivity, vanity, moodiness
Pink	sweetness, delicacy, refinement, sentimentality
Brown	stability, harmony, hearth, neutrality
Black	sophistication, simplicity, power
Gray	neutrality, boredom, coolness, safety, conservatism
White	purity, calm

The same color can have very different associations in different parts of the world. Black, for example, can be a good color for office furniture in Germany, where it is viewed as a strong color (in the office context), but not in the Middle East, where it is associated with women and weakness. Some specific cultural associations to colors, identified by Mubeen Aslam (2006), are as follows:

White represents
   purity and happiness to Anglo-Saxons
   death and mourning to Chinese, Japanese, Korean, and other East Asian people
Blue connotes
   high quality, dependability, trustworthiness, and masculinity in Anglo-Saxon communities
   femininity in Nordic countries (except Sweden) and the Netherlands
   warmth in the Netherlands and Germany
   coldness in Sweden, Japan, and Korea
   purity in India
Green represents
   good taste among Anglo-Saxons
   adventure in the United States
   sincerity, purity, and reliability in China
   love, happiness, good taste, and adventure in Japan
   purity and adventure in Korea
Yellow signifies
   happiness in Anglo-Saxon cultures and Korea
   warmth in the United States

purity, good taste, pleasantness, happiness, progressiveness, trustworthiness, royalty, and authority in China

good taste in Japan and Korea

Red is associated with

masculinity, love, lust, fear, and anger in Anglo-Saxon countries

masculinity in France and Latin cultures

bad luck in Germany

good luck in China, Denmark, and Argentina

love in China, Korea, Japan, and the United States

happiness in China

adventure and good taste in Korea

Purple means

authority and power in Anglo-Saxon countries

expensive in China, Japan, and South Korea

love in China, Korea, and the United States

sin and fear in Japan

Black represents

fear and grief in Anglo-Saxon countries

expensiveness in Anglo-Saxon countries, China, Japan, the United States, and Korea

grief and sorrow in the West

fear in Japan, Germany, Poland, Mexico, the United States, Latin cultures, and Slavic countries

power in China, Japan, the United States, and Korea

dependability, trustworthiness, and high quality in China

Other researchers have looked for consistency between perceptions of colors across countries. Associations to day and night seem to influence how white and black are generally perceived. White is consistently associated with good things and certainty, while black is associated with negative things and uncertainty. Gray has generally been found to have negative associations, like its more saturated cousin, black. Blue and green have generally been found to have good associations. Red is seen as active across most cultures.

Challenging

Different cultures have different preferred mental states, and place design can lead to particular mood states. Territories should, as appropriate, reflect those desired states. Asians feel that the ideal mood is a sort of peaceful Zen bliss—they value being relaxed (Tsai 2007). Americans, on the other hand, think that the ideal state is happy and excited—energized (Tsai 2007). These differences in ideal mental state mean that these different groups are interested in creating different sorts of spaces in their homes, workplaces, schools, healthcare facilities, and public places.

Complying

National cultures can be different in ways that have implications for the design of spaces where people accomplish needed tasks.

DIRECT AND INDIRECT COMMUNICATION

In some cultures, communication is more direct, and in others it is more indirect. Indirect cultures rely more on nonverbal communication and the context of the situation to convey information than straightforward verbal declarations. People from Asian cultures, such as Korea and Japan, and from eastern Europe and Latin America tend to be more indirect in the way that they communicate. People from more individualistic cultures, such as the United States, tend to rely less on context and nonverbal communication to convey information and to speak more directly. In more indirect cultures, communications tend to become particularly oblique in situations in which it would be unpleasant to lose face, such as professional and other formal situations. In indirect cultures, communication is clearer and less veiled in nonwork situations. In informal spaces within the work environment, cultural concerns about avoiding discussion of difficult workplace issues may be weaker. Incorporating casual spaces into office buildings in indirect cultures is thus potentially useful.

> **DESIGN IMPLICATION**
>
> In cultures where communication is often indirect, be certain that spaces created convey appropriate nonverbal information and incorporate informal meeting spaces into environments whenever possible.

APPROACH TO SCHEDULING TIME

Another way that national cultures differ is the way that they use time, and this has repercussions for the design of the physical environment (Schein 1992). In monochronic cultures, people schedule their time so that they can complete one task without disruption before they go on to the next. In polychronic cultures, people may be doing several things at once, and one of those things is generally socializing with others. People from northern Europe tend to be monochronic and people from southern Europe and Latin America tend to be polychronic. Monochronic people are stressed if they are compelled to multitask and in that situation may feel that they are "not getting anything done." They are more effective when they can complete different activities in separate spaces. Monochronites value efficiency and the privacy that they feel produces it. When they want to socialize with their neighbors, people from polychronic cultures value plazas while those from monochronic cultures are more apt to favor longer main streets. Polychronics work best when several things can happen at the same time in a space. Businesspeople in polychronic cultures can be very effective when they have physical contact with each other: for example, when they are seated on a sofa as opposed to on either side of a desk.

WORKPLACE DESIGN IN GENERAL

Workplaces are spaces where accomplishing specific tasks is the highest priority, so the appropriate influences of national culture on workplace design are the ultimate examples of how well-designed spaces help people comply with their agenda.

National culture continues to have a large influence on workplace design, even as some firms and industries become global. Culture should play an important role in workplace design for some time because people's sense of who they are, which is intensely linked to their national culture, is deeply tied to how they earn a living. It is not uncommon to find offices in Europe that look exactly like offices in Asia that look exactly like offices in North or South America. The similarity in the design of these offices only means that they resemble each other; it does not mean that the people in them are working successfully. There are a number of documented situations in which people from different national cultures sharing a workplace have had space-based conflicts. These problems have arisen from violations of personal space, differing concepts of privacy, and basic disagreements as to the appropriate use of space.

A workspace communicates nonverbally what a person wants others to know about himself personally and professionally, and while communicating to others it also reminds him who he is or wishes to be. The messages to be communicated are socially determined. For example, in India, it is likely that employees will bring their families to their workplace to show them the caliber of the company that they work for. Some families have veto power over the employment decisions of their members, and the workplace design influences those potential vetoes, so in India, workplaces need to be designed with these visits in mind. The criteria that are used to assess workplaces vary from country to country. In North America, working at the top of a tall building in a penthouse has traditionally been a sign of relatively high status; the same is not true in India. Electrical power is not as reliable in some parts of India as in the United States, so in India executives often work near ground level so that they do not have to climb too many stairs if the elevator can't operate.

In some cultures and industries, individuals may be motivated to present a different image to the world in their homes and their workplaces. For example, at home a person may be very interested in appearing to be a child-focused family man, while at work, he may be interested in being perceived as a cold-hearted bond trader. In other cultures a father might want to present himself as a focused leader in both locations. The worker's national culture has nonverbal symbols that can be called up to present each image—photos at home of children cavorting about versus posted graphs of bond returns at work. A home office can be tricky to design—how much of the work shark should the kiddies see? This question is easier to answer before you recognize that those nonverbal clues communicate not only to visitors but also to the person using the space. It is harder to be ruthless when looking at a picture of Junior and his chubby cheeks than when looking at a graph or last year's sales award.

Some differences in workplace design between countries are mandated by laws, but those laws were developed based on culture-specific concerns for worker welfare. Workers in Germany, Sweden, the Netherlands, and France must have access to window views, which indicates the value that these national cultures place on restorative experiences for workers. Although in France people generally maintain relatively close personal distances, the law mandates that the minimum allowed distances between two people sitting at facing desks is four meters, which indicates a concern for the maintenance of at least a minimum amount of privacy.

Jurian van Meel (2000) has prepared an insightful analysis of how, in Europe, national culture combines with market conditions resulting in the office space ultimately used by workers. He concludes that workspaces in the United Kingdom are more similar to those in the United States than offices on the European continent and that cost-effectiveness and flexibility are important criteria used to assess office plans in the United Kingdom. Although the British national culture is consistent with placing workers in individual cellular offices, status distinctions in the workplace can be defined if some workers sit in open spaces and some do not—and this is also valued by the British. Other reports indicate that the floor plans of British workspaces are very dense.

Van Meel sees different workplace design practices in the rest of Europe. Although in the United Kingdom and the United States there are many open-plan offices (areas where many workers will sit in an open space, separated by short petitions), in continental Europe, cellular offices with floor-to-ceiling walls and doors have traditionally been more popular. In Germany these cellular offices may be shared, and that is also the case in the Netherlands. Environmental issues are very important in Germany, as are openable windows. Sturdy furniture is valued in Germany, but aesthetics hold sway in Italy. In Sweden every employee has a private office with a window—an administrative assistant has the same basic space as the person he assists. In Sweden, workers are also very attached to their work group, so there is a lot of design attention focused on group spaces and break areas.

Offices in Asia have traditionally been very different from those in Europe. Historically, in Asia group members sit around large tables that may have short partitions a few inches tall between each workspace. The manager of the group traditionally sits at a small table slightly separated from the table where lower ranking group members toil. Western-style privacy is nonexistent. This office design form is still common in Asia.

Standardized global real estate plans are dangerous. A cross-cultural committee that agrees to a flexible workplace design, customized to each location, is creating a useful work environment for each national group.

■ CONCLUSION

When people design places without considering cultural issues of importance to the people who will use those places, spaces that are culturally unacceptable and unusable can result. For example, hospitals that have been designed by North Americans ignoring national cultures have often not considered the large number of visitors/companions that a patient may have, and the resulting crowds of people can make emergency transportation of patients through hallways impossible and procedure waiting rooms very difficult places to be or use. Hospitals that have been built on a high-tech model without concern for local healing practices also forego the potential effects (even if they are only placebo) that come from recognizing a range of types of medical treatments.

Culture-specific forms of architecture continue to be used not only because they are consistent with the local national culture and its values, but also because they help us maintain our identity as individuals and members of particular groups. In addition, familiarity with a particular sort of architectural form increases its attractiveness and desirability.

Differences in culture can lead to different responses to the same spaces. National cultures are mixing more throughout the world, and people are becoming more aware of how their national culture is distinct from others. Recognizing and responding to place-relevant national cultural differences in the design of homes, schools, hospitals, stores, and offices is thus becoming more important as well as more difficult. If we recognize these differences, and design for them, the spaces we create can enhance the lives of a larger and more varied assortment of people.

9

PREDOMINANT ACTIVITY AND THE DESIGN OF PHYSICAL ENVIRONMENTS

The physical space we're in influences the mental state we're in. Different mental states are more appropriate for different kinds of activities. Our physical environments also affect the amount of mental energy that's at our disposal.

Human beings draw energy from the physical environment that surrounds them as well as whatever they are doing (Wohlwill 1966). There is a sweet spot energy level at which we function very well. More or less energy than this and things do not go as well—we are not as competent, comfortable, or satisfied with the situation. When we're under- or overstimulated we have difficulty focusing on something or concentrating on what we're supposed to be doing. If we are working on a more mentally stimulating task, we do a better job at it if we get less stimulation from our environments, and vice versa. Concentrating and doing more complicated tasks provides more mental energy than doing simpler tasks. Things that we've practiced more are generally simpler, but some tasks remain stubbornly in the complicated category no matter how many times we've done them. The tasks that remain complicated include things like analyzing data, writing reports, and solving problems creatively.

Different spaces can sometimes work better for us at different times. When we're doing a simple task, such as sorting something or writing perfunctory responses to e-mail messages, we like a more stimulating place—for example, we like to play lots of vocal music and chat with our friends while we get the job done. In that case what we're doing generates little mental energy, so we have plenty of capacity left for stimuli from our physical environment. When we're concentrating, for example, when we're studying or trying to solve a professional dilemma, we nix the others and play music without words—or no music at all. We're getting a lot of energy from the work we're doing, and if our environment sends us too much stimulation to deal with, we're overloaded and stop doing anything well. When we're at work in a sea of cubicles and someone starts to talk in the next cubicle—with their wife or about an upcoming project—even the most introverted of us is too social a beast to be able to ignore what is being said, if it is being said in a language

FIGURE 9-1 ■ This person is regulating her stimulation level by isolating herself in a meeting room. She has turned her back to passersby to avoid interactions with others and partially closed the blinds so that people can see the room is occupied, but the person in it prefers to be alone.
Copyright © iStockPhoto/Nilgun Bostanci.

with which we have any familiarity. Undesirable tasks seem to be pretty mentally stimulating as well, so we do better at things we don't like to do if we have fewer distractions.

If we are understimulated, we try to find something—an object or a place, for example—that jazzes up our life. That new place or object may be unusual or complicated, and that provides a jolt of energy to our life. In the reverse situation, we make an attempt to rid ourselves of some sources of stimulation—suddenly the simple and predictable seem like the best choice.

The amount of information we are processing at any one time determines our stimulation level at that moment—if a place give us more to think about because there is a lot of variety in the objects within it, that space is more stimulating to us. A place is particularly stimulating if we cannot predict what we will experience next. Places can create an air of unexpectedness if the path through the space wanders or if artwork in it is changed regularly, for example. Environmental stimulation comes in many forms: For example, people close to us or watching us are stimulating, and so is loud or fast or varied music, a strong scent, an unusual scent, bright lights, or a complicated image. When an experience is more intense (for example, sharper contrasts between colors in a space), the experience of being around it is more stimulating.

Unfortunately, there's no neat equation to tell us how much mental stimulation we are getting from any particular task and environmental input. It is important to work with users to determine these "sweet spots." Questions provided in Chapter 11 will help you investigate this issue.

People adapt to the stimulation levels of places where they most frequently are. A person from a big city such as New York wants a higher level of stimulation from her environment and whatever she is doing than a person from the countryside does.

Different mental states are more appropriate for different sorts of activities (Cote 1999; Fredrickson and Branigan 2005). When we're in a pleasant or good mood, we do better at innovative and creative and strategic tasks because we think more broadly. We are better at solving problems and making decisions when we are in a good mood; we are also more flexible, thorough, and efficient when

DESIGN IMPLICATION

Considering that people may be doing complicated tasks now, but simpler tasks later, it is best to create a moderately stimulating work environment. When users are doing a task that is easy or one that they have done in the past, they can make the space more complex by changing the music, for example. When they're working on something more complicated, a chair that pivots so that the more visually complex sections of the room are not visible, for example, will make the same space useful in this new situation.

thinking about topics that interest us. When we're in a good mood, we're better public citizens, are more constructive and cooperative bargainers, are more generous, show more social responsibility and interpersonal under-standing, make more constructive suggestions to others, and seem to better comprehend our own strengths and weaknesses.

Sometimes it is good to be in a bad mood, and a place can help gener-ate that negative mood just as it can help create the good mood. A nega-tive mood has a lot of influences on us that are not the opposite of a good mood, but it is true that a good mood causes us to think more broadly and a bad mood causes us to think more narrowly. Bad moods are best in situa-tions when flexibility, creativity, sociability, etc., are not so important and operating on automatic pilot is desirable. This is very handy in an emergency situation when strict remediation plans need to be followed or when some other routine task must be accomplished in one specific way (Norman 2004).

DESIGN IMPLICATION

Using design to create the appropriate mood in a space, either positive or negative, can be key to the success of that place.

Predominant activity should significantly influence the design of a space.

10

INTEGRATED APPLICATIONS OF PSYCHOLOGY-BASED PLACE DESIGN PRINCIPLES

There is no one right space for all people at all times—but you can create the right space for a person at any particular moment. This chapter introduces a model I have developed for using information from earlier chapters about how we respond to spaces. Apply it to help the people who will use the places you are developing achieve personal and professional objectives.

Some of the things that we do every day we do alone, and some we do with other people. Some things focus us inward; they are more thoughtful and have a more internal, mental, intangible outcome (we learn something) as opposed to being higher-energy activities (we do something, such as paint a dining room). So at different times during each day we are an intellectual (low energy and nonsocial living), an artisan (still nonsocial, but high energy), a teammate (social and doing something that's high energy), and a sophisticate (social and engaged in a low-energy activity). Each of these "people" has a particular sort of place in which it thrives, but you should temper the general points that follow about what works best for each in light of your spaces users' dominant senses, personalities, and cultures (see Chapters 7 and 8).

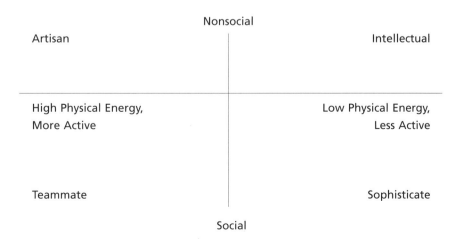

Daily life is complicated to unravel, and we can streamline our discussion of it using a chart. Each of our activities can be categorized into one of the quadrants of the diagram on the previous page, which breaks our actions into those that are social and nonsocial as well as those that are more active and require more physical energy and those that are less active and require less physical energy. This categorization will organize our generic applications of place science.

Some examples will make this discussion a little clearer. Learning something mental (as opposed to physical), reading for fun, listening to music, or completing a crossword puzzle is intellectual. People learning a new language or calculus or doing the solo work involved in creating a new advertising campaign or strategic plan are being intellectuals. As artisans, we may be cooking or cleaning alone or doing any sort of solitary hobby with a physical outcome, such as building model boats. If someone joins us while we're cooking, we become teammates—the same happens when someone begins to work on any hobby with us (quilting alone versus quilting at a bee). We're sophisticates while attending a symphony performance. A quiet conversation is also part of our life as sophisticates.

By modifying smells, using movable furniture, or changing the colors of lightbulbs and other features of a space, a single place can be used to live several "lives." It is possible, for example, to provide users with opportunities to reorient themselves to look at different things by including several seating choices in an area with a variety of wall treatments. You can provide different experiences by varying scents with electrical scent diffusers. Each of these sorts of options creates opportunities for a different response to the space.

When you are putting together a place, think about the most general use of the space and focus your attention on the design features as they relate to that function. For example, when you are working on a bedroom space, the color of the sheets and the firmness of the mattress will have a more significant influence on your experience of the bedroom than the color behind the headboard of the bed or the imagery in the painting hanging above the bed.

The national and organizational culture in which the space you are working on will be experienced should be considered as you design a place—whether you choose to embrace or reject it. If you are developing a workplace in a region in which education is respected and you wish to be respected by your coworkers, work articles from your alma mater into your office décor. If you are working in a place where meals are casual, and sometimes boisterous, and you want your users' neighbors to feel comfortable when they eat in the dining room you are designing, enhance it with more vibrantly colored walls and more relaxed furniture, not the pale walls and more formal design that would be seen in a region where eating is a more somber event.

Another thing to consider as you develop a space is the level of sensory stimulation people are used to in their daily life. Different people, with different life experiences, have different optimal stimulation set points—a person from New York City has a higher desirable base stimulation level than a person from a rural community, all else being equal. Keep this in mind as you develop spaces, and you will create places with the level of complexity or input from the environment that is appropriate for the person who will use the space.

Places communicate to their owners and the people who visit them. The messages that they send are something that you should consider as well when designing a space. A person must show himself and others who he is as an individual in the design and furnishings of his home, for example, if he is going to be happy there. The strength with which places silently communicate our image is why we're so concerned about the choices of individual pieces of furniture or the specific art we hang on our walls.

Any sort of activity can take place in any space, but we can make some generalizations about where people live each of their lives. The following provides more specific information about living the "quadrants" of our lives.

■ INTELLECTUAL LIVING

Spaces for **intellectual living** should induce contemplation, and most desirable environments for intellectual life provide enough stimulation to prevent counterproductive boredom. The real "action" in this life is mental, and restrained input from the physical environment allows mental life to flourish.

We generally live our intellectual life in offices, studies, fine arts studios, libraries, and bedrooms. Why bedrooms? The process of falling asleep, like writing a novel, is a nonsocial mental activity.

There is a single optimal level of mental stimulation no matter what we're doing. If our physical environment is exciting, varied, or novel and we're doing a task that also provides a lot of mental stimulation, we'll be overenergized and underperform. Those exciting, varied, and novel aspects of the environment keep us from focusing on a complex task at hand. This is why it is better to do a thoughtful task in a more relaxing, simpler environment and a less-thoughtful task in a more physically energizing space. Loud noises, bright lights, unusual or strong smells, and particular colors (see Chapter 5) increase stimulation as do people who are physically closer to us or who can see us against our wishes, for example. We can be understimulated by an environment just as we can be overstimulated—imagine a simple, monochromatic space—with the same negative results.

Visual effects: Colors used on walls, upholstery, and furnishings should be moderately relaxing and should blend well in spaces where we are intellectuals. Dramatic contrasts between colors shouldn't be used in these spaces; the colors selected should all blend delicately together. Avoid beige or white monochromatic environments—they can make individuals so introspective that they become unproductively tense. Using multiple shades of other colors together in monochromatic environments can be restful.

Colors should be less saturated and brighter in these spaces. Cooler colors that meet those criteria, coupled with lower levels of illumination, help us concentrate by increasing our focus on our own thoughts and decreasing our level of physical activity. Even traces of red should be avoided in intellectual spaces; the use of red in academic and professional environments has been linked to lower intellectual performance. Ceilings painted sky blue would be a nice touch in these spaces—sky blue ceilings have been associated with higher scores on IQ tests. Brighter colors on the walls make a space seem larger, which reduces distracting feelings of claustrophobia.

Intellectual spaces should not be visually or physically cluttered. Fewer and simpler patterns should be used on upholstery, curtains, wallpaper, etc. Seeing curved, symmetric, or harmonious forms is relaxing. Plants of any kind, particularly those with rounded leaves, are also a nice addition to these spaces.

Lighting color and level are important space design considerations. Less light in a space is associated with more relaxing places. If lighting levels in these spaces get so low that they seem dim, creativity will be adversely affected. Cool white light compared to warm white light impairs the long-term memory recall of novel information, so it should be used with care in these spaces. People perform better on short-term memory and problem-solving tasks in warm (3,000 K, more reddish) than in cool (4,000 K, more bluish) white light and artificial daylight (5,500 K, even more bluish). In addition, people exposed to warm white light (3,000 K) report stronger preferences for resolving interpersonal conflicts through collaboration and weaker preferences for resolving conflicts through avoidance than people exposed to cool white light (4,200 K). Many lightbulbs are labeled with their temperature (or K level) or an adjective indicating whether they emit warm or cool light.

Sounds: Low pitches are deeply relaxing. Midrange sounds (harp, acoustic guitar, chamber music) are moderately relaxing. Consonant, simple, and predictable harmonies in major keys are calming. Natural sounds (moving water, rustling leaves, etc.) are peaceful, as are acoustic music and soft, gentle, tonal sounds. More complex music requires more processing than simpler music, so it should be avoided when people will be trying to concentrate. If concentration, decision making, or creativity is required, noise levels should be below 55 dB, which is the volume of a normal conversation.

A regular, slow, legato (smooth) tempo or rhythm is soothing. Play slower, quieter music in the background at a low volume in these spaces. Around 50–70 beats per minute would work well.

Silence is a lot like a monochromatic color scheme from a psychological perspective and will only aid the concentration of rare individuals.

Tactile inputs: Textural input from the visual and tactile senses should be limited. A range of textures is exciting; remember that here we are trying to focus inner energy and encourage concentration, not generate physical excitement. More finishes should be matte than shiny. Spaces for intellectual activities should be slightly cooler than a standard environment to prevent too much relaxation and sleepiness. They should not be noticeably cold.

Smells: A space that smells like vanilla or lavender will keep people from being too numb or too frantic to focus on the mental task at hand. Any of the relaxing scents from Chapter 5 are useful in these spaces. Lemon scents are also good for mental workouts.

Spatial details: Seating should be arranged so individuals do not necessarily catch the eye of other people, whether the space for intellectual living is located in a home or a public place, such as an office or a library. Imagine a row of chairs all facing in the same, or just slightly different, directions. Many people are inherently social, and if they catch each other's eye they will interact (particularly extraverts), which is not desirable during intellectual living.

People who are working on a thoughtful task require bigger personal spaces than other people. Too many people too close increases the energy level, and when a person is working on a thoughtful mental task, they shouldn't be physically energized.

A clearly defined personal territory will also help users focus. Humans are not that different from their primitive ancestors, and when we feel that our territory may be infringed upon, we must stop and check out this potential intrusion—which distracts us from a mental task. Territories can be defined with walls, carpets on the floor, and color changes, for example.

For the same reason that you must have a clearly defined territory, you need privacy for intellectual living. If people do not have appropriate privacy, they will make an effort to achieve it—and all that effort diverts energy that could be used to think great thoughts! We all define privacy differently at different times; for some, privacy is being completely alone, but that is not true for other people at other times. In a private situation a person feels properly isolated from other people.

Opportunities for mental rejuvenation or restoration are refreshing (and important) while working on a thoughtful task. Make sure people can see something restorative (outside, fish, a fire) while living their intellectual life.

▓ ARTISAN LIVING

Artisan life is very different from intellectual life. The contemplative peacefulness of the space where people live their intellectual life is not the kind of space in which they can best live their artisan life. Being an artisan, like being an intellectual, is usually not social, but while living as an artisan you are physically active.

People generally live artisan lives in spaces where they prepare food (if they do it alone), do laundry, exercise alone, and engage in active hobbies, for example.

Visual effects: More saturated, moderately bright colors should be used in an environment geared to accomplishing physical tasks because they will spur activity and discourage daydreaming. Warmer colors coupled with high levels of light lead us to focus on the environment outside ourselves and to engage in physical activity. Using relatively brighter colors on the walls of productive spaces makes these areas feel bigger, which also helps you be more productive. Complimentary color schemes (one color and the color opposite it on a color wheel) feel lively and active.

More complex patterns on upholstery, curtains, wallpaper, etc., should be used in these spaces. These spaces can be enhanced by multiple complex patterns. Angled, geometric, asymmetric forms and those with moderate variety are appropriately invigorating.

Sounds: Faster, louder music than the soundtracks used in intellectual environments will promote artisan living. A fast, staccato (short, clipped), allegro (lively) tempo is appropriately invigorating as are high pitches (woodwinds, violins). Disconsonant, complex, and novel/unpredictable harmonies in minor keys are invigorating. To keep people more alert, vary music types and tempos to prevent their brains from habituating to any particular sound. Noise levels should not go above 70 dB for repetitive activities or above 85 dB under any conditions. If you are standing 10 feet from the average operating vacuum cleaner, you are experiencing 70 dB; 85 dB is the sound level of a garbage disposal from 3 feet away.

Tactile inputs: More textures should be used in this sort of space than in the spaces for intellectual living because more textures spur activity. More shiny surfaces than matte finishes should be incorporated into these places.

Smells: Peppermint is a great scent to smell while you are being physically productive. Peppermint diminishes perceptions of apparent physical exertion and provides energy for doing mental tasks as well. Any of the energizing smells from Chapter 5 are useful here.

Spatial details: Since this life segment is focused on accomplishing specific, physical tasks, a seating arrangement in which people can't see each other's eyes should be used, whether these spaces are inside or outside the home. If people are not making eye contact with each other, they will be less likely to be distracted from what they're doing.

To keep them physically productive, don't let artisans be crowded by others or let others encroach on their territory; they will expend some of the mental resources at their disposal responding to the presence of these other people—and that is energy that won't be available to accomplish whatever their primary objective is. Feeling that they have an appropriate level of privacy (something that only they can judge for themselves) is crucial for obtaining the highest levels of productivity. Appropriate levels of both visual and audio privacy are necessary for people to do their best work.

▪ TEAMMATE LIFE

A different sort of space is best for being a **teammate.** The spaces for artisan and intellectual life are places where people function alone, teamates are interacting with others. When people are functioning as a member of a community or group, their space needs change.

People are teammates in dining rooms (if they are eating with others), family rooms, their kitchen (if they cook with others), and sports/fitness areas in which people interact, such as the area around a family pool.

Visual effects: Less bright, more saturated colors and dramatic color contrasts are great for team settings—these places even benefit from splashes of the ultraenergizing reds. These reds cannot be the dominant color in a community setting, however. Red can make people become aggressive, so it is important to use it with discretion in a team setting. (See Chapters 5 and 8 for additional information on the psychological and cultural responses to colors.)

Warmer colors coupled with high levels of light lead us to focus on the environment outside ourselves, be more social, and spur physical activity. Warm white light also improves our mood.

More complex patterns on upholstery, curtains, wallpaper, etc., should be used in these spaces. They can be enhanced by multiple complex patterns.

Angled, geometric, asymmetric forms, particularly in a mix with moderate variety, are invigorating, and they should be used in these spaces.

Sounds: A soundtrack of fast, upbeat music is a great audio background for teammate life—it will provide appropriate positive energy. Louder music will create more of an impact, but the soundtrack for teammate life cannot be so loud that it drowns out interaction. A fast, staccato, allegro tempo and high pitches (woodwinds, violins) are invigorating. Disconsonant, complex, and novel/unpredictable harmonies in minor keys are invigorating. To keep users more alert, vary music types and tempos to keep people from habituating to any particular sound. Noise level limits match those of artisan spaces.

Tactile inputs: Varied textures are appropriately energizing in these environments. Finishes that are shinier than matte should be used.

These environments can be warmer than other spaces—slightly warmer temperatures encourage social interactions.

Smells: Basil, cloves, and rosemary scents—since they are energizing and culturally associated with eating, a community activity—are particularly useful in teammate spaces. The energizing scents from Chapter 5 are appropriate here.

Spatial details: You should lay out a space for teammate life so that teammates can make eye contact with everyone present, if desired. Chairs arranged so that teammates are at 90-degree angles from each other are great—when sitting in them people can look at each other or away from each other as desired, without awkwardness. To help people live as teammates, the space should allow them to nonchalantly look out of a window or into the distance if they need a break from an intense social interaction.

In spaces for teaming life, interpersonal distances become slightly smaller and less clearly defined territories become much more acceptable. Some personal privacy can be foregone in these environments.

■ SOPHISTICATE LIVING

Sophisticate living is social and low in physical activity.

Sophisticate living takes place in parlors, living rooms, music rooms, and conference rooms. Specific rules apply to spaces for brainstorming, and they are discussed in Chapter 13.

Visual effects: The environments for cultural life are generally more subdued and require muted colors of lower saturation and higher brightness should predominate with less dramatic contrasts between colors. Many of these spaces productively use neutral shades with accent colors.

Less saturated, brighter colors, coupled with lower levels of illumination, increase our focus on our thoughts and decrease our level of physical activity.

Darker wall coverings will make rooms appear somewhat smaller and encourage social interaction, if necessary.

Fewer and simpler patterns should be used in these spaces to prevent them from becoming too energizing.

Seeing curved, symmetric, or harmonious forms is relaxing. These forms should be used in sophisticated living spaces.

Sounds: A regular, slow, legato tempo or rhythm (50–70 beats per minute) is relaxing. Low pitches are deeply relaxing and midrange pitches are moderately relaxing, as are consonant, simple, and predictable harmonies in major keys. Natural sounds (moving water, rustling leaves, etc.) are relaxing, as are acoustic music and soft, gentle, tonal sounds. If concentration, decision making, or creativity is required, noise levels should be below 55 dB. More non-right angles in the room shapes of these spaces will make them seem less noisy, just as they quiet intellectual spaces.

Tactile inputs: Fewer textures (more of which should be matte than shiny) should be used in spaces for sophisticated living. The temperature in these environments should be appropriate for the event.

Smells: Jasmine is an appropriate smell for these sorts of spaces.

Spatial details: For certain cultural events it is better to be able to make eye contact with others, and for some it is not appropriate. Less eye contact is desirable at a concert, where we need to avoid conversation, but more eye contact is beneficial during many quiet conversations.

Personal space can be reduced in these environments, and territories and privacy may be less defined.

▧ RECOGNIZING INDIVIDUAL DIFFERENCES

When designing a space to be used by a small group (generally four or fewer people), determine the dominant sense of the people who will use the space you are "sense scaping" and then use discretion as you intentionally stimulate that sense. If you do not have the opportunity to learn about the dominant sense of the users of the space, keep in mind that vision is the primary sensory channel of most people in the Western world and that smells generate instinctual responses in people. Instinctual responses are different from dominant responses: an instinctual response means that we can't help but be influenced by something; a dominant response means that something is emotionally compelling. Responses to sound, except at the basic beats-per-minute level, are more generally culturally determined.

Personality also influences the optimal design of the spaces. Make sure to consider the personalities of the people who will use a space, and the information presented in Chapter 7 about what that should mean for place design. If people are more extraverted, make their physical environments more sensorially intense than if they are introverted, for example. Cultural influences on optimal place design must also be recognized in the spaces you develop.

If you think about the four lives people lead every day and the related place science guidelines, the spaces you create will efficiently and effectively help their users achieve their personal and professional objectives.

11

RESEARCH METHODS FOR PLACE DESIGNERS

You can't design spaces in which people will thrive without having information about the people who will use the spaces and what they'll be doing there. Research questions are included in other chapters when they are crucial to the discussions there, but the focus of this chapter is collecting design-useful information. I have developed the questions and the protocols presented here so that you can do just that. To learn about identifying individual personality and organizational culture see Chapter 7; refer to Chapter 5 for Nasar's methods for developing visual quality; turn to Chapter 14 to learn more about programming retail spaces.

Sometimes there are more time and resources available to do research than other times. From the research options outlined below, choose those that mesh with your schedule and collect the information you need to learn for a specific project. Each of the following sections is a brief introduction to the technique mentioned; the data-gathering methodologies presented have been comprehensively addressed in many different textbooks.

The most important thing to remember when you're using any of these research techniques is that the people who are using the space that you will develop may not be like you—they may work/play/live differently than you do, they may value different things than you do—and all of those differences should be respected. Do not create a space for others that would be great for you; create a space that's great for the people who will see it. If you create a space that ignores the needs and requirements of the ultimate users of that space, it will be a failure—using it people may be distracted, confused, bored, or worse.

There is a fundamental rule among place-design researchers—don't ask people for information and then ignore what they tell you. This makes them angry and unhappy with the spaces developed. Always acknowledge that you have registered users' concerns, even if you cannot respond to them in the space. You might, for example, need to tell the users who have worked with you that you do understand their concerns about the open layout of the office furniture currently in place in their company and all of the acoustic distractions they experience, but that the furniture can't be replaced due to budget constraints. Hopefully, after uttering that sentence, the next one you speak is about a modification to the white noise system at the firm that will begin to rectify the lack of acoustic privacy in the space, to continue with the example. It is important to users that you as a researcher listen to their concerns, value their opinions, and respond to the issues outlined to the best of your ability.

Sometimes, the general design of a new space has been preordained. For example, the management of a firm may have decided that all of its employees will work at long refractory tables to "break down communication barriers" (see Chapter 13 for insights on how well this plan will probably work). If that's the case and additional information will not influence management opinion, don't research any issues related to a place's design. That effort will only frustrate everyone involved.

If you are honest with people during the research and design phases of a project, the change management phase of a project runs smoothly—as a matter of fact, it doesn't really need to be "managed" at all, except to the extent that mechanical details, such as who prints to what printer and what medicines are stocked at each nursing station, need to be worked out. If you are not honest with users about the design of a new space and why it will take that form, the change management portion of a project is impossible. Users aren't stupid, and it's pretty hard to convince them that a space that doesn't meet their needs actually does.

■ RESEARCH OVERVIEW

The first step in any research project is to decide what needs to be learned. You might need to find out more about an organization's culture so a space can be developed that's consistent with that culture. You may need to get some idea about what employees really do (or should do) all day so you can make sure that they have the spatial tools they need in the future. Do you need to understand who the organization feels they will be in five years to ensure their new facility continues to meet their needs? The research bottom line is that you need to know what people need to accomplish in a space and how they would feel most comfortable (psychoanalytically and physically) accomplishing those things. The traditional list of journalists' questions (who, what, where, when, why, and how) covers the same ground that you must explore to design an effective space.

You will probably need to answer quite a few questions during the research phase of any project (if it seems as though there are only one or a few outstanding questions, re-evaluate your list of queries). It is best to prioritize the relevant questions based on how much influence each answer should have on the space design and try to answer the most significant questions first—that way (hopefully) if research resources evaporate, the most crucial information has been collected.

This chapter addresses several ways that you can collect needed information:

Written surveys

Individual interviews

Group discussions

Observation

You can combine these techniques to meet your needs and feel free to improvise new ones—just don't abandon the general guidelines laid out below.

It is a good idea to use several tools in the course of any project because different tools are useful in different ways for collecting particular types of information.

Written surveys are a good choice when the research budget is limited and the issues to be investigated can be addressed with multiple-choice questions (survey takers select the appropriate answer from among those provided). Written surveys can be administered using an online surveying tool, such as Survey Monkey or Zoomerang. If Survey Monkey or Zoomerang are used, the information collected can be analyzed with readily available tools, such as Excel. Providing the appropriate response options for the multiple-choice questions requires some prior knowledge of the situation being investigated.

Individual interviews are the tool to use when you think that you might want to probe responses to some of the questions you're asking or you would like to ask some questions that can't be beaten into the form of a multiple-choice question. An interview is a good way to get a nuanced impression of how an organization might change in the future, for example. Interviews and group discussions can be time consuming to schedule and conduct, and participants can be concerned about discussing sensitive topics during interviews.

Sometimes, the best way to collect information is if several users are in a room with you and those users respond to each other's statements directly. For example, if different groups have divergent views of the future, gathering members of those groups into one discussion may reveal that there are more (or fewer) consistencies between their views of the future than might have been clear otherwise. Also, when design features need to be prioritized (because of lack of space, resources, etc.), group discussions can be very useful.

Observation is useful when users can't answer questions because they don't have any practice thinking about the issues that you need to address, or they are too involved in a situation to discuss it objectively. For example, team members may "know" exactly how they feel they should work together and may report that as their current modus operandi, if asked. Observation may reveal that a team works (perhaps very successfully) in a completely different way. Learning how people do things now may point out problems that can be eliminated in the design of a new space—it is hard to forget other people sit near you and speak loudly on the telephone (potentially a current problem) when you can see the shadowy forms of nearby coworkers through frosted glass partitions, for example (potentially a future solution). It can also indicate how new spaces should be like existing ones. Observation also reveals ways users have modified their environments to make them work better, which can be valuable info when new spaces are being developed. If employees have a collection of "Do Not Disturb" signs ready to display at the doorways to their cubicles, that collection provides important information about the best work conditions for those employees. Sometimes observation gathers information about topics you would not have known a priori needed to be considered during the design of a new space, such as subtle nuances in the relative status of various users. Observations ideally continue until no new information is being collected, but in applied research, a certain time period usually needs to be set aside for observations to be done.

If at all possible, it can be good to collect information from written surveys first so you have some idea what a place is like. Observation next helps you to further understand a space, and perhaps to unravel puzzling patterns in the answers to survey questions. Following up with individual interviews and group discussions allows you to probe any remaining outstanding issues. If it is possible to complete another round of observation after the final discussions, additional insights can be obtained.

Each of the research tools is best used in particular types of situations. Sometimes, those situations are not viable. For example, it is difficult to do observation at a government site if no research team members have the security clearances required to enter the study area.

■ WRITTEN SURVEYS

Putting together a good written survey is difficult. Many times, information needs to be collected through indirect questions—you can't just ask users about some topics because they are too sensitive or because users don't have the background and skills needed to answer direct questions. Writing indirect questions is hard. It is also challenging to write questions that don't prejudice the way they are answered.

Remember that the questions that you'll ask will get at people's perceptions of their experiences. If you ask people about noise, they will be telling you about how noisy a space seems to them. If you need absolute noise levels, don't ask space users; take readings with a sound meter. People's perceptions are their reality—that's the sort of reason why placebo drugs can work so well—so it's best never to tell people that their perceptions are incorrect.

All of the kinds of survey questions we'll be discussing here collect information that can be analyzed using Excel—for meaningful data it is only necessary to tally the frequency with which each response has been provided and to convert that frequency into a percent of all of the people who answered the survey. Although it is useful to analyze data at an organization-wide level in many cases, it's often important to also look at the answers given by particular groups of people within an organization. An organization's culture can be useful to determine the overall form of a corporate headquarters, but when the space for the accounting staff is being developed, it's silly not to consider information from the accountants about the culture of their group.

After you write a survey, it's best if you have a few people take it who are similar to the people who will ultimately complete the survey. Look at the data you collect from this collection of 10 or so people and make sure that there's nothing odd about it (the average age of a work group being 92, ideal homes without places to sleep, etc.). The answers provided by this test group will show you whether your questions are appropriate. Testing the survey also gives you an idea how long it takes to complete it—people will rarely spend more than 10 minutes answering questions unless highly motivated to do so by the topic of the survey or a prize drawing. It can be particularly useful to have a couple of survey testers "narrate" what they're doing while they take the survey (e.g., "This question is asking me about [whatever], so I'll pick this answer because [reason]").

Any written questionnaire should begin with a brief cover note. That note should tell participants that all the information collected will remain confidential (if it will), how to complete the survey, and about how long it will take to answer all of the questions. If you tell people realistically how long it will take for them to answer all of a survey's questions, they will set aside a reasonable amount of time to complete it, which results in more thoughtful responses and a higher number of completed questionnaires. Any survey cover letter should also thank people for taking the time to answer your questions.

Distribute surveys to as many people in an organization as possible. Never collect information only from people who volunteer to complete a survey. Often volunteers want to lead the research toward particular outcomes.

Analyzing data from a group when less than one-third of its members (or 10 people, whichever is larger) have returned surveys means you run the risk of coming to conclusions based on an unusual subset of the whole group you are interested in speaking with. When groups of interest are very small (less than 10 members or so), all members of the group need to be encouraged (regularly) to return their surveys.

If you are not able to collect responses to use—related questions from about 10 users of each type who will regularly access the new space—supplement the information you collect from people who do answer questions with data from informed facility managers (if they are employed/used). A fast way to collect information from overworked facilities managers is to prepare a checklist of any reasonable possible options and have the facilities managers respond using that list.

Never report data that are supposed to be confidential in a way that makes it possible to identify who said what—if there is only one female African American employee in a group over the age of 50, don't report separately the data for female African American employees over the age of 50.

When you are writing survey questions, keep the following in mind:

Questions should be asked in a neutral way. Don't ask people how much they enjoy their new chair; ask more broadly about their attitude toward their chair or their experience sitting in it. Similarly, make sure that the responses provided to multiple choice questions permit participants to express any one of a full range of possible opinions (i.e., allow people to both strongly like and dislike an aspect of a space).

Don't use jargon in the questions. Few laypeople know what "circulation" is, for example.

Use multiple-choice questions unless there are enough resources available to look for themes in the answers to open-ended questions (participants answer questions in their own words instead of selecting from among the answer options provided). If you do ask open-ended questions, bear in mind that people will not write long answers (no matter how important the question is to you) and often the answers they do supply will be difficult to understand.

Don't presume or make assumptions about what people do or emotions they might have. For example, don't assume there are any positive features about a chair before you start to investigate them.

Each set of questions should be accompanied by directions (e.g., "Please answer the next five questions using a scale of 1 to 10, with 10 being the most positive possible rating and 1 the least positive rating and all the numbers in between represent ratings between the most positive possible rating and the least positive possible rating."). The wording of these directions may seem somewhat stiff, but all possible responses must be explicitly described.

The answers that you provide for multiple-choice questions should cover all of the possible options, and it should not be possible for people to select two options unless that was the plan when the question was written. If the response options are numerical this is particularly important (e.g., options of under 10, 10–50, 51–100, etc.; not 10 and under, 10–50, 50–100, etc.).

FIGURE C-1 ■ Comforting prospect and refuge can be created in modern interior spaces, as evidenced by this library space. Humans feel secure in darker spaces with lower ceilings (refuge) that are adjacent to more brightly lit spaces with higher ceilings (prospect). Copyright © iStockPhoto/Teun van den Dries.

FIGURE C-2 ■ This living room conveys a lot of information about its owner—as he or she consciously or unconsciously intended. Copyright © iStockPhoto/K. Inozemtsev.

FIGURE C-3 ■ Psychologists and others often organize colors using a wheel such as this one. Individual colors influence us psychologically, as do sets of colors used together. When colors that are across from each other on the color wheel are combined in equal amounts in a space, the effect is very energizing. Copyright © iStockPhoto/bluestocking.

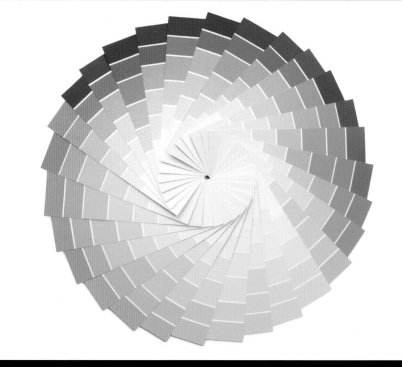

FIGURE C-4 ■ This visually complex space provides so much stimulation that it is nearly overwhelming. Copyright © iStockPhoto/Olaf Loose.

FIGURE C-5 ■ Formal, calming balance makes this hotel lobby a refuge for travelers. Copyright © iStockPhoto/Nick Free.

FIGURE C-6 ■ The red color used on the walls in this space and the reflective coatings on the surfaces make this a highly energizing space. Copyright © iStockPhoto/Olga Mirenska.

FIGURE C-8 ■ Palette A. The interior palette preferred by the Japanese, and the second most preferred by Koreans, but the least preferred by the English. These results are consistent with the fact that the preferred psychological state of Asians is relaxed, while North Americans prefer to be energized. *Journal of Interior Design*, Vol. 28, Issue 1, 2002.

FIGURE C-9 ■ Palette C. The collection of colors that Western cultures found most desirable in an interior environment (and the third most preferred by Eastern cultures) is colorful, using reds, blues, greens, and yellows, albeit subtly. This collection was the set of colors selected as most desirable by American citizens. It was the second most desirable to the English and Japanese, and the least desirable set of colors to Koreans. *Journal of Interior Design*, Vol. 28, Issue 1, 2002.

FIGURE C-10 ■ Palette E. Koreans found most desirable a collection of neutral hues with a fairly even split between warm and cool colors (some obviously red and blue), midrange brightness and low saturation overall (with comparable numbers of colors with strong and moderate levels of saturation), and high contrasts in saturation between adjacent colors and middle levels of brightness contrasts. The Japanese also found this collection of colors highly desirable for interior environments. *Journal of Interior Design*, Vol. 28, Issue 1, 2002.

FIGURE C-11 ■ Palette F. The British found most desirable, and Americans' second most desirable, a collection of warm colors of moderate brightness and saturation, with moderate brightness contrasts and low saturation contrasts between adjacent colors. *Journal of Interior Design*, Vol. 28, Issue 1, 2002.

FIGURE C-12 ■ Palette D. The palette least preferred by all of the cultures tested had bright but unsaturated neutral colors and high brightness and medium saturation contrasts between adjacent colors. *Journal of Interior Design*, Vol. 28, Issue 1, 2002.

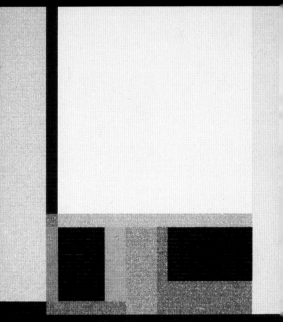

FIGURE C-14 ■ People communicate information about themselves through the way they personalize their homes. Each of these front doors communicates information that people from the same cultures as the homeowners who customized the doors can understand. Copyright © iStockPhoto/Peter Austin Photography.

FIGURE C-15 ■ Children have special place-based needs. For example, they need a variety of forms of stimulation to aid their cognitive development. Copyright ©iStockPhoto/Galina Barskaya.

FIGURE C-16 ■ The fireplace in this shop reminds shoppers of relaxing sojourns around their home fireplaces. Humans are calmed by looking at flames, just as they are by looking at aquariums. It is important that retailers create spaces with the appropriate energy level. For example, if people in this space become too relaxed, they may not leave and may also stop buying additional food and beverages. Jim Brozek Photography, Smith Brothers Coffee—Fireplace Seating Area, Copyright 2007, courtesy of Kahler Slater.

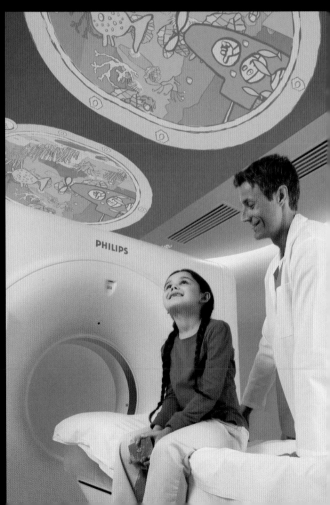

FIGURE C-18 ■ The Philips Ambient Experience combines animations with sounds to reduce stress for patients undergoing an assortment of different exams or procedures. Photo courtesy of Philips Healthcare.

Sometimes you will want to ask people how strongly they agree or disagree with a statement using a set of response options that run from strongly disagree to strongly agree. If you provide an odd number of options (5 or 7), people can be neutral by choosing the middle number; they cannot do this if you provide an even number of options. There is a philosophical debate in social science research about how likely it is that people are actually neutral on many topics. Space design research should use an even number of response options in place-related questions. People rarely have neutral opinions on place-related topics.

Any question should probe only one topic—don't ask people a "double-barreled" question about levels of light and temperature, for example. Double-barreled questions are cumbersome to answer and to write appropriately.

Be wary of the answers you get to questions about the future or the past (before last week)—people are not (generally) accurate prophets and they have bad memories.

The most important questions should be placed at the beginning of a survey (in case people stop answering questions). Demographic questions should be at the end of the survey because sometimes demographic questions make respondents unduly concerned about confidentiality and that influences their answers to subsequent questions.

Written questionnaires are a good way to answer many of the questions posed by journalists (who, what, where, when, how, and why—although how and why are often best addressed in interviews or discussion groups) about workspaces, family areas, classrooms, etc. It is convenient to use questionnaires to get at issues such as what activities take place in a group space and in individual cubicles, and whether information management tools (e.g., electronic and mechanical tools such as whiteboards and tackboards) are being used. Any question whose answer you would want to follow up with the questions "Why?" or "How come?" should be asked during an interview or group discussion. It is often useful to follow up a question about an "ideal" space with "why" or "how come," for example.

What happens (or should happen) in a space during any month are the activities that a space should facilitate. In a workplace, the tables, chairs, and desks for these activities can be specified to suit different work styles (ways of acting to complete work tasks). To determine work styles, you can ask the following question to users: "*For you to do your current job well, which of the following should the space you work in be more like: Santa's elves' workshop, with places to build and tinker; bank vault where you are sealed in every morning with your computer and papers and work uninterrupted; booth at a great restaurant where people drop by to discuss issues throughout the day (unfortunately, this option would have to come without the food); Quaker religious service—at Quaker services people silently ponder important questions and speak aloud when they have something significant to say; airline club where amenities are available when you drop in to use them?"* The option selected by the majority of group members provides clear guidance on the design direction for each team's work areas.

Some issues that you need to learn about should be approached indirectly, because people don't know the answers to related direct questions, or because they feel that there is a particular way that they should answer questions on that topic. So, the reasons that indirect questions are used are similar in some ways to the reason observation is used—but information can be collected more quickly and efficiently with written surveys than through observation.

One of the best ways to collect information indirectly is to ask people how others are responding—the information gathered doesn't actually tell you much about how the other people are actually feeling, but it does give you a good idea of what the person filling out the form thinks (e.g., *"Do other employees find it difficult to concentrate while they're working?"*).

Sometimes it's necessary to be a little cleverer. For example, it is important for you to understand the complexity of the work of people who will use a workspace you might be designing. That information gives you an idea of how much visual and acoustical shielding they require. To get at this issue, you could ask, *"When you are working and someone drops by your workspace to ask you a question, are you more likely to try to spend the last few seconds before they begin to speak making a note so you can return to your train of thought more easily or deciding how to greet them?"* The first response would indicate a more complex task. Or you could ask, *"Which of the following is most like how you spend your day at work: solving a new puzzle; performing a play that you've acted in before; teaching a class you have taught before to a class of students who occasionally ask thought-provoking questions?"* People who select the first response are doing the most complex tasks while those who choose the second are working on the least complex ones.

People cannot reliably describe their absolute level of performance in various spaces. They can, however, be asked to discuss their relative performance in several places because any ways in which they might distort their perceptions of their performance will be consistent and not be an issue when their assessments are compared. If they have decided that their performance was at level 5 in one space and level 7 in another, the difference in assessments is 2—if these individual assessments were each overstated by 1 (they should have been 4 and 6), the difference is still 2. Since people answering survey questions have bad memories and are poor prophets, this is a good question to ask as part of a post-occupancy evaluation (described later in this chapter).

Hill, Brierley, and MacDougall (2003) have described a very straight-forward methodology for determining how satisfied or unsatisfied people are with spaces and, since people are never completely satisfied with any space, which aspects of it should be changed first. Hill and his colleagues, however, don't think of their technique so much as a space analysis tool but view it as a way to measure customer satisfaction. To use their tool, you should first develop a list of features of the physical environment that you would like to learn about—such as sound levels in classrooms or group spaces, or the distance of team rooms from the individual workstations of the team members.

Next, ask participants to tell you how important or unimportant each of those features is to them using a 10-point scale that ranges from "of no importance at all" (1) to "extremely important" (10).

After people are queried about the importance of each feature, they should be asked how satisfied or unsatisfied they are with the same set of physical features using a 10-point scale that ranges from "totally dissatisfied" to "totally satisfied."

Anytime the averaged importance ranking is one or more points above the averaged satisfaction ranking, steps should be taken to alleviate negative situations. It may be, however, that so many gaps above one are present that you will need to prioritize your suggestions for change based on available resources, general feasibility of making a change, and other similar issues.

You can also ask people to select adjectives from a list you provide to describe current, ideal, or proposed spaces. By reviewing these lists, you'll get some idea of how well or poorly a current or proposed space meets, or would meet, various sorts of user needs. It is important that the adjectives on these lists are words that the people completing the survey would actually use. The terms that are reasonable to include vary by space-usage, geography, and education level, for example. Each list should have about 50 words on it in random order. It is important that each time you add one word to the list, you also add the opposite word to the list (but arrange the words in a random order overall). This means that if the word *pleasant* is on the list, the word *unpleasant* should also be there.

The issues that you will want to probe with the adjectives on the list are pleasantness, influence on activity level (e.g., calming), desirability, level of social interaction, aesthetic factors, appropriateness for activity (e.g., convenient), formality, intellectual response (e.g., interesting), mood (e.g., cheerful), uniqueness, and ambient aspects of the environment (e.g., noisy). Other types of adjectives might be useful if unusual current or potential spaces are being assessed.

▪ INDIVIDUAL INTERVIEWS

When you ask people questions orally in individual interviews, you can follow up their initial responses with subsequent questions (often "Why?" or "How come?"). These additional questions allow you to more fully understand the information that is being collected.

The following rules improve the quality of the information collected during interviews:

Reread the rules for written questions, and apply those tenets here—don't ask leading questions, for example.

Interview randomly selected people in the space you are talking about, if at all possible. If you are working on a workplace design project, interview people in their workspaces. Being in the sort of place being discussed can remind the people being interviewed of relevant issues and it allows them to point to specific items in a space to illustrate their statements. Interviewing in the space being discussed also gives you, as the interviewer, a clearer understanding of physical conditions being described, which can help you make comparisons between different interviews later.

Don't be a slave to the order, format, or content of interview questions. It is a good idea to write interview questions in advance and read them over and over until you are very familiar with them so that you won't be tongue-tied during the interview (it's even better if you can practice the interview with a colleague). However, if conversation naturally begins to flow while you are asking one question and the interviewee spontaneously starts to provide information that is relevant to a different question, don't stop him. Breaking the flow of discussion destroys the interview dynamic. Return to questions that get skipped at a natural point in the discussion. Also, if the person being interviewed spontaneously starts to provide information that you find useful, but that is not in direct response to any of your questions, let him keep talking! The point of interviewing is to learn useful material, not to march purposefully from one question to the next to complete some sort of interview ritual.

Tape-record interviews with a digital recorder. It is easy to share digital files with others. Also, you cannot possibly write down all of the interesting material provided during an interview and ask the right follow-up questions. Always ask interviewees if it is okay for you to record your discussion with them. Occasionally, an interviewee will say that she prefers the interview not be recorded, so always have a pen and paper handy. Always have a digital camera present during an interview. Occasionally an interviewee will show you something that you will want a photograph of later. Also, it can be useful to walk through a space during an interview, as particular questions come up, and you may need photos of what was being discussed later as you analyze the interview data. Videotaping makes some people nervous, so if at all possible, the digital camera and recorder duo should be used in its place.

Ideally only you and the interviewee should be at the interview. Sometimes, someone else involved in the design process somehow (perhaps the client who will ultimately pay to create a structure or pay your fee) will demand to attend interviews. Having other people present distorts the interview, particularly if some sensitive information might otherwise be revealed. Never allow more than one other person to be within earshot when you are conducting an interview. There is one exception to this rule: Do not interview children alone—under any circumstances. Having another adult present during the entire interview is the only way to ensure that there are no issues raised later related to inappropriate behavior.

Interviews should last no more than 30–45 minutes—after that everyone is tired and little new useful information is collected.

Dress like the people you will be interviewing or a tad more formally; this will establish camaraderie with each person being interviewed.

A spontaneous, irrelevant warm-up question about an easy-to-discuss topic should lead off an interview—an example might be "What a cool plant [pointing to a plant in her cubicle]. What's it called?" Once the ice has been broken and people have spoken, the conversation will start to flow.

The best way to encourage an interviewee to speak is to be silent. If you are quiet, the interviewee will speak. If he doesn't (after a count of about 30), ask if there is a reason he doesn't want to answer the question and reassure him that his opinion is valued. Perhaps there is something going on that you should know about before you proceed, or perhaps you have unintentionally done something rude. It is also possible that the interviewee is worried about his answers remaining confidential.

During the interview, look and act pleasant, but do not in any way respond to an answer in a way that indicates that you are pleased with the information presented—people like to make other people happy, and if an interviewee consciously or subconsciously feels that you are pleased with one sort of material, he will make an effort to supply more that is similar. Gentle probes such as "Can you tell me more about that?" "What else?" and "What about [relate the current topic of conversation to a prior topic]?" are appropriate. People are also likely to continue talking if you repeat what they have just said. If people get off topic into information that is not useful to you, you can verbally reassure them that they are providing important material and that you hope to return to that information later, but at this time . . .

At the end of the interview, be ready. Often after you have turned off the tape recorder, all sorts of useful and relevant information starts to spill out of the interviewee.

People from all groups who will be using the space being developed should be interviewed—this can include homeowners, retail customers, and patients. Ideally, interview at least 10 people from each user group. If less than 10 people will use a space, all of them should be interviewed.

Individual interviews are a good way to collect programming information because collecting use-related process information in a written format requires many cumbersome questions, and apparent inconsistencies in answers can't be investigated.

Straightforward programming questions are often useful. Consider the following:

"Describe one of your typical workdays."

"Describe a time when you were working really well. What did you accomplish? Where were you? What were you doing?"

"If I were a fly on a wall during one of your group meetings, what would I see?"

"If I gave you $1,000 to invest in [name of space], what would you spend it on? Why?"

You can ask even more specific questions about the primary activity planned for the space being created:

"What will happen in the space being created? What should happen in the space being created?"

"What will a usual day in the life of the space be like? How about an unusual day?"

"Who will use the new space?"

"When?"

"For what?"

"Why?"

Answers to the two questions that follow will show you how the room you are creating will fit into the activity matrix in Chapter 10:

"Is the primary use planned for the space social or nonsocial? Will the primary user of the space spend a lot of time there interacting with other people or alone?"

"Does the primary use planned for the space result in a tangible, physical output, or a more intangible, mental product? Will people be writing books there or cooking meals, for example?"

Questions about the future of the family/firm/group are best asked in person. Multiple-choice questions to collect all required information would be cumbersome, and if these questions are asked in writing, follow-up questions cannot be added.

Other potentially interesting issues can be probed during interviews. People can be asked questions such as *"What surprised you most on your first day here?"* which investigates issues related to culture, how work gets done, and corporate identity. Questions such as *"What is the one thing about your workplace (home, etc.) that I shouldn't change? Why?"* help you understand how a space really gets used by an organization or person. If a question of this type is asked after camaraderie has developed between you and the interviewee, he will feel free to say that you should change every feature of it. Other similar interesting questions include *"How do you know if you are doing your job well?"* and *"What's it like here during* [name a relevant organization-specific sort of crisis, such as the software that's just been delivered to the major client deletes all their company records or a major accident nearby fills all patient beds]?" You can also ask, *"Have you ever seen (in person or on TV) a workplace* [or home, if you are creating a residence, etc.] *that is more appropriate for what you do now than your current workspace? How was it more appropriate?"* or *"What three adjectives would you use to describe the ideal* [name of place]? *Your current* [name of place]? *Why?"*

The essence of the space that you are creating will be clear if you ask users questions about the space being developed such as the following:

"If the [space being designed] were a person, what kind of person would they be?"

"What kind of person should they be?"

"What would they do for a living?"

"What kind of clothes would they wear?"

"What would they choose for their last meal?"

"What would their hobbies be?"

"How old are they?"

The answers to these questions are very useful and if a group or person is functioning well, they should guide the design process. A space whose last meal would bekung pao chicken is very different from one whose last meal would be steak and a baked potato. If the user group is not functioning well, the information collected provides important insights about the new, more appropriate, modus operandi you will attempt to encourage via design of physical environments. Current state information can facilitate the development of spaces that can evolve over time to support the various phases a group will move through as it travels to its ultimate, and desired, social forms.

In the course of any design project (particularly when you are creating a space for one particular user), it is good to collect answers to the following questions, which are easier to ask during an interview than on paper:

"Why are you interested in redesigning this space?" This question will ensure that you clearly identify aspects of the current space that are significant to the user.

"What is the most wonderful [space] you've ever been in?" At an early conceptual project stage, this question can be used in this general form. The space described might be a museum, a home, a store, a boat, an office, a garden, or somewhere else. Follow up questions include: "Where was it located? What was the purpose of the space? What colors do you remember? What was the light like there? What sort of furniture was in it? How was the furniture arranged? What did the space smell like? What textures do you remember? What do you remember about the soundscape of that place? What other memories do you have of that space?" This line of discussion can also be used to learn more about experiences in a place of the sort being developed. Asking these questions in the general and more specific form can generate a particularly rich set of insights. In addition, it is helpful to think not only about the best place people have ever been in, but also the worst. This series of questions will help you understand your users' place histories (Israel 2003). In Chapter 1, we discussed the importance of recognizing users' past experience in places when creating a new space.

"Are there things [furniture, wall colors, etc.] that you would like to continue to use in the redesigned room? What are they? Why would you like to reuse them?" Recognizing objects to be reused early in the design process streamlines space design, particularly if those things relate to place history or budget.

One good way to get people to open up and talk about difficult topics is to show them photographs and have them respond to the images. This is not a kind of Rorschach test and there are no incorrect responses. Collect a set of photographs (from magazines, iStockphoto, or wherever) that seem to represent the full range of human emotions—positive and negative, high energy and low energy. Images included could range from exciting in a pleasant way or calm in a pleasant way to calm in an unpleasant way (boring) or exciting in an unpleasant way (threatening). Concentrate on the more pleasant emotions (but do also include images related to the negative ones) and collect about 50 images. They might be of mud puddles, anthills, dewdrops, sand dunes, traffic signals, or birds flying in formation—just not the sort of spaces that are the topic of your discussion or close-ups of human or animal faces. Make sure that the pictures are all in color, all the same size, and all mounted to cardstock.

Lay the cards out on a horizontal surface in front of the person who will use the space and make a request such as "Pick three or four of these cards that give you the same feeling as being in this [workspace/hospital room/ etc.]" or "Pick three or four of these cards that give you the same feeling you would like to have in the ideal [workspace, etc.]" or "Pick three or four of these cards that describe [living in this house/living in your ideal house/ etc.]." Carefully place the selected cards to one side and ask the interviewee why she selected each card. This is the real information of interest. Why people have selected the images will show their emotional response to their current space or the response that they would like to have to a new space. Both are of interest. Hopefully, if interviewees are asked about existing locations you will have visited the current space, so you can learn how one particular group of people, the users you are working with, responds to the particular physical elements in place. Other chapters describe how to create particular emotional effects in a space, and these techniques can be used in new spaces in a way that is informed by any new knowledge you might gain about any unexpected ways that the user group responds to the physical environment. You might learn, for example, that the main competitor uses a certain color in its logo, and that seeing this color makes your user group tense; hence it's a bad color to include in a break area even if it would generally create the desired psychological effect.

Interviewees can also be asked to create some sort of visual representation of an ideal form of whatever sort of space you are designing. To avoid having these images be completely detached from reality, you should ask people to create an ideal space for them to do their current job well/for them and their family today/for them to treat their current patients with the best current technology available/etc. The problem with having people simply create the ideal office for them to treat their patients is that the doctor, in this example, may stop thinking about the ideal space to remove bunions in his current small town (how the space will actually be used) and dream about the ideal space for him to do plastic surgery on famous actors on Rodeo Drive in Los Angeles.

People are often embarrassed to draw or diagram anything in front of other people—apparently we all had the same judgmental elementary school art teacher. If you ask people to draw an ideal space on graph paper with thick markers (which hide many sins), they will be a lot less tense drawing in front of you. You can also ask people to maneuver cutout shapes that represent pieces of furniture or architectural features of a space into the appropriate position, but then you restrict people's imagination to the particular kit of parts you supply. If the space being created is limited in size, make sure that the interviewee creates a space of the same size. That will help you understand how she prioritizes elements in the space. It is important that interviewees narrate what they are doing as they create the images so that you know why they are creating those particular spaces. Those "whys" are key here—the whole purpose of this exercise is to learn more about what's going on in the interviewee's head, not to see how good an artist they are. Another reason why it's important for you to have people narrate what they are incorporating into the space is that sometimes the judgmental elementary school art teacher was right, and there's no way to tell what has been depicted from looking at the image.

People who will live or work in a space you are developing can also be asked to collect images that give them the same sort of feeling that they want to have in the developed space, for example. These images can be collected from any sources the interviewees encounter—magazines, websites, shoe catalogs—or they can take photographs on their own. You can talk with the interviewees generally about what motivated them to select the collection of images that they did, and in more detail about specific images or elements of images that they find particularly significant.

During an interview, people can be shown images of current spaces or potential design solutions and asked for their responses to the spaces using the adjective checklist method, described in the "Written Surveys" section, to begin a conversation. Subsequent questions can ask them to describe what the experience of being in the illustrated space would be like. Do not use floor plans in this exercise; most people who are not architects or interior designers cannot interpret them.

■ GROUP DISCUSSIONS

A lot of spaces have been designed using information collected during group discussions. Group discussions have, however, fallen out of favor with social science researchers because it is too easy for one very opinionated person to dominate the discussion and for other aspects of group dynamics to distort the data-gathering process. Group discussions can, however, be an efficient way to collect information if scheduling the session does not become too complicated. During a group discussion, information may be gathered from several people. The same sort of questions that are addressed during individual interviews can be probed during group discussions. Also, group members may make comments that build on the statements of other participants, creating a much richer data set for later analysis. Because of the open dialogue that takes place during group sessions, they are best for exploratory discussions and are not as useful for systematically examining information.

Group discussions are much like individual interviews, with a different ratio between interviewers and group participants (again, there should never be more than two interviewers visible). The rules for individual interviews outlined earlier are relevant here, along with the following additional parameters:

Group discussions should have from 6 to 10 participants (randomly selected from the groups who will use a new space). Groups about this size keep everyone talking. So does arranging the chairs in a circle so that everyone in the session room is looking at everyone else.

Within any one discussion group, all the participants should be similar to each other in ways that seem to matter for the research being done—for example, similar job level, job type, role in the new space to be created—but each discussion group held should differ on these same parameters. This mixture of groups ensures that a broad range of information will be collected and that people will feel free to participate in each group. It is particularly important that all of the people in a workplace design group discussion be of the same job level (all executives, all middle managers, all clerical staff, etc.) because if status levels are mixed in a group, participants of lower status are not apt to speak freely.

Group discussions work best when focus group participants are strangers to each other because people who have known each other may share unspoken information that you as the interviewer might not be familiar with.

Group discussion moderators should make sure all participants are actively involved during the session. The moderator can keep one person from dominating the conversation through techniques such as not looking at the dominating person or making statements such as "X, we're familiar with your opinion, so let's involve some other people in this conversation." Nonparticipants can conversely be motivated to speak by asking them for their opinions or looking at them. Conversations on particular topics of interest (the moderator must be very familiar with all of the research questions before the group starts) can be encouraged by rephrasing earlier comments of the group or asking a participant to clarify or expand a particular point. The moderator needs to ensure that the group does not splinter into a number of smaller conversations, which makes it difficult to keep on topic and to pick up all of the important information on the audio (or video) recordings.

A research discussion is not a random conversation; it should be carefully organized to probe topics of interest. Since the sessions are exploratory, it should not be possible to answer any of the questions raised with yes or no responses.

If discussion groups are longer than 90 minutes, the energy levels of both the participants and the moderator start to lag.

Usually, at least three group discussions should be conducted on any given topic, with different kinds of space users, if time and resources permit.

It can be particularly effective to ask group participants to react to pairs of images, none of which are of the same type of space as the one being developed. Ideally the images would be similar to the sets described in the individual interview section of this chapter. Projecting images on a screen breaks the question-asking routine, and responding to those images is interesting to many group members because they do not often do visual things. Participants can be asked questions related to the visual images, such as the following:

"Which image is a better representation of what it's like to work around here? Why?" or "How come?"

"Which image is a better representation of what it should be like to work around here? Why?"

"Which of these animals would be a better mascot for this organization? Why?"

"Which of these images would you show to a person newly hired to do your job here to explain what your job is like? Why?"

"Which of these tools would be most useful in your workspace? Why?" (Show two objects not related to working in an office, etc., such as a fire extinguisher and a backhoe.)

"Which of these images best captures the essence of what it's like to be a patient here? Why?"

■ OBSERVATION

Observation research is a great way to learn more about how a group of people that interests you is interacting with the world around them. Doing observation is useful when people may not know how they use or respond to a space, or they may not have the vocabulary to provide the information you need to design a space for their use. Doing observation is also handy when people may feel that there are socially appropriate answers to design related questions you might like to pose. There is some information that can only be collected via observation, such as how people tend to move in a space, how individuals respond to afternoon glare, and how long most people spend talking to each other over (or through) cubicle walls each day. A lot of the information that you collect from observations is difficult to understand without speaking to people using the spaces you are observing. You may get the feeling that some sort of object is valued when you are observing, but you may not be able to figure out why, for example. That's why it is handy to schedule observations before individual interviews and group discussions.

Observations are carefully planned; they are not "hanging out in a space." To streamline the observation process, a form can be developed to record the frequency of activities of interest, leaving plenty of space to record information in addition to these tallies. True observation is much more than simply counting specific activities; it involves watching and analyzing information related to a design project. Some behaviors are analyzed in any observation project (who is in a space, what are they doing [basically]). Generally answering the journalism questions helps you understand how a group or individual currently uses space: Who does what? With whom? When? Where? How? and (to the extent it is possible to determine) Why? What is the apparent emotion among people in the space?

Sometimes there are more specialized issues to be investigated: What seems to be causing people to act so bizarrely in the conference rooms? What informal rules have developed for use of the conference rooms? Where do patient families go for privacy? How often do members of two groups— whom management would like to interact because it seems that the results of those interactions would be creative solutions to problems—actually talk with each other?

It is also possible to observe things that might aid in interpretation of information collected through other means. For example, through observation, you can determine the level of privacy that retail employees have during their breaks or that nurses have while they're trying to concentrate on notations they are making on patient charts. This information could be usefully paired with participant perceptions of their stress levels or the quality of their current work. When you are observing, you can determine how individuals have modified their environments to meet their needs. This can be useful information as you create new spaces for the same sorts of people.

The academic anthropologist rule book says that observations should take place until everything observed could be predicted from what has been learned during earlier observations—but applied researchers often cannot devote that much time to a project. Since any space you are creating will be used at different times of the day and on different days of the week, you should make observations during all of these different times of the day and on different days of the week. All of the sorts of spaces that you will design should be observed (hallways, individual spaces, group spaces, specialized work zones, exhibit spaces, cafeterias, lobbies, etc.). Several of each type of space should be observed, if possible. It can be interesting to observe regular and "extreme" examples of different spaces—for example, workspaces in the middle of a sea of cubicles and workspaces on the edge of that sea right inside the front door. Contrasts between what you see in each of these spaces can be useful.

Generally, people will wonder what you're up to when you arrive to begin observing. Be prepared to tell them that you are going to be observing for the next few days (that's the usual amount of time available to do observations in a space, regardless of the anthropology rule book) to learn more about what it's like to be in the space. If you lie about what you're doing, you'll get caught. Eventually, people start to behave more naturally as you observe them. Usually this takes a day, or so. You will never become invisible, but if you avoid doing attention-getting things, such as clicking the top of your pen or chewing gum, you will be less conspicuous. Ethical observers sit in a natural position in a space and do not hide.

People doing observations should bring a camera with them to record things of interest that they see. Also, they should take notes. At the end of the day, it's difficult to spontaneously recall dozens of insightful thoughts you've had during the day. Save any interpretations until observation sessions are completed; be open-minded during the observation process.

Videotapes of user activity can also be analyzed, just as direct observations are assessed. All people being videotaped should be aware that you are recording their activities.

Whenever research data can be collected before and after changes are made to an environment or a space is created, you have the opportunity to learn how effectively the spaces you have created meet user needs. This is called a post-occupancy evaluation. No post-change research should be conducted until six months after a project has been completed—the dust needs to settle and people need to learn where the bathrooms are before you gather their opinions.

Using the techniques outlined in this chapter, you will get to know the people who will use the spaces you are creating, and that means that you will be able to more effectively apply the information in Chapters 3–9.

12

SPECIAL FOCUS: HOMES

People's homes are sanctuaries, retreats that provide physical and mental shelter and support.

In their homes, people can control their interactions with others and their sensory experience, as well as restock their mental energy. Even people without much money can create home spaces where they show themselves and others who they are. Although cultural norms influence what's displayed in a home, employers don't, so home spaces can be truer expressions of who their owners really are than workspaces. Some spaces in homes are more private than others, and it's in those most private spaces where people have the most design options. We live our evolving lives in homes, and the same space has different duties at different times, even during a single phase of our life—people can eat and study in the same dining room at different times of the same day.

Homes have all of the attributes of a well-designed place. They are

- Comforting
- Communicating
- Complying
- Challenging
- Continuing

■ COMFORTING

We re-create past place experiences we treasure in our homes (Israel 2003). Sometimes we get the chance to do the same thing where we work, but not often. If you are designing a home, it is particularly important for you to use the questions in Chapter 11 to learn about people's past place experiences. People form deep emotional attachments to their homes and want them to be just as psychologically comfortable as they are physically comfortable. That's why people are so determined to have their homes be similar to other places that have been satisfying. Smelling the sorts of smells that we remember from desirable spaces, seeing the sorts of colors we remember from those settings, and feeling the same sorts of surfaces under our feet (the list could go on and on) make our lives more pleasant through tiny sensory flashbacks.

The fact that McMansions (the large, impersonal homes being created around the United States) don't have the sorts of features that the population remembers is one of the reasons why they seem so desolate and emotionally unsatisfying for the people who live in them. Although McMansions meet some of their owners' needs to indicate to others that they are financially comfortable, in many cases they are also impersonally designed to respond to the physical and emotional needs of an unidentified family. So they don't actually respond to the needs of any family.

Some of the design features in these McMansions are just plain wrong. Think about the cavernous ceiling heights in many of their family rooms. They are so high that they make these spaces seem formal, which is at odds with the intimate family gatherings that many hope for in these settings. (See Chapter 6 for more details on ceiling heights.) McMansions also often isolate family members into special purpose rooms, or their own private bedroom suites, so that only the most introverted families would be comfortable liv-

FIGURE 12-1 ■ Territories are not necessarily private. This balcony is clearly visible to passersby, but only the residents of the space through which it is entered can use it. More public territories give people who control them the opportunity to express who they are to a wider range of other people. Copyright © iStockPhoto/ red_moon_rise.

ing there. Dining room space is often sacrificed in these homes, although mammoth kitchens contain spaces in which people can dine. Eating in a kitchen is distracting, however. People dining in kitchens are distressed by the visual clutter of all of the appliances and tools used to prepare a meal—although the increasing amount of takeout food consumed at home may reduce the amount of visual clutter present in a kitchen.

The development of soulless McMansions is coming at a particularly dangerous time. As the social contracts that have traditionally bound people to the organizations that employ them are evaporating, people who have neither a "home place" nor a "work place" are left with few places where they feel comfortable and secure and where they can represent themselves through place design.

Women and men have different comfort-related objectives for the places that they control. Women are generally more attuned to relationships between people and are interested in creating spaces that support those relationships. Men usually focus on the functionality of objects and spaces and value efficient spaces where particular tasks can be performed. When house shopping, a heterosexual couple standing in a kitchen will be attuned to different aspects of the same scene—the woman will focus on the breakfast nook to make sure it is large enough to accommodate a table at which all family members can gather, while the man will make sure that the work triangle seems efficient.

Keeley and Edney (1983) have thoroughly investigated models of hypothetical and desirable homes created by men and women who were not professional designers. Women created homes that were more original, while the homes created by men tended to have more traditional bilateral symmetry. Homes designed by women tended to be smaller overall (also the rooms were smaller) and have more communal areas and more curved walls than the homes designed by men.

Noise, daylight, and views of nature are important in homes, just as they are in other sorts of places. Noise while we are sleeping can cause problems, even if the noise is not loud enough to wake us up. When we hear noises louder than 35 decibels while we are asleep—whether they are from an airplane or someone snoring—our blood pressure and heart rate increase.

> **DESIGN IMPLICATION**
>
> Homes need to meet residents' needs for psychological comfort and support.

■ COMMUNICATING

When asked by researchers, parents are quite clear about the appropriate design of a space where family members interact; this sort of place would generally be termed a "family room" (Miller and Maxwell 2003). Parents would

FIGURE 12-2 ■ This is a calming residential space. The colors, furniture arrangement, and views help people restock their mental energy and relax. Copyright © iStockPhoto/Galina Barskaya.

like it to be a relatively large space with higher ceilings (vaulting not necessary), adjacent to the kitchen (but without a direct view of the cooking areas in the kitchen from the family room eating spaces), that has multiple entrances. Several different activities should be able to take place in the space and ideally it would be zoned into subsections with groups of comfortable chairs or a table at which people could eat, do homework, or in a particularly bucolic vision of the home, play board games and assemble jigsaw puzzles together. People in this room should be able to go directly into the backyard and large windows should overlook the yard, according to the people interviewed by Miller and Maxwell. Interviewees also felt that this space should have built-in storage and bookshelves.

When living rooms or family rooms have a fireplace, it can serve as the focal point required to develop the rhythm and balance discussed in Chapter 5. Worldwide, a fireplace also symbolizes the security of a home. Even though many fireplaces serve only a symbolic function now, that function is so important that most people would still like to have one in their home (Miller and Maxwell 2003).

Painting walls colors that individuals feel are particularly desirable, or taking the more drastic steps of moving walls around, makes a place more closely meet user physical and psychological needs. The recent increase in do-it-yourself (DIY) programs on television and products for DIYers seem to be responding to the needs of many individuals to create places that reflect what they feel are important aspects of who they are as a person. These efforts at differentiation are often the cause of DIY activities among people who are comfortable financially and who live in adequate homes that simply say the wrong thing to visitors and residents—people get just as clean in a traditional bathtub as they do in a Jacuzzi tub, but the Jacuzzi tub says something—even about homeowners who never use them (and most don't). Customizing a home also allows people to take full possession of it. The functionally "unnecessary" activities that take possession of a home are much like the steps that diners take in a restaurant when their food arrives—to claim their food, they will touch the edges of their plates, even if they've been warned that they're hot.

Not every home is lived in by traditional families whose ancestors reached America on the Mayflower, although advertisements of home design products in the United States rarely recognize that fact. For example, religious Jews who observe the Halacha religious code choose not to do many things on the Sabbath and often design their homes to recognize those restrictions. For example, because they are not permitted to use electricity on the Sabbath, some choose to automate the lighting systems in their homes so that darkness does not become an issue. Many people can be involved in the preparation of Indian meals, and larger kitchens permit all of their work to flow smoothly. Some Moslems would prefer to live in homes where men and women can socialize separately. Latino families, which are often large and close-knit, soon overflow conventionally sized living rooms.

DESIGN IMPLICATION

Homes must recognize cultural differences in how residents prefer to use this space.

■ COMPLYING

Special Space Needs

Most of this book has focused on how young and middle-aged adults (ages 18 or so to about 65) interact with the spaces that surround them. Children and people over 65, as well as people with psychological challenges, also need, and have, homes.

CHILDREN'S EXPERIENCE OF PLACES

Children experience social and physical environments as they grow. The physical environment can aid the cognitive development of young children if it contains a variety of sensation-rich objects and places for them to explore from the time they are infants. This collection of objects and places should stimulate, collectively, all of the toddlers' senses, and in a variety of ways (e.g., not all of the visual stimulation should be through variations in color, but shape and size should change as well). Regularly changing the mix of children's experiences is a good idea. Redecorating the rooms of 15- to 17-month-old children has been associated with higher levels of cognitive development later in childhood.

If the environments that preschool children experience are moderately stimulating, say with several different ceiling heights, children are more cooperative than they are in environments that are either more energizing (a variety of both ceiling heights and wall colors) or less energizing (only one ceiling height or wall color).

Young children are very quick to appraise the spaces in which they find themselves. They are particularly attuned to psychologically significant spaces, such as where they say good-bye to their parents when they arrive at school and where they are taken at school when they do not feel well.

In many ways children *are* short adults; both children and adults have many of the same psychological needs. Privacy is important to children. Children as young as two need a place in the home to which they can retreat. Children can use times when they have privacy to sort out the events of their day and begin to understand who they are. Children who are in day care seek out spaces where they have prospect and refuge. Starting at three, children benefit psychologically from having a room (or clearly demarcated section of a room) that they can claim as their own and that they can control and personalize.

Children between 8 and 12 are particularly keen on having a "place of their own" that they can use to show off who they are, but that can be difficult if they share bedrooms. Needing privacy sometimes does not make children tiny recluses, as they also need spaces where they can socialize with their friends without parental scrutiny—both being alone and socializing can take place in the same room at different times. A desire for privacy has made many a teenager's car a prized territory.

Being able to look out over nature is not only important for adults; children as young as one also benefit from taking a look out over something green. Viewing nature as a very small child is directly related to faster cognitive development.

Boyatzis and Varghese (1994) have found that children have positive and negative associations with light and dark colors. Positive emotions are associated with light colors and negative emotions are associated with dark colors.

Until they are around eight, children don't integrate the information that they receive through their different senses, which can lead them to have different responses to a situation than adults.

Children and young adults today are much more design savvy than previous generations. Children and teenagers today are being exposed to more complex colors than previous generations have been. They are also seeing more colors in use in human applications than previous generations. Younger people are particularly receptive to the use of interesting materials, such as those that are metallic, translucent, or pearlescent.

Today's young adults have more clearly defined design preferences than members of previous generations have had. Target, for example, promotes lines of products by designers in their stores with an energy that was previously reserved for products with endorsements by celebrity entertainers. Children and young adults are often the targets of these campaigns. Colleges are finding that they can use buildings on their campuses by celebrity architects to entice students to enroll at their schools.

DESIGN IMPLICATION

Design homes (and schools) with the special needs of children in mind.

SPACES WHERE THE PSYCHOLOGICALLY CHALLENGED WILL THRIVE

Creating spaces in which physically challenged people can successfully live and work is a relatively well-established practice compared to creating spaces in which psychologically challenged individuals can thrive. Larger numbers of people with autism and Attention Deficit Disorder/Attention Deficit Hyperactivity Disorder (ADD/ADHD) are being identified in the population, and researchers and designers are beginning to identify ways to design environments in which they can live successfully.

DESIGN IMPLICATION

Interior designers working with healthcare professionals have identified clear requirements for spaces that will be used by autistic children. Since autistic children can focus too intensely on details in the spaces around themselves, it is best not to use geometric patterns on floors and carpets in spaces with autistic users. It is particularly important that any patterns used have few "countable" details because autistics can become intent on the counting things. Colors that are generally relaxing, as described in Chapter 5, should be used in spaces with concentrations of autistic users to prevent overstimulation. It is also better to hide sinks and sources of water as well as electrical switches and trash cans in areas used by autistic people to prevent them from being disturbed. Waterproof fabrics and beveled edges on furniture and woodwork also prevent damage to property and people.

Chapter 15 contains a discussion of learning spaces for autistic children.

Spaces can also be designed to be more accommodating to people with ADD/ADHD. Professionals who work with ADD/ADHD patients have suggestions that can be applied in homes, classrooms, study areas, and workplaces. Exercising—at a fitness center or by walking down a corridor or up a flight of stairs (or even doing calisthenics in that stairwell)—helps to burn off excess energy and keeps people with ADD/ADHD focused on the mental tasks before them. Noise at moderate levels, along with moderately stimulating colors, scents, and textures, seem to help hyperactive children learn. White noise or self-selected music can be used in spaces where hyperactive people need to concentrate, whether those spaces are at home, school, or the workplace. People with ADD/ADHD also see a reduction in symptoms when they have a view of nature while they are working, but everyone ultimately benefits from having a view of nature. Desk and paper management systems that help people to focus on the task at hand—by eliminating non-task-related material from view and making it easy to switch from one task to another—are also useful to people with ADD/ADHD. A surface that pulls out from under other work surfaces can be handy for this purpose.

SPACES FOR OLDER ADULTS

Adults don't develop different place-related psychological needs as they get older. They still need a home that is a well-designed place. This is true whether they are living in a house that's been part of their lives since their children were small or a retirement community or a nursing home that they entered six months ago. Many nursing homes, in particular, don't provide the people living there with privacy, control over their environment, or the ability to personalize their living space so that it represents who they are. People with senile dementia and Alzheimer's disease can find the ability to personalize their physical environment particularly beneficial.

The lenses in our eyes yellow as we age, so colors in spaces for older individuals should be adjusted in ways that are consistent with this effect. Unfortunately, there is no neat formula that will let you know how much colors need to be adjusted for a particular person. To judge how much to adjust colors, it's best to gauge reactions to individual

---

DESIGN IMPLICATION

Older adults need to live in well-designed places.

colors by asking people what particular colors remind them of and why they elicit those memories.

■ CHALLENGING

Homes are the only places where people have complete freedom to pursue their personal goals. Even people whose ambitions (e.g., be an extraordinary mountain climber) may be difficult to fully achieve in their home can engage in activities there that are consistent with their objectives (e.g., improve their physical condition; chart their course up Mount Everest). Backstage areas of homes (not seen by casual acquaintances) are particularly useful for this purpose.

■ CONTINUING

Future Homes

There is a robust movement in the United States disparaging McMansions (large homes generally built without much concern for individual homeowner differences) and encouraging smaller homes that reflect homeowner differences. Susan Susanka drew a lot of attention to this design philosophy in 1998 when she wrote the first of her many similarly themed books, titled *The Not So Big House*. Not-so-big homes use client-focused home design to efficiently provide the sorts of spaces required by owners. These homes are not necessarily less expensive than McMansions because their creators focus a great deal of attention on finish details and meeting precise lifestyle needs.

Susanka has written that effective smaller homes consider movement and views through (and outside) the home, acoustic dampening, segmented or segmentable spaces (some with prospect and refuge), the mood-evoking properties of design features such as lighting, and thoughtful recognition of the owners' personalities when spaces are designed, detailed, and finished. These physical features of not-so-big homes are consistent with the principles of good place design outlined throughout this book.

Green homes have been popular outside the United States for some time and are now becoming increasingly prevalent in the United States as well. The sorts of architecture that are traditional in different parts of the world are generally green; they have evolved to cool or heat without modern, energy-consuming HVAC systems, for example. Often, looking to these structures provides answers to questions such as environmentally responsible ceiling height (higher in hotter climates to capture heated air), window design to encourage air flow and solar shielding (or exposure, depending on the climate), and locally sourced building materials (i.e., the prevalence of homes made of stone in areas where there are lots of rocks on the ground). Decisions made about energy sources in green homes can influence other design decisions, such as window location/size and room size/placement.

There is also a growing concern about exposure to environmental toxins and germs that is spurring many people to move into green homes.

When people who want to live in green homes actually do, they feel that their home more accurately reflects who they feel they are, they feel more attached to their home, and they feel more comfortable living there than they did before moving into the green home. Living in a green home also gives people the feeling that they are exercising some control over their own destiny by minimizing environmental damage to the planet.

A single technological advance can have a tremendous influence on spaces we create. Think about the changes made possible by affordable flat screen monitors. Work areas no longer need to be able to accommodate deep, heavy monitors. In homes and hotels, armoires are disappearing—the televisions that used to live in them have been eliminated and flat screen monitors hang on the walls. Many of the flat screens can be programmed to display art when they're not being used to broadcast television programs or other video feeds, which can be an aesthetic enhancement to a space. When video conferencing allows home workers to tie into meetings, a whole new market for desirable conference backdrops may develop.

Technology is becoming more prevalent in all environments, including residential ones. Technology will not stop evolving, and homes that are going to be continually satisfying to their owners have to be able to evolve to take advantage of new technology forms. Incorporating more technology into the home is becoming inevitable as homes are becoming white-collar workplaces for their adult owners and sophisticated learning labs for their child residents.

Smart homes have built-in technology that performs activities formerly done by humans—at least on a good day—such as turning out lights in vacant rooms. Other technology that may be embedded in these systems is more exotic—it might enable people to monitor their home when they are not present or it might note who specifically is entering a room and adjust the environmental conditions in line with the ambient preferences they have entered into system memory banks.

People are very concerned about losing the essence of their home experience as more and more technology is built into these structures. Welcome smart systems fade into the background of people's homes; they need to silently and automatically complete the tasks that their owners have asked them to do. People are particularly concerned about giving up control to these systems, although in an ideal situation, people feel the systems should be able to respond to the changing situation in the home.

Technology is making it possible for individuals to create mini-territories that they move with themselves as they travel through any space. People can be listening to music that no one else can hear as they walk though a home kitchen and can be watching a video that no one else can see as they stand in line at a store. This sort of space control creates an expectation of control that can make not adding technology stimuli to a space seem odd. A developing backlash to the prevalence of technology in spaces can be seen in the increasing number of signal-blocking devices in use in various structures.

Members of the general public have become much more aware of design issues, and this is reflected in, and is a consequence of, the home product assortments now available to them. Designers, who formerly created products only for the elite, now create lines that are featured at mid-price department stores. It is reasonable to hypothesize that this interest in design will escalate among the general public.

The growing individualism of Americans is reflected in their push to make their homes more private and to more accurately reflect who they feel they are as a person (see this discussion earlier on the DIY movement).

Racial diversity is increasing within the United States and evolving home design practices reflect those changes. In Chapter 5, color preferences of various racial and ethnic groups were discussed. Those preferences are reflected in the palettes used in homes and commercial settings. The influence of increasing multiculturalism extends far beyond a diversifying color mix. Different cultures use home spaces in different ways and judge housing using different criteria. Houses and offices being created today for the population at large need to reflect as many of those changes as possible. Many homes in the United States now incorporate feng shui principles and provide gathering areas within the home for large families, for example.

Millions of people across the planet believe they are spiritual, although they do not necessarily attend religious services. This has given rise to spaces for in-home meditation. This interest in spirituality and related spaces seems to be increasing.

More people are living alone, and the stigmas associated with living without a partner have lessened. In the United States, there are now more single-person households than married couples with children living together—and the first group is increasing at a faster rate than the second. The increasing number of people living alone means that homes of different sizes and configurations will be desirable in the future. In single-family homes, for example, privacy is a very different issue than when several people live together. The increasing numbers of people living alone will encourage the provision of different amenities at work and in home neighborhoods, and also lead to the creation of more places outside the home where people can mix casually with others.

Even when several people are living in the same home, there is increasing attention to creating spaces within that house where people can be alone. These places include smaller spaces where people can surf the Internet by themselves and separate studies/offices for husbands and wives. Homes with more private space are not necessarily any larger than those with lots of group space in family rooms, etc. The private spaces are being substituted for communal areas.

People are getting heavier. This will require the use of bariatric furniture even in homes and increases the need for patient lifts in hospitals. It is also already causing architects and urban planners to create spaces that encourage people to move and burn off extra calories. Stairwells are being made inviting, for example. Often new staircases are being designed to be lighter, more interesting places to be. In many public spaces, new staircases have windows to exterior views and changing art displays. This is consistent with society's changing focus from thinness to wellness.

Homeschooling is increasing, and that may influence home design as special classroom-type spaces may join the home office as must-have home spaces.

The physical world has been designed for streamlined operation by right-handed people, but the number of left-handed people in the population is increasing fast. This trend will influence home, workspaces, school, and healthcare design.

Much of the public's discussion of future places is based on generational differences, and *American Demographics* reported comprehensively about the space-related preferences of various generations (Gardyn 2003).

Members of Generation X (born between 1965 and 1978) have shown clear patterns in their thoughts about places. They want to live in environmentally friendly homes (and they're willing to pay for them) with open floor plans that allow them to interact with their families. People in this age group are technologically savvy, however, and need spaces where they can use their computers, although a home office is not as desirable to them as the opportunity to use their computers wherever they desire in their home. Bathtubs are popular with this group.

Expressing their own character in their home is important to members of Generation X, but to them, expressing themselves seems to have less to do with impressing other people than it did for previous generations. Part of expressing who they are as people is the freedom to use many spaces in their homes in several different ways. Furnishings they value are designed in a casual, simple, functional style. This is true in both home and work environments, and in professional settings they are less concerned with having their space reflect their relative status and more concerned that it have the amenities, such as individual and team technical capabilities, that they desire.

Generation Y (born after 1978) is drawn to bold colors in home furnishings. They prefer solid colors and textures on surfaces, but when they do choose to use a pattern in a space, it is abstract. They prefer that surfaces be easy to clean and often select multipurpose furniture pieces, like Generation X, particularly if these pieces can be seen as art or design choices. They want their furniture to be flexible in location as well as purpose, and find furniture on wheels very convenient. Spaces for Generation Y must support telecommuting and blurring the line between personal and professional activities. Members of Generation Y want to be doing things that are meaningful and interesting, and they value personal growth both at home and at work. They enjoy learning in all of its forms, and spaces created for them must reflect this.

While future homes will continue to be important refuges for people, they will also evolve to meet their residents' physical and psychological needs. The factors that define well-designed places, in general, will remain relevant to effective home design.

13

SPECIAL FOCUS: WORKPLACES

Workplaces are aptly named; they are places where work needs to get done (and hopefully done well). The physical form of the workplace can make it more or less probable that this will happen. When people are satisfied with their workspace, they are likely to be more satisfied with their jobs (Veitch et al. 2007), and when people are more satisfied with their jobs, they are apt to do them better. In this book, *workplace* refers to the entire facility controlled by an organization while *workspace* refers to the area assigned to an individual worker centered around his or her own chair.

This chapter focuses on the design of office workplaces and workspaces and not factories. Designing factories well requires that specialized operations management and ergonomic factors to be considered.

Environmental determinism is strong when people are designing workplaces. Environmental determinism is the belief that you can change people's

FIGURE 13-1 ■ It's hard to concentrate in this office; there is not acoustic or visual shielding from other workers. This office design is not unusual. Copyright © iStockPhoto/Igor Terekhov.

behavior by modifying the places in which they behave, without changing anything else in their lives. Regularly, executives at major corporations decide that they want their workers to collaborate more and that they believe they will get this to happen by creating workplaces where each worker can see every other worker while he or she is seated in his or her desk chair. Workers do not become more collaborative just because they can see one another; in fact, they may become less collaborative. When people start to be rewarded financially for working together, along with being in a place that actually enhances collaboration (which is not an open space, as information to come will show), working in teams becomes more desirable.

How people perceive their professional success influences their perceptions of the design of their workspaces (Fischer, Tarquinio, and Vischer 2004). People who feel that they are professionally successful are generally more satisfied with their physical work environment than people who do not feel that they are professionally successful. People who feel successful are more likely to be satisfied with physical aspects of their workspace, such as its size, its aesthetic impression, and its perceived privacy. People who feel that they are more successful are also more likely to see their workspace as healthy. People who are more dissatisfied with the work that they are doing have more complaints about the environment in which they are doing it. The influence of worker feelings of success on workplace appraisals helps us understand the sometimes apparently contradictory information available about the appropriateness of various workspace design elements when location-specific programming research is underway.

Workers are asked to do several different kinds of tasks in the course of any workday. Their workspaces should be designed so that as many of them as possible can be done effectively and efficiently. Sometimes the sort of workspace design that is appropriate for one of those tasks is completely different from the workspace design that is appropriate for another. In that case, the workspace should be designed for the most crucial employee task, as defined by the organization. It's difficult, for example, for customer service employees both to figure out how to do their job better by overhearing what their coworkers are saying and to ignore the visual and audio distractions of what is going on around them when they respond to complex customer questions.

As with the other places we have discussed, well-designed workplaces are

- Communicating
- Comforting
- Complying
- Challenging
- Continuing

■ COMMUNICATING

Individuals have a lot of control over what their homes look like; they have much less influence on their workplaces. Many people find their memento-heavy, postmodern soul spending 50 hours a week in a no-knickknack modern workplace.

At home, people use design to communicate who they are as individuals to others, and at the same time remind themselves who they are. In workplaces, people personalize (add useful or decorative objects to) their workspaces to accomplish the same things, within the bounds established by their employers and the culture it rewards. At the same time, employees are also trying to understand what their colleagues are "saying" through their workspaces and what their company is trying to communicate about what it values through the physical form of its offices. (More information about how workers communicate through the design of their workplace is included in the next section.)

The physical form of the workplace can communicate a general level of concern for worker well-being. Green buildings, for example, signal to workers that an organization values its employees' long-term welfare, and that has positive repercussions. They also signal a concern for the public welfare to the general population, which has significant public relations value if the concern seems legitimate. People working in green buildings are more likely to feel that their workplace meets their needs than people working in other buildings, and they are also less likely to be negative when there is a problem with building operations (e.g., temperature, lighting, noise; Leaman and Bordass 2007).

Messages are sent via rules about how a workplace can be used, by where a company's headquarters are located, and by the sorts of furniture selected for the lobby. Even maintenance counts; poorly maintained spaces indicate a lack of regard for whatever happens in them whether those spaces are offices, classrooms, patient rooms, or somewhere else. The messages that an employer communicates through its physical environments influence employee satisfaction with their jobs, how well they're working, and their intentions to keep doing those jobs. When the messages sent by physical environments are inconsistent with the other messages being sent by the firm (through bonuses and mission statements, for example), the physically observed messages are seen as more true than the verbally expressed messages. Constructing a workplace requires that employers spend money, and those expenditures are seen as expressing the real soul of the firm (Becker and Steele 1995).

Sometimes all of this "discussion" gets further complicated because companies try to present their corporate brand in their workplaces. That brand may or may not be consistent with what the company values as an organization. For example, a fun family restaurant chain that gives its customers all sorts of freedom to create unique experiences as they eat may value precise adherence by its employees to an intricate behavioral code.

For organizations to be successful, the enduring statements made by a workplace and workspace design must be consistent with a the group's organizational culture, as discussed in Chapter 7.

It's important to remember that just as a workplace sends messages to the people who work there, it also sends messages to people who don't, who simply walk by on their way home from work. The messages sent to nonemployees originate from metaphors and forms that are spelled out by the national culture of the people walking by those offices because these nonemployees can't be invited in for a symbol explanation. When the messages sent to people outside the organization seem different from the messages sent to people inside the workplace, worker discontent is likely to result.

DESIGN IMPLICATION
Be acutely aware of the messages being communicated through workplace and workspace design.

It's hard for people who are not part of an organization, or who don't spend a lot of time observing it, to understand definitively what is being said in any place created by it. Even important symbols can be misinterpreted by outsiders. That is why it is important for you as a designer to interview and observe the people who will use the spaces you will create (see Chapter 11 for additional details).

The ways organizational symbols can be misconstrued are endless. Imagine a company with playground equipment in its lobby. That equipment could indicate that people who work there are free to be expressive without constraints or that management knows that sometimes for various reasons employees' kids will be in the office, and since they value the private lives and responsibilities of their employees, they want the kids to be amused during their visit. Or imagine a firm where board games are found prominently throughout the office space. You might think that means that employees enjoy hanging out together during breaks and that the culture is clannish. After interviewing employees you might find out that those board games are never used, they were placed around the office by management, and the employees find company officials manipulative.

■ COMFORTING

Workers are affected psychologically not only by all of this unspoken communication but also by the ambient nature of the places they find themselves.

Aesthetic elements of the brand used in workplaces and workspaces can actually be counterproductive. Color may be used in a workplace to communicate a brand, but the saturation and brightness of that color also have predictable and potentially negative effects, as discussed in Chapter 5. Adding a brand's red logo color to a workspace design can have negative influences, for example (see Chapter 5 for more information on red's influence on the performance of mental tasks).

Alternately, a stately auction house that carries the color scheme from its mid-saturation, mid-brightness logo to the room where professionals assess the authenticity of paintings has made it relatively easy for those professionals to concentrate on the task at hand while also reminding them of the long and distinguished history of their employer.

Mood has a big effect on what people do, and workers are not immune to its influence. The design of their workplace/workspace can put people into a positive or negative mood. The effect of place on mood is reviewed in Chapter 9, but to recap: When people are in a negative mood, they methodically work through whatever task is before them—which on occasion is a good thing. When people are in a positive mood, they are more likely to work persistently, think broadly and flexibly, and potentially be creative. They also do a better job at getting along with other people and resolving disputes through negotiation. When they are in a good mood, people will work to develop their own capabilities as well as those of their employer. People also remember positive things when they are in a good mood, and call up negative memories when they are in a bad mood. Although remembering negative situations can be helpful, often remembering positive situations can give workers the incentive necessary to accomplish great things.

In previous chapters, we've reviewed how particular smells, lighting levels, sounds, and other features of the physical environment influence mood, and all of that material is relevant when workplaces are designed.

People become stressed when there is an inconsistency between what they believe or what they want to do and thoughts/actions afforded by the physical environment in which they find themselves.

> **DESIGN IMPLICATION**
>
> Use aspects of the physical environment in workplaces/workspaces to create the most appropriate mood for the task at hand, or allow the environment to be modified by users to create a variety of moods if employees' professional performance would benefit from the ability to vary the emotional influences of office spaces.

Workers are often stressed. People become stressed when their work environment doesn't say the things about them that they want it to—for example, they may think their workspace seems to say that they have low status, but they feel that they do not. People are also stressed when their workspace is too loud for them to concentrate, too cold, or so bright that glare obscures their computer screen. They feel stressed when their neighbor's chair is too close to theirs.

When people are stressed, they divert part of their brainpower to trying to understand the stressful situation and determining how to eliminate it (Evans and Cohen 1987). If they are doing a task that is particularly complex, they

FIGURE 13-2 ■ Sunlit work areas have been linked to worker satisfaction. Copyright © 2008 Farshid Assassi, courtesy of BNIM.

may not have much brainpower available for diversion, so they cannot, as described earlier, do their jobs as well when stressed. Stress also puts people in a bad mood, which has negative cognitive and social consequences. When people experience physical stresses continuously, they can become unmotivated to keep trying to eliminate that stress and demoralized in general.

When people feel that they have control over whatever is distracting them, they are not as adversely influenced psychologically by it—even if they never actually change the negative situation. Odds are they will exercise that control sooner or later, as the angle of the sun, number of people meeting in the next office, etc., varies.

The professional demands placed on many workers means that even if their physical environment is not very physically stressful, they may be quite tense. This makes it particularly important that physical stressors be removed from workplaces. Spaces in which employees can decompress (or at least try to decompress) and restore their stock of mental energy are productivity-boosting workplace additions.

The relationship between how people feel about their job and how they feel about their workplaces is complicated. When people are not happy with their jobs, they are likely to be less happy with the workplaces and workspaces in which they are doing it, and to declare that they are less productive. Also, when judging their entire workplace, workers focus on the workspace that is assigned to them. That workspace will have more of an impact on their evaluation of their physical work environments than anything else on-site (Becker, Sims, and Schoss 2002).

■ COMPLYING

Sunlight. Nature views. They're important everywhere, including workplaces. They increase job satisfaction. Employers want their workers to be satisfied with their jobs because workers who are more satisfied with their jobs do them better (Edwards et al. 2008) and are less likely to move on to another employer.

Rachel Kaplan has researched people's responses to views of nature from their homes and from their offices (1993, 2001). Her research on views of nature from the home indicates that when people can see grass and other natural things from their windows, they are more satisfied with their neighborhood and generally feel better. She found that views of built environments from windows at home or views of just sky and weather didn't have the same effect. Her workplace research shows the same results—no matter where humans are, we respond to nature in the same way. Workers with a view of nature are less frustrated at work, more enthusiastic about their jobs, in better physical health, and more satisfied with their lives. People with views of nature are less motivated to quit because of job stress. Views of nature are calming, as discussed in the healthcare chapter (Chapter 16). Not just any nature views will do, however—a view into a difficult-to-walk-through, dark, jungly sort of nature is not very desirable. Humans relax when they look out over nature that has some water in it and some mown fields. There should be trees around the outside of the fields and in clumps within the fields.

Adding plants to offices, in individual pots or more substantial installed planters, is a cliché, but there is strong support for that cliché from scientific research—plants make people happier with their jobs and enhance their performance of those jobs. Plants in a workplace reduce workplace stress, even when people have only peripheral views of them. Seeing plants out of the corner of their eyes not only reduces workers' stress, but it also makes knowledge workers more effective at doing their jobs. Plants make people feel better about their work life in general. People think they are performing at a higher level when plants are present in their workplace, which gives them a nice psychological boost. Plants put people in better moods, and there are a lot of positive ramifications of those better moods, as discussed above. Plants seem to promote human creativity.

Plants are so calming that they should be removed from spaces where people do work that is repetitious. When a job is repetitive, but people do need to focus on what they are doing, plants may make the space so calming overall that performance suffers.

Putting plants in an office space makes it seem more attractive and comfortable to the people who use and visit it. Plants (yucca and lilies, particularly) are also physiologically good for an office—they remove carbon dioxide from the air, so people can concentrate better.

A moderate number of plants in offices seems best. In a study using plants the size of typical houseplants, the best effects on human mood and office attractiveness were seen in an approximately 130-square-foot cellular office space with 10 plants. Ten plants produced better results than no plants or 22 plants. Plants with rounded leaves are more relaxing and have a more positive influence on creativity, while plants with sharp, narrow leaves aren't as valuable an addition to a workplace.

Plants can only accomplish so much in a space—if there is a single plant in a generally energizing space, it may labor in vain to calm viewers.

Potted plants can reduce stress in workspaces without windows or with city views. Although potted plants do a lot of good things in offices, they are not substitutes for views of nature through windows—a view of nature trumps an office plant every time.

> **DESIGN IMPLICATION**
>
> Incorporate views of nature and potted plants into workplaces.

Aquariums in offices produce the same relaxing effects as plants. They calm the people looking at them. Aquariums are usually more difficult to install and maintain in a space than plants, but if the logistics make aquariums feasible, they can be placed in break rooms, lobbies where job candidates wait, cafeterias, and other office spaces where people may need some sort of help to relax.

Art is prevalent in office buildings. Chapter 16 describes the sort of art that is generally appropriate for healthcare environments, and similar pieces are good choices for offices. Abstract and other nonrepresentational art can, however, be used in offices, although it is undesirable in healthcare facilities. Any abstract art used should be accompanied by a short (50 words or so) description of the artist's style or a straightforward title—that short description makes healthy individuals feel that pieces of contemporary art are more meaningful and pleasing.

Students in classrooms with more daylight learn better than students in darker classrooms, and sunlight has similar beneficial effects in workplaces. Sunlight makes office workers happier with their jobs and improves their well-being in general. The bigger and closer the windows the better! Daylight also makes people more alert. Light shelves, horizontal blinds, light wells, skylights, interior windows, and clerestories can all be used to move daylight into a space. So can multistory light pipes made from panels of prismatic glass. Glare can be a problem in daylit spaces. Transparent window coatings and computer screen covers can eliminate the glare without ruining the view or distorting the colors of the sunlight.

DESIGN IMPLICATION

Daylight (but not glare) in workplaces should be maximized. The closer that windows are placed to the ceiling of a room, the more deeply daylight will travel into a space.

People who sit near a window are on task more than people who sit far from windows. Knowledge workers who sit near windows spend the same number of hours per week at work as their coworkers who are farther from the windows. However, people who sit near windows spend more hours during the week doing what they are paid to do than people in interior cubicles—specifically, people near windows use their computers more (and apparently for work-related purposes).

Daylight's intensity changes during the course of any workday, so it must be combined with artificial light in most workplaces. Combining daylight with a worker-controlled task light and indirect ambient lighting is comfortable and healthy for workers, and is associated with higher productivity levels than other lighting choices. When sophisticated lighting systems can be used that vary light levels in a structure, in the same way that exterior light levels change during the course of a day, employee mood and well-being are improved. Varying perceived light levels in an office during the day, to mimic the natural light cycle, helps keep employees' circadian rhythms in sync with other people living at the same longitude and latitude—which reduces stress.

Full-spectrum fluorescent lights do not simulate daylight closely enough to reproduce all of its great effects. Full-spectrum fluorescent light is not any healthier for workers, either psychologically or physically, than other sorts of currently used fluorescent light. The extra effort required to stock and use full-spectrum fluorescent bulbs is not justified. Fluorescent lighting has a bad reputation; people think it causes health problems, but carefully conducted research studies have shown that it does not.

The artificial lighting in a space has as much influence on how workers perform as the amount of daylight in a space. Both direct and indirect lighting increase the energy level in an office. More brightly lit rooms are seen as more cheerful, which boosts the moods of people in the space. However, if the light in two rooms is equally bright, the space with more indirect sources of light will seem more cheerful.

Offices that are brighter (lit to 2,000 lux) seem roomier than offices that are lit only to 500 lux. The same effect holds for offices with cooler light (4,000 K) as compared with warmer (2,700 K) lighting levels. Manav (2007) also found that people enjoyed experiencing warm- and cooler-colored lights simultaneously.

Lighting brightness matters. When people are in relatively darker spaces (150 lux), they are more creative and more amenable to rewarding the performance of others than when they are under relatively higher lighting levels (1,500 lux). When light levels are higher, workers are more apt to stay at their desks during breaks than if lighting levels are lower.

Humans in workplaces prefer the same sort of dappled light that is positively perceived in other spaces.

Light can be different colors, and those different colors influence how well workers perform certain tasks. Short-term memory and problem solving are better under warmer (3,000 K, more reddish) light than under cooler (4,000 K, 5,500 K, more bluish) light. When long-term memory comes into play, gender becomes important. Men do better at tasks requiring long-term memory in warm and cool white light (the 3,000 K and 4,000 K conditions), while women do better than men at tasks requiring long-term memory when the light gets very blue (5,500 K). This information on light color and gender is useful when single-sex environments are being created. When asked to recall novel information stored in their long-term memory, people in general did better in warm white light than in cool white light, which is interesting news to people creating brainstorming rooms. Warm white light is energizing and puts us in a good mood, while cool white light is more stressful for employees than full-spectrum light.

The color of light has other influences how people behave. Under warm white light (3,000 K), people are more interested in resolving interpersonal conflicts through collaboration and less motivated to avoid dealing with them than under cool white light (4,200 K). This information can be applied when designing offices for arbiters and lawyers. People assume higher levels of risk under warm white light than when they are experiencing any other light colors—which is useful information for stock brokers (and casino designers).

The color of office walls should be based on what sorts of work will be done there. People perform knowledge work best at a medium energy level; they need to be calm enough to concentrate, but not so de-energized that they are falling asleep. More mentally strenuous tasks should be done in spaces with more calming colors, and tasks that are repetitive and don't require much mental effort should happen in more energizing spaces. Chapter 5 reviews which colors are more energizing and which are more relaxing. Colored surfaces are always used in combination with some sort of light. When the surfaces are warm colors and light levels are higher, people focus on the world surrounding them; when lighting levels are lower and colors are cooler, people focus more on their own thoughts and it is easier for them to concentrate. Red reduces performance on cognitive tasks, as described in Chapter 5. When people are placed in rooms painted the same pink as Pepto-Bismol, they calm down quickly, which makes that color a good choice for spaces that agitated people might visit, such as holding cells at police stations or human resource departments where people are resolving employee conflicts, for example. Whenever you are selecting colors to be used in a workplace, remember the cultural associations to particular colors, which are described in Chapter 8.

Mahnke (1996) has thought a lot about the appropriate colors to use in office environments and offers many useful suggestions. As we discussed in Chapter 5, dark colors on walls make those walls seem to advance. Mahnke suggests that cubicles in the center of a sea of cubicles should have darker walls than cubicles on the periphery, so that people in those middle cubicles feel comfortable. Mahnke also suggests that less energizing colors should be used in noisier spaces. To keep people moving briskly along in circulation spaces, he suggests red, orange, and bright colors in general be used there.

Colors are generally used in combinations, which is a good thing. Uniformly gray, white, or beige offices provide so little stimulation that people in them have a chance to focus on their own thoughts. Focusing on those thoughts can be really stressful, depending on what sorts of concerns the worker has. People in monochromatic environments have difficulty concentrating on cognitive tasks. Monotonous and achromatic environments also lead many people (particularly extraverts) to look for energy somewhere else.

We use visual cues to keep track of what is currently important in our lives. Tackable and writable surfaces in workspaces (along with a moderate level

DESIGN IMPLICATION

Colors used in surfaces and lighting should be selected with care.

of visual complexity around those surfaces) help us organize environmental memory cues. It seems that when we are looking at something, such as our stapler, we are reminded of things we have learned while looking at it. That's why, as we talked about in Chapter 4, people do better on exams when they are given in the same room in which the material being tested was taught. People will perform their job better if they usually work in the same space. Research has also shown that we recall information better when we are in the same mood we were in when we learned it (Eich 1995) and physical environments can be designed to create specific moods.

Seeing things that we link closely to a sort of situation causes us (unconsciously) to behave in a way consistent with that situation—when people see money, a briefcase, or something that reminds them of their job, in artwork, for example, they sit farther apart (which is consistent with competition or tension or a formal setting) than if they are not reminded of their job. Similarly, when children see pictures that remind them of Santa Claus (seeing images of Santa Claus himself is not necessary), they are more likely to share candy with others.

Workers and others are generally most comfortable in uncluttered offices. These spaces are higher on order and lower on visual complexity than cluttered spaces. This makes them less arousing than cluttered spaces.

Views within offices can be almost as important as views outside to nature. Workers like the same sorts of views from a refuge into a more expansive, more brightly lit prospect area that were discussed in Chapter 2. People at work find that refuges are less stressful places to be, just as people at home and at school do.

Humans need to look into the distance every so often to relax their eyes. Being able to see at least 15–20 feet from some comfortable seated position in their office chair is particularly desirable for worker eye comfort. Sometimes interior windows from one space inside a building to another can be useful for this. Inside windows can also help move daylight, and sometimes views of nature, to people deep within a building.

Noise is energizing, so it is not surprising that it harms performance of the complex sorts of tasks that office-based knowledge workers are called on to do, but does not affect the performance of simpler tasks.

One of the reasons why noise can be distracting is that we try to make sense of it. Irregular noises are disturbing because we try to find a pattern in them. Conversations in a language we understand are particularly distracting because, inevitably, we become involved with what is being said and can't resist listening to the dialogue—no matter how strongly we have vowed to ignore it. All this focus on workplace conversations means we don't do the cognitive tasks we are paid to do as well as we would if there were less noise. Workers do not seem to become less stressed by office noise as they spend more time in noisy spaces, so the odds that "they'll adjust to the noise in their new space" seem very low.

Too much noise from other workers is often the reason that workers say they need privacy, and more noise is related to less satisfaction with a job. Noise from coworkers has been shown to directly influence stress levels, with more noise being linked to more stress. In general, when workers perceive that they are distracted, they become less satisfied with the physical environment in which they work.

Reductions in the noise in workplaces improve employees' opinions of their employers and their satisfaction with their jobs.

DESIGN IMPLICATION

Playing white noise in the spaces between dropped and true ceilings and raised and true floors (with the white noise initially directed toward the true ceiling and the true floor in each space, respectively) makes that white noise more effective than simply playing it in the spaces between the raised floors and dropped ceilings. White noise is a relatively inexpensive way to control office noise. It cannot be properly installed and calibrated without professional training.

Sixty-five-decibel pink noise (a white noise-like sound) effectively masks office-type noise and has been associated with improved memory function.

Sound transmission through a space is also reduced when interior walls extend beyond the dropped ceilings or raised floors to the true ceiling and floor in a space.

Solving workplace noise problems by creating spaces near their desks where employees can go when they need to concentrate is not necessarily a good idea. Moving from one space to another eliminates all the visual memory cues that have been created in the first space. Also, people must make an effort and move from their primary workspace to use these secondary spaces. To be effective, "concentration" spaces need to be soundproofed.

When it's noisy, we don't even bother to take simple steps that would make it easier for us to concentrate on the task at hand. Workstations and chairs that are not adjusted properly are distracting, but when people are working in noisy conditions (55–65 decibels), they are less likely to adjust them than people working in quiet conditions (40 decibels), according to one recent study. The people in this study who worked in these two different noise conditions didn't perceive that they were experiencing different levels of stress, and many people working in offices may not realize that noise makes them tense. This is particularly likely to be true of younger workers who have only worked in open offices.

Research has shown that people who nap briefly (30 minutes or so) at midday perform at a higher level than people who don't. The Japanese realized this long ago, and in many Japanese offices, the workplace lights are actually dimmed at lunchtime. Organizations are beginning to provide their workers with spaces where they can nap, if they wish.

The paths, or circulation routes, that people use to move through a workspace should follow the same rules as those that move through spaces in general. Paths are interesting, and spur people to move forward, when they curve away and the people traveling along them can assume that something new and desirable will be around the bend. Periodically changing the art visible around this bend can create a very pleasant workplace experience. Workplaces that are designed on diagonal axes (axes not necessarily aligned with the parallel walls in a space) also add a desirable level of complexity and activity to a workplace.

Workplaces can be designed to combat the obesity epidemic. One way that some firms are doing this is to make using the stairs more desirable and using elevators less desirable. Walking up stairs seems like a better choice when elevators are programmed to run slowly or are inconveniently located and when the music and artwork in the stairwells are enjoyable. Stairs that are clearly visible and centrally located are used more often. Open stairways in central spaces help remind workers about their colleagues on other floors and their areas of expertise because people traveling on the stairs have views into places where other people work. Covered walkways also encourage walking between several company buildings.

There is evidence that walking around while trying to reason out a solution to a problem is a good thing. Joyce Carol Oates, the acclaimed

FIGURE 13-3 ■ This pleasantly mysterious walkway spurs people to move forward. Copyright © iStockPhoto/pdtnc.

FIGURE 13-4 ■ This stairway is a pleasant place to be, which motivates people to use it to travel between floors instead of an elevator. Copyright © iStockPhoto/ Konstantin Sukhinin.

American writer, often walks when she needs to solve a problem, and so did Wordsworth, Thoreau, and Dickens, according to reports. Pleasant walkways (indoors or outdoors) would therefore seem to be useful at workplace campuses.

There is often considerable debate in a workplace about the appropriate temperature for the space. Different cultures, and their varying climate-based design traditions and clothing, make it difficult to state one appropriate temperature for offices around the world. Research by Vischer (1996) in the United States and Canada, however, indicates that temperatures between 68 and 72 degrees are best. Air should circulate at less than 40 fpm. Relative humidity between 30% and 60% is desirable in workplaces.

Spaces for Individuals and Spaces for Groups

Individual workers and groups of workers share many space-related design needs. For example, both individuals and groups of workers need to be able to work without distractions (acoustic privacy and visual privacy are good for this) when desired, they need to have a sense that they control their experiences as they work (they can change the lighting levels and control who is talking with them in their workspace, for example), and they need to feel that they can personalize and modify their territory to meet their needs.

INDIVIDUAL WORKSPACES

People thrive when they can show themselves and others who they are by placing pictures and objects that have meaning to them in the areas that they use regularly—and "personalizing" their workspaces also increases their satisfaction with their jobs and the physical environments in which they do them. Morale and the general social climate are better as well. People want to show others who they are not only as individuals ("I write poetry") but also as group members ("I am a Lithuanian" or "I am a member of a rock band"). This force is irresistible, so workspace design must allow for it to happen gracefully. As a matter of fact, the more public the space, the more likely that unsightly personal decorations will be visible if appropriate opportunities to decorate the space are not provided—the more a workspace is visible to others, the stronger the drive of its owner in it to decorate it. The drive to personalize is also stronger the more similar that one individual workspace is to the next.

People know that organizations and other people are also sending and receiving nonverbal messages. That's why the symbolic communication in a workplace is so important—people believe that much of the most important and most true information is

DESIGN IMPLICATION

The drive to personalize is irresistible; provide workers with the tools they need to do so.

never spoken aloud. Only the person who owns a workspace really knows what she's trying to express with the material she adds to it, but people from the same geographic area will generally have a pretty good idea about what's being "said."

Workers want their workspaces to communicate their value to the organization. People from different national and organizational cultures expect to find different sorts of activities valued by their employer, as discussed in Chapters 7–8. In more interdependent cultures, where group effort is valued, enhancements to group-level spaces are more appropriate ways to show that worker effort is recognized. In cultures that value independence, individual-level efforts and rewards will be most highly valued.

In many cultures, the idea of differentiating the status of workers is considered inappropriate. In the United States, to actually say, out loud, that one person is of higher rank than another and therefore *should* have a more desirable workspace than another person would be shocking. All this apparent equality is fine in theory, but in actuality, human beings are pack animals and in a pack, not all are equal.

For example: A new workplace was built without closets for workers' coats (Hatch and Cunliffe 2006). To give workers a place to hang their hats, coatracks were provided on a first-come, first-served basis. Within a short period of time, the coatracks migrated from their original random distribution to the workspaces of the higher-status employees. Certainly, all of the employees understood what the new coatrack distribution system meant, although it might take visitors a little while to figure it out.

We like to know the relative power of the people we are interacting with—that way we know what to do. Our behavior toward other people depends on their relative status. More desirable workspaces not only communicate to the people who visit them, but also to the people to whom they are assigned—how much their owners are valued by their employer. Different organizations choose to signal status in different ways—higher-ranking individuals might have "better desk" chairs than lower-ranking individuals at some companies, and at others the work surface materials might be the clue.

DESIGN IMPLICATION

Build status-based differences into any workspaces you design—the people who use the spaces you have created will if you don't, and they may not act in a way that's consistent with the design concepts you value.

People at work need privacy. When people are in a private space, they can take stock of what is going on, reflect on what it means to them, and decide how they will respond. Privacy (visual and acoustic) is important for regenerating stocks of mental energy, which can be quickly diminished in stressful situations. When people feel that their workspaces are more private, they are more satisfied with their jobs, so again, they do them better. When people don't have privacy, they are less likely to bond with coworkers, which makes it much easier to find employment elsewhere. Doors have the most

FIGURE 13-5 ■ Task lighting provides some environmental control to workers. Environmental control has important implications for worker satisfaction and performance. Copyright © iStockPhoto/ Alenjandro Raymond.

direct link to perceptions of privacy in workspaces; not being able to see their coworkers is the feature of their physical environment that is the second strongest predictor of whether people feel that their workspaces are private. The door is a lot better at establishing privacy than the view.

People communicate more or less depending on whether they think they are in a private space, and whether they feel in control of the communication-related situation. People in open, cubicle-filled workplaces, where everyone can hear all of the nearby conversations, are less likely to speak about information that they find personally important—although the amount of actual talking in an open space is higher. All that extra discussion is unlikely to be about anything related to work. Workers are particularly noisy in cubicles when they cannot see coworkers while seated at their desks because they seem to forget that other workers are present anywhere on the floor. They get louder and louder, which is particularly annoying when they are having a nonwork-related conversation.

Office workspaces are becoming smaller. The National Research Council of Canada (2004), Construction Division, determined that in 2002 the average clerical worker's workspace had an area of 71 square feet, professional/ technical staff members had 88 square feet, and managers had 178 square feet, on average (down from 79, 103, and 205, respectively in 1997). It is harder for people to establish and maintain privacy in spaces of these sizes, particularly since many of them are open.

DESIGN IMPLICATION

Create private spaces for workers (besides the bathroom).

FIGURE 13-6 ■ The doors on these workstations provide visual privacy to workers and also eliminate visual distractions. Jim Brozek Photography, Miller Brewing—Chicago Workstations, Copyright 2006, courtesy of Kahler Slater.

People value having control over conditions in their own workspace, and when they feel that they have that control, they are happier with their jobs and feel that they are more productive, comfortable, and healthy. They also have the feeling that their employer respects their opinion. When people feel that they aren't in control of their workspaces, their performance on planning and organizational tasks is impaired—when people feel they are out of control, they are less likely to take control over their own lives. A hidden benefit to giving workers control over the light levels in their workspaces is that from worker to worker there is a lot of difference of opinions about the appropriate light level for any task, and most employees do several tasks during the course of a day. When people have their own light, the odds increase that the light levels will be "appropriate" for workers.

Workers can come to feel that they are being judged about the way that they control their environment if others seem to monitor how they have calibrated their sensory experiences. It can also get to be a job in itself to monitor and realign all of the sensory aspects of a workspace. For that reason, it is best to provide workers with only a task light, something that can affect air ventilation in their workspace (such as a fan), and the ability to sit in different orientations in the workspace to do different tasks. As discussed in Chapter 7, workplaces also must be designed so that they are consistent with the cultures of work groups and organizations—and a work group does not necessarily have the same sort of culture as the organization it's a part of.

In some groups, for some jobs, people need to be able to concentrate to do their work well. In other groups, people doing other jobs don't need to concentrate. People who need to concentrate and people who don't need to concentrate work best in different sorts of places—but even people who are doing well-practiced tasks need access to places that are private. Questions to determine task complexity are included in Chapter 11.

People can sit in cubicles and offices so that they can see the people who are approaching them or so that they are not distracted by the passing traffic. The inner chipmunk in humans hates to sit with its back exposed—that's one of the reasons why booths are so popular in restaurants and the first seats taken in coffee shops are the ones against the walls.

In workplaces, people are torn—they want to protect their backs, but they also want to do a good job—they want to be able to concentrate. Facing out of their workspace if it has an open doorway protects their back, but facing in helps with concentration. In a cubicle, looking inward means looking at a cubicle wall from very close range, and this puts people in a negative mood and makes them feel less in control of their lives—which has bad repercussions that were discussed in Chapter 9. People who face oncoming individuals have more control of their conversations. Facing out is also more conducive to in-office meetings and is therefore associated with managers. Workers who display confidential information on their computer screen that could be read by people moving through their space must face out of their workspace. For other workers, it makes sense for them to be able to face into or out of their workspace as desired.

When people can see other workers because they are facing out of their workstations, they are less likely to forget that they are there. Whenever people working are aware that other people are nearby, they do mentally complex tasks more poorly but simple tasks better—it's almost as if when people have an audience they get nervous about making a good impression and fail to do difficult tasks well, while marshalling all of their resources to do high-quality work on easy tasks. Being visible to others is energizing to people; the more people, the more we are energized. Being visible to others at all times, and being able to see other people continuously, is distracting to knowledge workers. When people working alone can be observed by other people, they are less likely to be creative and entrepreneurial. When people can be observed by their boss, they don't develop the ability to act independently and make independent judgments.

Seeing their coworkers walking around is distracting to knowledge workers sitting in their workstations. The seated people wonder why people are walking around, whether they should be walking around too, whether they are missing out on something they should be involved in doing. The best way to answer these questions is to get up and see what is going on—which means that whatever was getting done at their desk stops happening.

DESIGN IMPLICATION

Provide visual screening for workers.

GROUP SPACES

Individual workers need a territory, and so do groups (Wineman and Serrato 1999). A group space should be designed to meet the needs of the team that will use it—not all groups thrive in the same sort of space.

Groups with a clearly defined territory are more productive. Teams need their own dedicated spaces to become really cohesive. Being cohesive is important because groups work better when they are unified and focused. Making a group more cohesive increases the intensity of emotions being felt, which is not always a good thing. A group that is a little disgruntled will become very unhappy as its members become more unified.

DESIGN IMPLICATION

Create territories for groups as well as individuals. Walls around group territories definitively delineate them, but changes in ceiling heights and partition fabrics and carpet colors can also set these places apart. Changes in carpet textures, carpet contrasts, and carpet pattern offsets also make spaces appear larger and may be used to distinguish team areas. Enclosing a group in its own walled space is the best way to ensure that its members will become a united, motivated, high-performing team because it also gives them the real privacy required to directly confront difficult issues. Groups also need to concentrate (together) to get things done, and enclosed group rooms (separate from individual workspaces) make group concentration possible.

Group spaces, such as dedicated conference rooms and other shared spaces, should be close to the workspaces of the people who will actually use them. When these shared spaces are far from the workspaces assigned to team members, they are used less and people are more likely to get distracted from whatever caused them to move to the group space while they travel to it. Group spaces should also be placed midway along circulation routes and not at their ends. When they are placed at the end of hallways, they are more apt to be used for independent work than for group work.

Group spaces should be designed to permit team members to place all sorts of group-meaningful stuff in the space. These might be work products or a stuffed octopus that's a mascot. These objects help a group bond and develop a common identity. This identity enhances intra- and intergroup performance. Intragroup performance improves when information is posted in group spaces because that material helps people understand how what they are doing relates to the activities of the group.

When groups have an identity, intergroup interaction is more effective—everyone knows what group she is a member of and what the responsibilities of each group are.

Seeing information from other groups as they pass through the building helps people understand the organization itself better. This sort of "activity log" can be presented electronically via websites, but it is particularly compelling when it is presented in physical form along the outside of group spaces that line common circulation paths.

Displayed thinking or displayed achievements take on special significance when they can, in some form, be presented to members of the general public in an organization's lobby and other reception spaces.

Group spaces do not eliminate the need for individual spaces. Group members also need personal territories to bond with the organization and to feel satisfied. Workers focus more on their own workspace than the organization's campus when assessing their satisfaction with their workplace. So although the design of shared spaces matters to employees, having their own workspace and being satisfied with its design matter more.

COLLABORATIVE SPACES

Group spaces are assigned to particular work teams and are just one type of space where people can collaborate. Collaborative spaces are another. These areas can be used by any group. Collaborative spaces of different sizes are necessary because collections of people work best in spaces in which they are neither crowded nor spread apart over unnaturally large distances (see Chapters 6 and 8 for information on culturally appropriate personal space zones). The physical dimensions of conference rooms are determined by the sizes of the relevant interpersonal space zones of the people who will use the space.

In meetings, people want to sit in particular ways, as described in Chapter 6. National and organizational cultures influence preferred table shapes, with more egalitarian and people-focused cultures preferring round tables and more hierarchical and process-focused cultures preferring more rectangular tables (so the leader can sit on one of the short sides of the table).

In an effective collaborative space, all group members need to be able to respond to what is being discussed at any one time, so whiteboards and computer display tools need to be present. People not currently in meetings need to be able to see into group rooms to verify the presence of individuals or even if a meeting is in session. When doors are opened and closed to determine whether someone is in a room, the concentration of people in that space is broken.

Group meetings at which people stand are shorter than meetings at which attendees sit down, but physical conditions of some attendees (such as bad backs) may preclude stand-up meetings. People are more likely to engage in work-related conversations if they can stand or lean to one side in a space, without sitting down. Sitting down makes a commitment to the conversation—and a quick getaway impossible.

It is naïve to think that all collaboration happens in places set aside for that purpose. Most meetings take place in, or directly outside, individuals' workspaces, which increasingly means in individual cubicles. Most of these sessions are actual meetings about work—not just casual conversations about lunch.

Group spaces are also distinct from informal gathering spaces, such as coffee bars. Unstructured interaction in informal spaces allows people to get to know each other more personally, which is good for forming friendships and a sense of community. Informal spaces also permit the sort of off-topic conversations that can lead to serendipitous cross-fertilization of ideas. These spaces work best if they are convenient for all workers and visibly connected to travel routes through the building. To reduce stress, they should have a range of different sorts of seating areas so that groups of different sizes, or solitary individuals, can use the space. Gathering spaces not owned by any particular group should be centrally located and not placed within any work group's perceived territory.

Any gathering spaces that are too open visually and spatially will not be used. They make people feel exposed and vulnerable. People forced to meet in them will be tense and distracted. People like to sit in more protected sorts of places, preferably with their backs against a wall of some sort.

People and groups who work together (or should work together) need to have workspaces near each other. Even in the era of electronic communication, the frequency with which people communicate (in person or electronically) decreases dramatically as their workspaces get farther apart. By the time they sit more than 50 meters away from each other, the odds that they will interact are very low. Even after recognizing factors such as a shared knowledge base and common team membership, people who sit closer together interact more than people who sit farther from each other (Allen and Henn 2007).

Moving from one floor to another to communicate with people is also a significant hurdle to be overcome.

Middle-level managers in organizations know what other teams their groups work with regularly and which of those interactions are most crucial to the health of the firm. These managers' input should guide the placement of groups within a space. It is also important to recognize when groups should be interacting, but are not, and locate them close to each other (Allen and Henn 2007). Management needs to identify these groups—they might be teams that could be expected to develop creative solutions to problems if they worked together, for example.

FIGURE 13-7 ▦ Workers traveling between floors on open, central staircases can see into the workspaces of other teams, which can spur communication and knowledge sharing (Allen and Henn 2007).
Copyright © 2008 Farshid Assassi, courtesy of BNIM.

DESIGN IMPLICATION

In a workplace, create both collaborative spaces and areas for informal interaction among coworkers.

Distributed work arrangements are not eliminating the need for corporate campuses. They are, however, changing the function of corporate campuses to spaces where people bond to the firm as opposed to places where more specific concrete tasks are performed. Although technology exists for us to be in contact when we are separated, physical copresence is an important way for human beings to communicate and bond. As Edward Hallowell (1999) described in the *Harvard Business Review,* humans have a continuing need for face-to-face contact, even though technologically enhanced copresence is increasingly possible. We do not communicate fully and effectively and in-line with our own societal norms when we are not in the same place. How close people stand to each other, the details of their facial expressions, and what they smell like are all important ways that humans currently communicate—just as they have for thousands of generations and will for at least the next few hundred. The spaces that are created at a workplace take on a higher symbolic meaning when there are fewer of them.

People who do not have a desk of their own at their company's offices need to be able to concentrate when they are on campus, just as workers with assigned workspaces do.

Home offices must meet the same psychological standards as effective out-of-home workspaces. Many recently built homes have spaces that were designed specifically as home offices, so they are isolated from noisy

DESIGN IMPLICATION

The National Research Council of Canada NRC (2004) has quantified the design ramifications of many of the features of psychologically appropriate offices that have been discussed in this chapter. Through their empirical work, they have determined the following:

- Partitions between workspaces need to be at least 60 inches tall (on three sides of the cubicle) to provide any visual screening and 64–66 inches high to provide any acoustic shielding (higher may influence air circulation).
- Office noise louder than 45–50 decibels is annoying. To keep ambient sound at these levels in check, white noise of equal volume should be used.
- White noise alone can't do the trick. Sound-absorbing materials need to be installed in the ceilings, floors, and walls. NRC's recommendations are (STC = Sound Transmission Class; SAA = Sound Absorption Average] as follows:

- Exterior walls—STC 50
- Windows—STC 35
- Ceiling—SAA greater than .9
- Floors should be carpeted—STC 55
- Partitions between cubicles—SAA greater than .7 and STC 20
- Sound waves move in lovely straight lines and bounce off hard surfaces that they encounter and travel in other straight lines, although the direction of those waves is deflected from the direction of the wave that hit that surface originally. To reduce the possibility that those bouncing waves are annoying, the National Research Council of Canada recommends that partitions be placed between where the sound generation sources (mainly people) are located on an office floor and workers. It is also desirable to have those sound producers facing

areas of the home, which aids worker concentration. Employers who create workplaces that require all thoughtful work be done at home run the risk of shifting the site of this type of work to a space where it also cannot be accomplished, for example a home with young children, where it is difficult for parents to concentrate.

The National Research Council of Canada, Construction Division, provides several office design software packages to the public free of charge at http://irc. nrc-cnrc.gc.ca/ie/cope/index.html. Their COPE (Cost Effective Open Plan Environment) software determines the impact of various office features on worker experience. It assesses trade-offs between partition heights and lighting types in particular design situations, for example. COPE-ODE is an online calculator to estimate environmental conditions and occupant satisfaction in a particular office design; it also performs life-cycle cost analyses. COPE-ODE helps designers assess the repercussions of changing features of the workplace design and suggests potential modifications to the environment. COPE-Calc is a downloadable program to evaluate the acoustic experience in a particular workplace environment. The software provides advice about creating better acoustic spaces. In addition, users can access a program feature to hear, given the current design of an office, what an individual talking on the telephone in the next workspace would sound like to a worker in a workspace being analyzed. Additional software at the National Research Council of Canada site allows designers to simulate the ways that daylight will influence light levels in rooms with various sorts of windows (DAYSIM, SkyVision, and DAYlight 1-2-3).

DESIGN IMPLICATION CONTINUED

away from each other and into a sound-absorbing surface while they make noise or speak (although as discussed above, people need to be able to see into the distance to rest their eyes).

- If the window surface and the facing wall are both covered with materials that deaden the movement of sound waves, the workspace can be made considerably quieter. When hard surfaces, such as light covers, are removed from the ceiling as well, the results are even more dramatic.
- To reduce sound transmission, workspaces should have an area of at least 67 square feet.
- Noise-generating spaces, such as high-traffic circulation routes, should be isolated from workspaces.
- In general, to create a pleasant atmosphere, there should be more than 30-foot candles of light per square meter

bouncing off the walls in a workplace. The Illuminating Engineering Society of North America website (www .iesna.org) has tables of appropriate lighting levels for various tasks.

- To reduce the possibility of glare, all light sources should be shielded and placed perpendicularly to the locations where people will be working.
- To make spaces seem larger, 60% of the light should be indirect, but workers prefer that 40% of light be indirect.
- To move daylight back into a space, partitions through which the light can be transmitted are desirable as well as ceiling reflectances of 75 percent–90 percent and wall reflectances of 50 percent–70 percent. Horizontal light shelves, baffles, and light tubes are also useful ways to move daylight through space. (Report available at http://irc.nrc-cnrc.gc.ca/ie/cope/index.html.)

DESIGN IMPLICATION

Placing small cellular offices around a central group space can facilitate group work and individual tasks if the fronts of the individual offices are sliding glass doors (Brill, Weidemann, and the BOSTI Associates 2001). When the sliding doors are transparent glass, users can see when their teammates are gathering and determine when they should potentially join them, but effectively work on individual tasks at other times. These cellular offices can be as small as 50–60 square feet if the door on the front of the cubicle is transparent glass.

People who finance workplace design projects often seem to want to know if the new workplaces being constructed will make their employees more productive than the current offices. The primary jobs of today's knowledge workers rarely produce output that can easily be counted or categorized as "good" or "bad." Changes in the structure of a market, for example, can make a wonderful ad campaign fall flat.

A team of researchers from Georgia Tech and Steelcase came up with the sort of useful solution to this productivity management problem that can be emulated elsewhere (Peponis et al. 2007). They completed a project at a design firm where hours per project phase were carefully monitored. Modifications made to the firm's environment were projected to improve collaboration, and certain phases of the design process were known to be more collaboration intense than others. These researchers investigated whether more or less time was being spent on these design phases in the new or old environments and thereby determined the relative productivity of the two spaces. The sort of creative problem solving used by Georgia Tech and Steelcase can be applied elsewhere, although the exact metric that they used, time spent doing collaborative work, is only relevant to a small subset of all workplace projects completed.

■ CHALLENGING

Often employers want "creative spaces" in their offices. This demand ignores important differences in ways people can be creative and infers that a creativity "recipe" exists. Believing that plunking individuals down into a particular space will make them be creative is at best naïve. Plants have been associated with places where people are creative, but throwing a few plants into a space is not sufficient on its own to prompt creative behavior. A space can put people in a better mood, which broadens their thinking, for example, but if the individuals in a space lack subject-specific expertise or motivation of some sort, they will not be creative.

McCoy and Evans (2002) have, however, found certain design similarities in creative spaces. They determined that creativity is most likely in complex, visually detailed places that are built from natural materials, that look out over natural spaces. Amabile's (1986) research also indicates that people are more creative in cue-rich environments. In addition, rooms where people are less likely to be creative are painted cooler colors. In spaces where people are more creative, they are apt to be seated so that they are looking at each other. McCoy's (2002) dissertation research showed that highly creative teams modify their environments in ways they feel are appropriate, without regard for organization-wide rules. People seem to have a sense of freedom in spaces where they are creative. Creative spaces feel active and lively to the people in them.

Meyers-Levy and Zhu (2007) compared the thoughts of people sitting under 10-foot and 8-foot ceilings. More abstract and generally freer thinking was likely under the 10-foot ceiling while people thought more about specifics and details while sitting under 8-foot ceilings. These effects were only seen when people's attention was drawn to the ceiling by hanging lights from it.

Teams are also likely to be more creative if they are not distracted while they are working.

■ CONTINUING

The panacea of multitasking is influencing not only the design of workplaces and workspaces, but also the world of work in general. Multitasking is not a good idea (Rubenstein, Meyer, and Evans 2001). People who are multitasking are engaged in several activities—that is true—but they are not doing any of them well. When several tasks are done simultaneously, they are done more poorly than when people focus on each one individually.

Human beings' mental capabilities change slowly over time. Children whose parents required acoustic and visual shielding to concentrate cannot concentrate and work well in a cacophonous open space. Today, many people think that spaces in which members of Generation Y are asked to do thoughtful work can be designed like an open barn because younger people are "better at multitasking." That is wrong; members of Generation Y need the same sorts of conditions to concentrate and work well as their parents do. They also need the same access to privacy, a home base to show everyone who they are, a way to restock their mental energy . . . that previous generations do. Members of Generation Y have entered the workforce since the cubicle has reigned supreme. So many of them can't imagine working in any other sort of place, but that doesn't mean that they wouldn't do a better job if they did.

One of the professed advantages of the open office is that people working in them can multitask; they can be doing whatever they are paid to do (engineering airplanes, writing copy, filing corporate income taxes, etc.) while listening to the conversations of the people working nearby to learn important things that they should apply in their own work. These sorts of serendipitously overheard comments are actually quite rare, and since no two tasks done simultaneously are completed as effectively as when each is done individually, any such comments that might be made stand a good chance of being missed by the engineers, writers, and accountants mentioned earlier. When workers are distracted from whatever they are paid to do, they become stressed. In addition, conservative estimates indicate that it takes them 15 minutes to return to what they were doing before the distraction (some estimates put the time to return to task at 25 minutes; Mark, Gonzalez, and Harris 2005).

White-collar workers realize that they need to concentrate to do their jobs well. In a poll conducted over several years, workers stated that the workspace quality that had the biggest influence on their job satisfaction and individual and team performance was the ability to work without distraction on individual tasks (Brill, Weidemann, and the BOSTI Associates 2001). People do also realize the importance of group work; the second most important factor named in the research done by Brill and his colleagues was support for impromptu interactions while the third was the ability to hold meetings and do undisturbed group work. Brill and BOSTI's work has shown that people, on average, spend 25% of their day talking in their workstations, or very near to them, which adds up to a lot of potential distraction for people working nearby.

Future workplaces will reflect changing social dynamics:

- Current employees change jobs more frequently than previous groups of workers. They are also more apt to leave one form of employment and adopt one that is more personally meaningful for them. As people change jobs more frequently, the workplace/workspace is taking on increased importance as a recruiting aid. Potential employees "read" the physical environments at employers and place more weight on what they learn about life in the organization from those place designs than from statements in recruiting materials. Recruitment issues will be given even more importance in the future because of anticipated shortages of some sorts of highly desirable white-collar workers.

- As people change jobs more frequently, the physical environments in which they work must be designed to reduce the time needed to be working effectively after starting a new job. This may mean that there needs to be more standardization of workplace/workspace design— and potentially of home offices as well.

- There will be an increased demand for more and different sorts of learning spaces within and outside workspaces because of the increasing interest in continuing education shown by younger workers.

- The majority of college graduates are now women, and their increasing presence in the workplace means that offices must recognize women's amenity needs (such as for nursing stations, childcare, and dry cleaning, for example).

- Climate change may influence employee commute patterns and the need for workspaces in homes and third places, as well as the design of office spaces so that they are more environmentally responsible (affecting energy use, materials, and other related factors).

The design of effective workplaces requires careful consideration of many issues. Sensory inputs, organizational and national cultures, psychological needs for privacy . . . the list is long, but creating effective workplaces increases workers' satisfaction with their jobs, which is important for humanitarian and financial reasons.

14

SPECIAL FOCUS: RETAIL SPACES

Retail spaces are places in which money is exchanged for goods and services. Stores, restaurants, hotels, and casinos are all retail spaces. The discussion that follows generally names only stores to streamline the text, but design information relevant to stores is also appropriate for other sorts of retail spaces.

The people who own retail spaces have, since the first store went into business, been interested in learning more about how physical place design influences what shoppers do. Retailers have seized on the importance of place-based experience and, in their context, the influence it can have on profits. Their greatest focus is on how much money people spend in different spaces. Today, many retailers leave few aspects of shopper visits to their establishments to chance, sensory design has a significant influence on retailer success (Turley and Milliman 2000). Sights, sounds, scents, and tactile sensations are carefully integrated to create a desired impression and behavior. The supreme reward to a retailer for optimal space design is a large-ticket impulse purchase. Many factors influence consumer behavior (e.g., advertising of store products, location, and employees); no environment acts alone in determining the behavior of the people in it. Store design can influence some of these factors, such as employee behavior, but it does not dictate them.

Well-designed retail spaces satisfy the same general criteria as well-designed homes, workplaces, schools, and healthcare facilities.

◼ COMPLYING

One of the most important things to realize when doing retail design work is that there are three distinct groups of individuals who will respond to any store environment created: employees, recreational shoppers, and task-focused shoppers (Kaltcheva and Weitz 2006). The store environment influences retail employee experiences and behaviors in much the same way that an accountant's workplace influences his. The physical environment also affects what shoppers think about employees—stores that seem physically more pleasant to be in are staffed by people who are evaluated more positively. The responses of the two types of shoppers to store designs have influenced the actions of researchers and store owners much more than employee reactions to physical places, however.

Recreational shoppers and task-focused shoppers approach retail environments in very different ways. Recreational shoppers are shopping to enjoy themselves. When queried by a salesclerk, they can truthfully respond that they are "just looking." Task-focused shoppers have a mission to accomplish. They need to make a specific sort of purchase as quickly and efficiently as possible. The same person can be a recreational shopper some days and a task-focused shopper on other days or at different times on the same day. In a particular store, the majority of shoppers might be either recreational or task focused, or there might be a mix of types of shoppers present.

Recreational shoppers are out to be amused and enjoy a more arousing environment, while task-focused shoppers, who are already pretty energized by their need to complete their shopping tasks, would prefer a less energizing environment. When shoppers are task focused, they prefer to shop in a space with a more typical design—when running out to buy milk, shoppers want to be able to fly through the store, finding things in the sorts of places that they anticipate. Recreational shoppers, particularly those shopping in an emotional mood, prefer a store or restaurant with a more unusual design—when visiting a restaurant with an unusual chef, they would like the interior design to be unique.

A store that can be quickly reconfigured can be much more successful if the relative number of different shopper types changes in a predictable way. Stores that are frequented by both recreational and task-focused shoppers at different times can change some of the easy-to-modify aspects of the environment—such as lighting level and music tempo—from one time of day to another or from one department to another. If recreational shoppers and task-focused shoppers will be in the same store departments at the same time, it is best to design a moderately energizing environment, using moderately saturated and moderately bright colors on the walls, for example.

DESIGN IMPLICATION

Design in a way that's consistent with the type of shoppers that frequent a retail establishment, and, if appropriate, allow the space to be reconfigured to meet the needs of different types of shoppers at different times.

■ COMMUNICATING

People represent themselves to others through objects that they can, many of which are purchased. Objects take on different meanings depending on where they are purchased and the design of the places where people purchase expressions of their self-identity have to be consistent with the story told by the items purchased. Shoppers will select stores that are consistent with their general philosophy toward life—people who perceive themselves as environmentally responsible are more apt to frequent retailers they perceive to be environmentally responsible, for example.

One way to make sure that the retail places you are developing are consistent with the story told by the products sold there (and the stories shoppers would like to tell about themselves) is to ask potential shoppers some disguised questions. Asking target customers questions such as those that follow while they look at photo-realistic renderings (or photographs) of potential (or current) interiors can be extraordinarily useful.

1. Who would shop here?
2. What would they buy?
3. If this store/restaurant/hotel were a person, what would it be like? What would their hobbies be? What would their friends be like?

Follow up each of these questions asked with "Why?" "How come?" or "How so?" to learn more about how individual elements of the design are influencing responses.

Review the answers to these sorts of questions, looking for similarities between the responses and the lives of the people you're speaking with—the more consistency there is, the more the space designed communicates the right sort of information to the intended customers. Nonverbal communication is tied to the cultures of various groups (age, profession, etc.) and national cultures, so testing the store's design with each desired target group and in each country where it will be built out is very important.

People continually interpret and reinterpret what is happening around them. This behavior became ingrained in humans when they were living on the savanna and fighting to survive; habits tied to survival don't fade away quickly. Today, instead of focusing on a sound to determine whether it is the ominous noise of an approaching predator, we note whether it is the sort of music that we think says something about us that we want to acknowledge and others to know. Ideally, you should have potential shoppers assess what you will present through each sensory channel, but the picture-based method outlined in the last few paragraphs will generally be successful in Western society, where visual channels are used most frequently to transmit cultural information.

> **DESIGN IMPLICATION**
>
> Test the nonverbal messages being sent by current or potential retail settings to make sure that they are communicating valued information to target shoppers.

■ COMFORTING

In successful retail spaces, where products are sold at desired margins quickly to satisfied customers, shoppers are in just the right sort of mood. Except in unusual circumstances, the desired atmosphere is pleasant, and pleasant

FIGURE 14-1 ▪ The movement and sound of the water in this fountain will calm shoppers. That calming helps them to concentrate, which is desirable when certain goods (generally more expensive ones) are being purchased, but is not desirable at other times (when impulse purchases are important). Courtesy of Sally Augustin.

environments are straightforward to create, as described in previous chapters. People enjoy being in pleasant environments, and staying in a store longer has been linked to spending more money in that store.

It is more difficult to hit the appropriate energy level in a store design. The experience of being in a store must be exciting enough to spur action, but not so highly charged that individuals leave the premises without purchasing. Ways to appropriately energize shoppers are detailed in the paragraphs that follow. A store where curved circulation paths lead customers to expect intriguing new merchandise around the next corner is arousing in a way that is likely to keep customers in a store and exploring. A store that is energizing because it plays fast-paced, loud music is unlikely to create excitement without also inducing sensory overload and driving customers out of the store and into sensory peace. Also, the type of product being sold, from spa services to automobiles to music CDs, has an energy set point associated with it. That set point is largely determined by the importance of impulse and emotional factors in product selections, with impulse and lower-priced products selling best in higher-energy spaces, and more considered purchases being more frequent in medium-energy spaces.

Sound has a significant influence on how customers behave in a retail setting (Kellaris 2008). People take cues from the sounds that surround them regarding what sorts of products they will purchase. Even when customers are not consciously aware of the sort of music they are listening to, it influences their product selections—more French wine was sold in a wine department when French music could be heard and more German wine was sold in the same wine department when German music was played even though shoppers were not overtly aware of the music being played. In a similar study, more expensive bottles of wine were sold in a wine department when classical music was broadcast than when Top 40 music selections were played—classical music seems to be linked mentally to more expensive wines.

Music tempo influences listener behavior. They move through a store at a pace that matches the tempo of the music played—and if they are moving at a slower pace, they spend more money. When the music tempo is appropriate, desired behaviors will result—slower-tempo music (less than 72 beats per minute) should be played in expensive jewelry stores where clients should walk slowly between displays to focus on the relatively small-scale, high-price merchandise. In restaurants, diners eat more quickly or slowly depending on the tempo of the musical soundscape. More food is ordered in restaurant as when the pace of background music is slower. In bars, however, faster music increases drinking speed. Faster music has more than 94 beats per minute.

Since slower music is calming, when people hear slower-tempo music as they wait in line, they feel that they have spent less time in line.

People perceive that they have spent more time shopping when music is unfamiliar than when it is familiar, so more universally recognizable music should be played for task-focused shoppers or when people will be waiting in a line. When shoppers are listening to their preferred style of music, they have also been shown to spend more money than if they are not.

FIGURE 14-2 ■ Music tempo influences how quickly shoppers move through a store; faster tempos lead to faster traveling. Copyright © iStockPhoto/ ALEAIMAGE.

Since people concentrate best in moderately arousing spaces, sound levels can be modulated to encourage customers to concentrate on the desirability of potential purchases—or not ponder them—depending on the relative merits of the merchandise for sale. Music that is louder also causes shoppers to move faster. Sound levels over 75–79 decibels tend to impede conversations in restaurants, and diners will leave restaurants playing loud music sooner. Louder music increases the amount of alcohol consumed in bars; alcohol consumption is higher when music is played at 88 decibels than when it is played at 72 decibels.

The sorts of music to be played should be integrated with how many people will be in a store. Since the number of people in a store is directly related to how energized people are, when shopper density is high, slower, less energizing music (60 beats per minute) should be played, but when density is lower, faster music (96 beats per minute) can be played. These combinations keep shoppers from being overenergized by a store environment. The absolute number of people in a store required to reach perceived density levels varies based on national culture.

DESIGN IMPLICATION

Carefully soundscape retail settings.

The influence of scents on shopper behavior has been extensively researched, and a whole industry has been developed to disperse particular scents into retail spaces (Spangenberg, Crowley, and Henderson 1996). Even scents that do not draw shoppers' attention are useful. Scents that are consistent with the products being sold continue to influence shoppers, even if those same shoppers become aware of the scent and are determined not to let store design influence their product choices. Influences through other senses, such as sight or sound, seem to become less useful when customers become aware of them or when the shoppers are trying to make decisions independently of the store environment—in other words, when they are trying to avoid subliminal influences.

Scent can be dispensed in various ways and the related technology is rapidly evolving. Automatic scent dispensers are available that can present odors in conjunction with related products. In a less sophisticated approach, polymer pellets that are saturated with a particular smell can be placed in light fixtures so the heat of the lights vaporizes the scent. Scents are generally dispersed in stores through time-release atomizers or sophisticated heating and air conditioning systems. Muzak, a firm that long ago taught the world about atmospheric music, has developed a division that creates scentscapes to parallel musicscapes.

Pleasant scents put humans in a good mood, and these pleasant scents increase the likelihood that purchases will be made. They improve shoppers' evaluations of the merchandise in a store, the design of the store itself, how long shoppers spend looking around a store, and product sales. Citrus smells, for example, increase product sales. Appetizing aromas, such as the smell of chocolate chip cookies, can increase even unrelated impulse purchases (such as the sale of sweaters). The signature scents that are being used atmospherically in hotels, airlines, and stores around the world will, because they are pleasant, have the effect of leading customers to positive associations with those hotels, airlines, and stores. After stores establish particular scents as "their smell," they should make an effort to ensure that their store continues to smell the same way because *their* smell becomes associated with past pleasant memories (return customers are assumed to have pleasant store associations). These positive scent memory associations will put shoppers into a good mood. Starbucks modified its morning sandwiches to prevent the smell of eggs (bad smell) from overwhelming the smell of coffee (good, signature smell) in its stores. Like music, a pleasurable scent can be expected to have the most positive influence on sales when the other sensations in the store's physical environment are not very stimulating.

To be most effective, scents used in retailing should be logically consistent with the merchandise displayed—the part of the store selling artificial Christmas trees should smell like pine, not lemon. Scents that a national culture associates with women will increase sales of products for women (and vice versa for scents associated with men) among shoppers of that national culture.

People smelling pleasant scents perceive that time has passed more quickly and that they have spent less time waiting than people who are not in scented environments, so scent dispensers near cash wrap stations or other places where people will need to wait can be useful. People who smelled pleasant scents while selecting products from catalogs spent more time shopping than people asked to do the same shopping task in an unscented space, so pleasant scents may increase in-store shopping time. Using pleasant scents in casinos near banks of slot machines has been found to increase the income that casino owners earn from slot machines.

Ways that particular scents influence human behavior are discussed in Chapter 5.

Visual stimuli are extremely important influences on how shoppers behave.

In Chapter 5, light levels' influence on activity was discussed, and the relationships presented there can be applied in retail settings. Retailers can regulate travel speed and attention in different parts of their stores with light. People move more slowly in spaces that are more dimly lit, and their attention is focused on items that are spotlit. Bright lighting leads shoppers to look at and touch more merchandise, but not, alas, to buy more of it or to spend more time in the store. Since people tend to walk closer to light sources, pathways through retail spaces can be reliably choreographed.

When lights spotlight individual tables in restaurants, each table becomes a tiny territory, that tends to increase the time that people spend at that table—which is great if the restaurant sells coffee, desserts, and alcoholic beverages.

Sunlight, the potent force for psychological good in home, healthcare, workplace, and academic environments, also has strong positive influences in retail environments. Stores with skylights sell more merchandise than stores without skylights. Retail environments with skylights seem more spacious and cleaner to shoppers.

FIGURE 14-3 ■ The lamps on these restaurant tables create tiny territories for each pair of diners. Those territories can inspire people to linger, which is desirable in restaurants that serve after-dinner drinks and desserts.
Copyright © iStockPhoto/Xavi Arnau.

Color choices can influence behavior (purchases) in retail settings. Products being sold may interject color into any place, and that color will influence the resulting mood. A florist shop filled with red roses right before Valentine's Day will have a different emotional influence on shoppers than the same shop filled with white lilies just before Easter—in one case the space will be exciting and in the other serene. Colors also bring associations to mind—when thirsty customers see orange Halloween decorations, they are more likely to think about buying an orange-colored soda than when they see red Valentine's Day decorations. Other environmental cues can have similar effects on purchase behavior.

Color can be used to move people through a space, just as light can be used, with light ultimately having a larger influence on movement than color. Warm colors, such as orange (think of a shade the same color as the fruit), attract shoppers and cause them to make more rapid decisions than cooler colors, such as green. In an office products store, orange would be a good color to draw people to the back of the space and to encourage purchase of items that don't require much thought, such as printer paper. Drawing shoppers to the back of a store is beneficial because the trip there and back to the cash wraps at the front of the store moves consumers by a lot of products.

Spaces in the store around items that require more careful consideration, such as the printers section of the same office products store, should be predominantly less energizing, less saturated, brighter, cooler colors (such as a soft green) so that shoppers can effectively review product options. When shoppers feel unable to focus on the attributes of a product whose purchase requires consideration, they will postpone purchase of that item.

Some retail spaces should definitely be colored with warm shades. People looking at a warm color tend to find that time has passed more quickly and feel that they have spent less time waiting, so colors shoppers view as they wait should be warm.

Food displayed in environments designed with warm colors also tends to appear more appetizing.

Our peripheral vision has always been important for our survival. Today, men have keener peripheral vision than women, but in both sexes activity seen on the periphery of our visual field influences our impressions of the energy level of a space.

Management of peripheral view is particularly important in restaurants, where customers can reliably be expected to have a fixed orientation. When more activity is seen in peripheral vision, such as more waiters walking, a space seems busier and to have a higher energy level. This can be better for table turn, but it can be worse for selling high-profit items like after-dinner coffees and desserts. In general, people are more interested in eating in a restaurant that seems busy as opposed to one that seems deserted, however.

Screening dining room areas, for example, can be an effective way to get the right number of diners into a restaurant and to encourage them to run up large tabs.

Areas with moderate complexity and high order attract people. When shoppers see thoughtfully displayed (as opposed to haphazardly displayed) merchandise, a store seems more visually complex and less ordered. This increases the energy level consumers experience in the store and is generally pleasant. Too much visual complexity and too little order (disheveled/chaotic displays) are unpleasant. Assessments of pleasure are made by individual shopper groups in particular spaces, so complexity and order need to be investigated with user groups or determined by experts.

Signage is important in many public places. When signs use easy-to-read fonts, the places named on them are perceived to be closer than when place names appear in more difficult-to-read fonts. This relationship is independent of the colors used in the signage.

DESIGN IMPLICATION

The visual experiences of people in retail settings need to be carefully considered.

Sensory experiences do combine to create a general energy level, and when purchases requiring a lot of thought are planned for a space, the sensory stimulation that buyers will experience should be rather low. If people will be engaged in the hard mental work of making a choice between several products, and thereby generating a lot of mental energy, getting a lot of energy from the environment will throw them into an overstimulated state that leads them to leave a store before making a purchase. The reverse is true when products that do not involve sophisticated choices are being sold, Overall, these environments should be more energizing.

DESIGN IMPLICATION

Experiment with easily modifiable components of a space, such as scents and music, to fine-tune a space design.

The sorts of sensory experiences that are being delivered to consumers in retail environments should be consistent with each other. For example, energizing or seasonally consistent scents should be paired with energizing or seasonally consistent music if both are to be presented to consumers (e.g., cinnamony Christmas scents used when Christmas music is being played). This consistency increases how positively a retail environment is perceived. When a space seems more consistent, more purchases are made and customers are happier with the entire shopping experience.

Different sorts of sensory input seem to have different sorts of effects on people as well, and retailers should deploy sensory influencers based on the kind of product that they are selling (Donovan et al. 1994). Information obtained through some sensory channels affects us more emotionally, while information from other sensory channels influences us more cognitively. Smells seem to have more of a cognitive effect (although we do have emotional associations with them), while sounds, such as music, influence us more emotionally. Scents help us integrate new information with existing information and shop more efficiently. They aid with effective mental product comparisons or wayfinding, or example. Sounds, particularly music, change our mood as opposed to helping us process information more effectively.

As Donovan and Rossiter pointed out in 1982, sometimes it is best to acknowledge when the store that you are working with is just not very pleasant, and will never be a pleasant place. Making a store that's just not very nice to be in for various reasons (e.g., it has a traditional rough-and-ready warehouse design and is now open to the general public) energizing will actually drive customers from the store. In this case, adding fast music to a store or energizing colors to the décor can be a huge mistake. In some stores, calming music and colors are best, regardless of the product line.

People in retail environments exhibit all the human spatial needs that they do when they're in other places. Paco Underhill (1999), for example, found that when the personal spaces of shoppers are compromised, they become stressed and distracted from making a purchase. Shoppers also occasionally need privacy and may flee to dressing rooms or restrooms for a few moments of solitude. Crowding in retail spaces can intensify prevailing emotions, as described in Chapter 6, which can be good for retailers if the prevailing mood is positive. That increases the number of happy purchasers. It's not good for retailers if the prevailing mood is negative, which would increase the number of unhappy customers; unhappy customers leave the store.

Shoppers have patterns of behavior. When they first enter a store, they take a moment to get their bearings, so merchandise presented during the time that they are transitioning into the store environment is ignored. Once in a store they move in a counterclockwise direction—people entering museum galleries also generally tend to turn right and move in a counterclockwise direction. (In general, when they need to decide which way to turn, people turn toward their right if they drive on the right side of the road and toward the left if they drive on the left side of the road.) Merchandise halfway down aisles is easily missed because shoppers often do not walk the entire length of an aisle after they find what they are looking for—they return to the main route through a store. Shoppers take the shortest possible route from one place to another, so items placed between spaces where shoppers will probably travel are more likely to be viewed. Shoppers' speed picks up as they get closer to checkout counters. Products that are displayed at eye level also sell more briskly than those displayed at waist height. Display higher-margin products at eye level.

DESIGN IMPLICATION

Recognize how shoppers will move through a space—changing established travel behaviors is difficult and frustrating to shoppers.

People like to feel secure and relaxed when they are eating, and one of the ways that they can do that is by sitting with their back to something secure, such as the back of a booth and looking at their fellow diners. Seats with "protected backs" that have the widest views inside and outside the restaurant are the most popular.

One of the ways to make a restaurant more energizing is to let people see more of the food preparation work. We pick up the energy level of people we are watching. Energized people often leave more quickly, however.

People shopping in groups spend more money than people shopping alone. This is because the way merchandise is communicating nonverbally can be immediately corroborated when people with valued opinions are present—reducing communication doubt loosens purse strings. Shopping is also something we have done a lot of in the past, and when we have mastered an activity, we do it better in the company of others—that company keeps us from getting bored.

When people spend a lot of time in a retail space, such as in "their" coffee shop, they come to feel that it is an extension of their home territory. That, in turn, increases loyalty to that particular retail establishment.

People in retail spaces need to restock their mental energy from time to time, as people do in other spaces, particularly if they have been making a complex purchase. Views of nature, fish tanks and the natural fractal patterns described in Chapter 5 help shoppers mentally refresh.

Prospect and refuge are valued in retail spaces just as they are in other places.

People in retail spaces like to feel in control of their environment, just as people do when they are in other sorts of places, and will leave crowded stores quickly and in a negative mood, with few intentions to return to that crowded environment where they felt out of control. Crowding is a perception, however, and the use of lighter colors on walls and more windows and mirrors, for example, decreases feelings of crowding.

To create effective retail settings designers must consider instore sensory experiences that shoppers will have and calibrate them so that they are appropriate for the product being sold and the selling situation.

15

SPECIAL FOCUS: LEARNING ENVIRONMENTS

Learning and developing are high priorities for human beings (Lawrence and Nohria 2002).

Good places to learn share certain physical and symbolic characteristics, whether they are spots where children are mastering reading during primary school, or where adults are probing the secrets of a fine cabernet in a continuing education session. They also satisfy the criteria for well-designed spaces outlined in Chapter 4.

■ COMMUNICATING

Educational environments communicate to students, just as workplaces communicate to employees. When spaces look designed, as opposed to haphazardly thrown together, both students and teachers feel that the people who have created the spaces really value what is going on in them. Spaces that do not seem well-maintained tell pupils and instructors that whoever is financing the classes in session is not very concerned that students actually learn the material being presented.

Educators, except those at the university level, generally are not well respected by the societies whose youth they are training, as evidenced by their low pay scales. Effective school design is one way to show teachers that their contributions to society are valued.

> **DESIGN IMPLICATION**
>
> Communicate the value of education through school design.

■ COMPLYING

The success of classrooms is measured in what is learned there and the experience of teaching in them. Some aspects of what is learned in classrooms are easy to measure by traditional knowledge tests—do students know more at the conclusion of a set of classes than they did at the beginning? Classroom design can influence the scores on these academic tests. Classroom design can also affect the social experience of students and teachers, and those social experiences train young people to live in the adult world. It's more difficult to determine whether schools effectively train children to be well-socialized adults than it is to see whether they are teaching them to pass academic tests. The emotional influence of classrooms on the people in them is in part responsible for educators' success in either endeavor.

Classrooms are the workplaces of teachers and administrators, and they respond psychologically to their workplaces just as other workers do. The design of an academic environment must be consistent with the educational philosophy of its academic administrators, just as the design of any workplace must be consistent with an organization's culture.

People learn best if they are moderately energized. That means the colors used in classrooms and similar learning spaces should be in the midrange of saturation and brightness, and neither energizing nor relaxing scents should be used in these spaces. Even though lighter, less saturated greens have gotten a bad reputation for being "institutional," they do put people exposed to them in the appropriate mood to learn. In many classrooms, the learning materials inject many small bits of color into the space. Learning spaces should never be painted red, and red should not be used as an accent color in classrooms either. Red inhibits our ability to learn new material and use information we have already learned. Contrasts between the colors used in academic spaces should not be energizing. Moderate variety in the number of different textures, shapes, and types of symmetry used in these spaces also lead to the creation of a moderately and appropriately energizing space. Environments that are very complex are particularly challenging for young children. Lighting levels should also be moderately energizing. Chapter 5 includes a discussion of lighting design to achieve various psychological effects.

DESIGN IMPLICATION

Create moderately energizing learning environments.

Spaces outside classrooms also work best if they are painted particular sorts of colors. Energizing colors (saturated and less bright colors, see Chapter 5) should be used in hallways and other circulation spaces. Blue tones should not be used in cafeterias, as they are appetite suppressants. Warm colors stimulate the appetite.

Lighting affects not only what people see—at a basic level it enables them to see details in the world around them—but it also influences how they move through a space. Light draws individuals forward, so if the ends of hallways are more brightly lit (via artificial lights or windows), students will be kept moving toward them. People also try to walk as close to sources of light as possible, so if efficiently moving large numbers of students through a set of hallways is important (e.g., when pupils are moving from one class session to the next) light fixtures should be placed on hallway walls. If they're mounted on the walls, as opposed to the ceiling, the lights will keep one group of students moving efficiently down one side of the hallway and another group moving along the facing wall.

Different colors of light have been linked to better performance on different sorts of mental activities (as described in Chapter 5), so classroom lighting systems that allow light color and intensity to be varied are ideal.

Windows and daylight are important in academic environments (Heschong, Wright, and Okuta 2002a). Learning and teaching are mentally exhausting, and both students and teachers need to be able to restock their mental energy by looking out the windows of their school onto nature scenes. If nature views are not available green, leafy plants should be added to classrooms. Even when leafy plants are placed at the back of a classroom out of visual range, junior high school students are better behaved than when plants are not present in the classroom.

Sunlight in classrooms helps learners keep their circadian rhythms properly regulated, which reduces stress. Pupils learn better in classrooms with more daylight, whether it comes from windows embedded in walls or from skylights. Visitors to classrooms with large windows often find the shades drawn to reduce problems with glare. A glare-reducing window film, particularly if it is clear, dramatically reduces this problem, and so does initially siting schools off of an east-west axis. Skylights and clerestory windows are great sources of daylight, but windows placed low enough on the walls so that students can see out of them while sitting at their desks deliver two psychological benefits at the same time—they reduce both student and teacher mental exhaustion and stress. Full-spectrum lightbulbs do not have the same psychological benefits as sunlight. Buying full-spectrum lightbulbs is good for lightbulb manufacturers, but the bulbs don't provide any psychological advantages for the people sitting under them.

DESIGN IMPLICATION

Make sure students have access to daylight and views of nature.

Temperature significantly influences student and teacher experience in a space. Although students like classrooms to be a little cooler than teachers do, maintaining them at about 68–74 degrees Fahrenheit (40 percent to 70 percent relative humidity) generally keeps both groups relatively happy and neither energized or de-energized by thermal conditions. The air in classrooms should recirculate 1.5 times per hour. That air circulation can be through artificial means, such as air conditioning, or through natural means, such as openable windows, or via a combination of natural and artificial means. Even if air-conditioning is in place, openable windows are often found in spaces where students learn better.

It can be really loud in classrooms, and not all of that din is positively related to the lesson underway. Some of it is distracting. Minimizing distracting noises is as important in educational environments as it is in workplaces.

FIGURE 15-1 ■ Pupils learn better in classrooms with more sunlight.
Photo provided by Fielding Nair International, Architects and Change Agents for Education (www. fieldingnair.com).

Noise (defined as unwanted sound) from both outside and inside the school building that creeps into classrooms is undesirable. Students learn better in quieter spaces, just as office workers concentrate better in them. Trying to learn in a space where it is possible to hear people talking about topics not related to the lessons being taught is a lot like trying to concentrate in an office where it is possible to overhear other people talking. In both situations, overhearing people speaking influences performance of a verbal task, in this case learning.

Noise in educational environments can influence students' health and has been linked to higher blood pressure in students.

Gifford (2007, page 353) reviewed information from multiple studies and found that for students of all ages, "classroom involvement is greatest at moderate density . . . this would be about 30–40 square feet or 2.8 to 3.7 square meters per student." Other research has shown that classrooms for toddlers must provide five square meters of space per pupil or the children experience stress. When students are packed too densely together, they grow tense, and this results in poorer classroom performance and higher energy levels. It is unlikely that ambient features of the environment, such as calming colors on surfaces or relaxing scents, could ever overcome the negative repercussions of high-density classrooms.

DESIGN IMPLICATION

To bounce sound to the back of the room, a sound-reflecting surface should be placed above the area where the teacher normally speaks.

Sections of schools that are unavoidably noisy, such as cafeterias, auditoriums, and gymnasiums, should not be placed near classrooms and libraries. Interior and exterior walls should contain acoustical insulation and reach from the floor to the true ceiling, not a suspended ceiling.

The number of square feet of sound-absorbent material in the classroom should equal the area of the floor, but it should be clustered on the back ceiling and in a band around the room at the same height above the floor as the noise producing activities that must be damped.

Classrooms can be designed to minimize acoustical problems that originate within the room itself (Lang 1996). Softer surfaces, such as carpet, tackable surfaces, and acoustic ceiling tiles, reduce sound bounce.

Sound ricochets back and forth between hard surfaces when they are parallel to each other, so windows across from doors and marker boards are a noisy combination. Adding open storage areas to the walls parallel to the windows reduces sound reverberation. When walls are not perfectly parallel, even if their deviation from parallel is as little as five degrees, there is less echoing within a classroom space.

Ceilings should be lower than 12 feet to minimize sound reverberation and higher at the front of the classroom than at the back.

Doors should be staggered along hallways so that they are not directly across from each other.

Drywall of different thicknesses (5/8 inch and ¾ inch) should be used on the same wall because each thickness absorbs different sound frequencies; their joint use prevents transmission of sounds of a wide range of pitches.

Different classroom shapes promote varied learning experiences (Amadeo and Dyck 2003). In rectangular or square classrooms, a teacher can easily supervise everything that is happening in the space. Square and rectangular rooms focus all educational activities toward the front of the classroom. Teachers who use more traditional educational methods will be comfortable with this classroom shape. Teachers, in general, feel that nonrectangular/square classroom shapes allow multiple uses of the classroom space. Nonrectangular/square shapes are preferred by teachers who encourage small-group work, individual projects, hands-on learning, and lesson spontaneity. Other potential classroom shapes are a +, a fat T, and a fat L shape. These alternate shapes also create spaces where students can be in somewhat private settings.

DESIGN IMPLICATION

Room shape should be consistent with the teaching methods used by an organization.

Different sorts of spaces are conducive to different sorts of learning activities—spaces in which children will read silently to themselves should be different from ones where students will work together on a mathematics project, for example. When learners need to work alone, traditional rows are useful, but for group projects furniture arrangements where people can catch each other's eyes are more appropriate. When people can see into each other's faces easily, conversation and group work can flow naturally. Students are less disruptive when they are seated in rows than in arrangements where they can see into each other's faces easily, so during rowdy periods, teachers may want to have students move their chairs into this configuration. When

FIGURE 15-2 ■ Flexible seating allows meetings of different types to occur in the same space. Using the same space for multiple purposes can better serve user needs while reducing the assortment of spaces that must be constructed.
Photo provided by Fielding Nair International, Architects and Change Agents for Education (www.fieldingnair.com).

students can make easy eye contact with other students, if they are not really motivated, they will divert their attention from the educational task at hand. The teacher can maintain controlling eye contact with students sitting in rows.

Classrooms must be adjustable to adapt to different teaching situations, and also so that they can be changed just for the sake of change. We become bored with a space when we experience it in the same way day after day. Spaces need to change so that students continue to be stimulated by them to the desired level—remember that too little stimulation is just as bad as too much. If the amount of stimulation that they receive from their environment falls from its desirable level, and the total amount of stimulation from what they are doing remains the same, students and teachers may have a harder time keeping involved with their educational work.

DESIGN IMPLICATION

Develop seating options for classrooms that are appropriate for the learning activities underway. Furniture in educational spaces must be easy to move so that the space can be used for several different activities, and the classroom space should be free of single-purpose immovable objects (such as storage cabinets that are not pushed flat against walls).

School settings that are more homelike are better spaces for children to learn in because similarity to familiar environments is relaxing (Tanner & Lackney 2006). An educational space is more homelike if the furniture and materials used in it are similar to those found in a home and if the general layout of the space is like that of a home. A homelike school layout positions bathrooms so they are readily accessible and creates sheltered outdoor spaces that are reminiscent of residential backyards. A school is also more homelike if it is built in the general architectural style of the community in which it is found—a school built in the Arts and Crafts style is appropriate for a community of Arts and Crafts homes.

Pleasant mystery, the idea of something unknown but interesting placed out of sight ahead, can be incorporated into educational environments. For bonus points, that mysterious object can also be educational.

Boys and girls respond differently to the spaces in which they find themselves (Sax 2005). Boys, generally, do not hear as well as girls, so if you are creating a space where just boys will learn, make sure that it is well protected from sounds that are not related to the curriculum and that the space does not echo.

All the differences in how boys and girls respond to classrooms cannot be tied back to their ears. Boys and girls in kindergarten and first grade prefer different sorts of spaces: while boys find larger classrooms more desirable, girls prefer settings that are more complex, with more textures, shapes, and colors visible.

Teachers working with girls and boys ideally would also sit in different places. When they are working with a girl, teachers should sit across from her; when working with a boy, they should sit beside him (Sax 2005). If an educational space is going to be used exclusively by learners of one sex, the appropriate sort of seating should be provided, and in coeducational classrooms, both sorts of seating configurations should be available.

Mostafa (2007) has identified the sorts of spaces where autistic children will learn best. First, she recommends that spaces in which autistic children need to focus (such as speech therapy rooms) should be soundproofed to varying degrees. Skills can initially be taught in more soundproofed areas, but then practiced in spaces with less and less soundproofing to more closely re-create real-world conditions. Mostafa also recommends that neutral sensory environments be created in schools with autistic students. Students can use these spaces to regain emotional control. Since the spaces contain only neutral stimuli, they can be used as is by autistic children who are hyper-auditory, hyper-olfactory, hyper-visual, or hyper-tactile, or speedily modified with music for the hypo-auditory, with moving images for the hypo-visual, etc. Since autistic people like to follow routines, educational spaces they will use should be compartmentalized—compartmentalizing makes it easier to follow routines and promotes focus.

▨ COMFORTING

Students and teachers in educational environments have the same fundamental space-related needs as people in other spaces.

Children and adults are both more relaxed and in a mood that is conducive to learning new things and interacting pleasantly with each other when they are in a sheltered refuge, with a lower ceiling and a slightly lower lighting level than a brighter space with a higher ceiling. Brighter places with higher ceilings are perceived as more public, while darker spaces with lower ceilings are felt to be more private. (See Chapter 2 for more information on prospect and refuge in a space.) It is natural for people to cycle from public to more private spaces, so modifications of ceiling heights and lighting levels can be used to move people through an educational space or any other environment.

Children of preschool age are more cooperative and friendlier when they are in a space with variable ceiling heights. The variations in ceiling heights may promote feelings of comfort, which can encourage friendly behavior. Preschool-age children are more likely to be less friendly and cooperative with other children when they cannot see adults than when they can. Preschool spaces should be designed so that children always remain in visual contact with adults.

Students and teachers need to be able to maintain comfortable distances from each other, create territories through personalization, and have privacy when they want it. The interaction distances that a national culture finds appropriate are also relevant for classroom interactions. When teachers in North America are more than 12 feet from their nearest students, the students will be less focused on what the teacher has to say, just as many people at formal events (where larger interaction distances are used) are not completely focused on what a speaker is saying. Teachers should be less than 12 feet from their students, which is possible in most classrooms if the pupils' desks are not arranged in traditional rows. A teacher with a group of young students, or groups of young students alone, will stand or sit closer to each other than a group of adults, for example. Teachers generally have larger territories to personalize than students, but each group is more likely to bond with their school if they do have a place that they feel belongs to them.

Children bond more tightly with their school, which causes them to devote more energy to learning, when they have permanently personalized a space in it. Elementary school children who create a piece of art, such as a decorative tile, that is permanently mounted in a public place in their school feel a tighter link to their school than students who do not have the same opportunity. It's also important for teachers to display student work in classrooms—displaying work builds self-esteem.

Spaces that are scaled for children are ergonomically appropriate. They also help children to focus so they can learn necessary skills and to exercise some control over their own lives. Feelings of personal control make children feel more satisfied with the situations in which they find themselves, just as the ability to control the lighting or temperature in their workplace enhances the satisfaction that office workers feel. Appropriate scaling increases children's feelings of self-empowerment. Use of the proper scale in spaces

FIGURE 15-3 ■ Nature views at school help both students and teachers restock their mental energy levels.
Photo provided by Fielding Nair International, Architects and Change Agents for Education (www.fieldingnair.com).

ensures that students will be able to experience a space as the designers intend. For example, windowsills should be low enough so seated children have the intended access to outside views. When the sills are correctly placed, the scale of the structure is correct.

Students seem to learn better in environmentally responsible, or green, schools (Kats 2006). A 2005 survey by Turner Construction reported by Kats indicates that students attending green schools miss fewer days of class and perform better on academic exams. Incorporating more daylight into interior spaces makes a school greener, and so does building with less toxic materials—but there are many ways to "green" a school and Turner included schools with many sorts of environmentally responsible features in their study. Teachers in green schools are out of school sick on fewer days, and a study in Washington State indicates that teacher turnover is 5% lower in green schools than in other schools.

A seminar is not the same event if it is held in a different setting. Sommer (1983) learned that more university students participated in seminar sessions, and each student made more comments, when he made some simple changes in the room in which he taught. Students were more involved in class sessions when they sat on cushioned semicircular benches, a small carpet was placed on the classroom floor, and some mobiles were hung from the ceiling. Student test performance also improved in the modified classroom when compared to the performance of students who learned in a more traditionally institutional classroom. Sommer's work shows that when adult learners, at least, are in a more comfortable and casual setting, they learn more.

Mittleman and his colleagues have developed design recommendations for technology-enhanced classrooms (Mittleman et al. 2003). Wide aisles through technology-rich classrooms (four to five feet wide) make it comfortable for professors to move through a space and approach any of the students in the room. Similarly, if classrooms are generally shallow and wide, as opposed to narrow and deep, it is easier for the instructor to make eye contact with more of the students in the space. A shallow-wide layout also minimizes the distance between that instructor and his or her students. Teachers need ready control of all of the lights in a high-tech classroom; switches should be placed near where they will stand. They also need easy access to a phone system to call for assistance if (when) the technology in the room fails. Even though there may be lots of technology in use in the room, it must be possible to rearrange the seating for varied learning activities. Some students are inevitably late to class (or need to leave early); a door at the back of the classroom allows them to enter, disrupting the minimum number of other students. A table should be located near that rear door so that those late students can pick up handouts and other materials.

■ CREATING GREAT PLACES FOR TEACHERS TO WORK

Schools are teachers' workplaces, and school buildings have to provide the same sort of psychological support to them that office buildings provide to the accountants and lawyers who work in them. Teachers need a space that they can personalize with items that show others, and remind themselves, who they are as people. They also need to have privacy from time to time, as other workers do. Primary school teachers may be able to place photos on their desks and other similar personalizing items in a classroom that they use throughout the day, but their classroom desk is not in a private space. People teaching higher grades and adults often use different classrooms at different times. Their private spaces and spaces for self-expression can coincide or not, as space allows. A single space for teacher self-identification and privacy is more desirable and cost-effective than two individual spaces.

DESIGN IMPLICATION

Teachers work in learning environments. Make sure that some of the spaces that they use can satisfy the same psychological needs as other workplaces.

Noise seems to be more stressful for teachers than for students, so using sound-absorbing materials in the walls that surround their private areas is important.

Effective learning environments are important for the societies in which they are located. They can and must be designed to satisfy the physical and psychological needs of both students and teachers.

SPECIAL FOCUS: HEALTHCARE FACILITIES

16

Designing healthcare environments is tough. The process of getting healthy, or helping someone get healthy, is not easy mentally or physically and creating a space that optimizes healing experiences requires intense focus and empathy.

Healthcare environments seethe with tension. People who are sick can be psychologically stressed by the symptoms of their disease, the diagnosis and treatment process, and the places where those diagnoses and treatments are taking place. Friends and family members experience many of the same physical environments, as well as the uncertainty and unpleasantness of the diagnosis and treatment process. People working in healthcare environments with patients face many professional challenges. Many healthcare tasks are very intellectually demanding, often people's lives depend on completing them exactly correctly—and they are done in the same spaces that can evoke tension in patients. Workers need comfort as much as patients. Caregivers also have the unusual vocational stress of regularly being concerned about becoming ill by treating patients. In addition, today sophisticated machines are playing an increasingly prominent role in the diagnosis and treatment process and all of the technology depersonalizes patients and caregivers. Designing healthcare environments is further complicated by the need to control the spread of disease. Textures that can harbor germs are out, for example, even if they would create the perfect psychological effect.

Many of the stresses that patients, the people who support them emotionally, and healthcare professionals experience are inevitable when someone is ill. Tension added to the mix by the physical environment can be avoided, however, and healthcare environments can be designed so that they enhance the processes of healing and providing care (Ulrich et al. 2008). Healthcare environments are becoming more homelike (and hotel-like) for just this reason.

In the United States, healthcare providers are often paid a flat fee for treating people with a particular condition, so they are really motivated to make sick people healthy again as quickly as possible. When a care provider is paid a flat fee for treating a condition, and that fee is based on keeping the patient in the hospital for, say, four days, if the patient is released sooner than that, say in three days, profit margins increase. These set payment levels have made healthcare businesspeople interested in learning more about physical environments that speed physical recovery. High staff turnover rates, employee shortages, and the costs of replacing employees have made the same businesspeople take note of aspects of the physical work environment that make healthcare workplaces more pleasant and desirable places to be.

Healthcare providers working both inside and outside hospitals have also recognized the importance of the design of the physical environments in which they work. Dentists, for example, are aware that many people get very tense just thinking about paying them a visit. There is a movement among dentists in the United States to make their offices less stressful places to be. Dentists who are part of the "soothing care" movement are redesigning their offices to include aquariums and plants, as well as soothing images and colors. Some are even experimenting with calming scents.

■ COMMUNICATING

The impressions that people draw from physical environments are particularly important in healthcare settings because it is often difficult to judge the quality of healthcare services. Many variables influence the final outcome of any sort of healthcare procedure. Even if a procedure is completed correctly, results may be other than those desired because of some unanticipated or unanticipatable factor, for example. Healthcare facilities that seem to be thoughtfully designed, that minimize stress, and that provide psychological support for healing and caregiving send desirable messages about the quality of medical care provided.

Research by Harris et al. (2002) has determined that hospital interior design, architecture, housekeeping, privacy, and ambient environment are significantly related to environmental satisfaction, and that environmental satisfaction is a significant predictor of overall hospital satisfaction.

Patients whose hospital rooms are less institutional, and designed more like hotel rooms, have more positive impressions about their hospital stay and the quality of their care than people who stay in more institutional rooms. More institutional rooms, for example, lack artwork and do not have comfortable chairs for visitors.

Healthcare waiting areas speak directly to the people who visit them. Areas that are less institutional ease the people waiting into a more positive mood and reduce stress, all while generating important conclusions about the competency and humanity of the caregivers. Waiting rooms that are less institutional may include lamps, plants, decorative items, and multiple paintings (landscapes, as described below) that might be found in a home. If they find themselves in a waiting room that differs too much in design from other

FIGURE 16-1 ■ This waiting area uses homelike furniture and has a dropped ceiling, which differentiates this space from the rest of the lobby. These effects combine to make this a more desirable space for visitors to linger.
BJC Progress West, O'Fallon, MO. Courtesy of HOK.

waiting rooms they have experienced, patients become concerned. People, in general, feel more comfortable with places and things that are like the stereotypes they have developed for them.

Patients experience healthcare facilities in different ways than the medical professionals who work in them and also differently from the designers who develop them. Dramatically out of control, they may travel through hallways in wheelchairs or on gurneys. They may lie in stiff casts that prevent them from moving or that orient them to unnatural aspects of the space, such as the ceiling or only one wall. Sometimes when they are doing unusual things, such as lying perfectly still during an MRI, patients are under extreme stress. All of these events take place in a physical environment, and in all cases the design of that physical environment can profoundly influence the patients' psychological experience and the health-related repercussions of their care. Designers must recognize the ways patients will experience the environments that they create.

■ COMFORTING

Sensory stimuli significantly influence patients and caregivers.

Just as it does in workplaces, schools, and homes, exposure to nature in healthcare settings reduces stress and restocks mental energy. Postsurgical patients who can look out over nature from their hospital rooms recover from surgery more quickly than postsurgical patients without such views—even if those slower-healing patients had windows to the outdoors through

FIGURE 16-2 ▪ This patient room has a restorative nature view and a nature video on the monitor, all drenched in healing sunshine. These interactions with the natural world promote psychological and physical health. Image Courtesy of Anshen+Allen, © 2008.

which they saw brick walls, roofs, or other similar manmade objects. Patients with views of nature need smaller doses of pain medicine. In healthcare environments, windows should occupy from 20 percent to 30 percent of the exterior wall. Ideally, all patient rooms, treatment and testing areas, and waiting rooms should have views of nature. When this cannot be accomplished, nature images in art or virtual reality–type nature experiences can lesson perceptions of pain and reduce stress while increasing positive emotions. (See the next section for information on appropriate art for healthcare facilities.) Patients prefer the same sorts of views of nature that people in other spaces do—optimally, they look out over a meadow with relatively short grass, one or several collections of small plane-like trees, and a rim of woods. A peaceful, gentle water element may also be present in this optimal view. Views of nature should be placed where patients can see them, which might be on the ceiling if mirrors can be positioned accordingly. In addition, plants in healthcare facilities help patients relax.

The staff at healthcare facilities also benefit from views of nature. So do people who just happen to be inside the building. Blood donors had lower blood pressure when they were watching a nature video than when they were watching regular television programming or urban scenes on video.

The psychological ramifications of art have been more extensively analyzed by environmental psychologists in the context of healthcare environments than any other sorts of places. Researchers have learned that representational art showcasing open pastoral scenes with scattered trees and meadows that are rimmed

with a forest, tended gardens, and placid water are the three best sorts of images to use in healthcare environments (Ulrich and Gilpin 2003). These sorts of pictures distract patients and their companions from the situation that has brought them to the healthcare facility to begin with. Chemotherapy patients who can see art while being treated are 20 percent less anxious than patients who don't (and those exposed to live music are 32 percent are anxious).

Abstract or ambiguous paintings or sculptures are the very worst choices for a healthcare setting; it is better to use no artwork in a space than ambiguous, surreal, or abstract art—even if a piece is widely popular among the general public. The general public is not in a doctor's waiting room or a hospital. People who are concerned about their own or someone else's health are there, and they want to be reassured. Also, while under extreme stress or delusioned, people don't want to see images that have any possible negative associations or interpretations. Similarly, shiny surfaces on floors, walls, windows, etc., can generate odd and scary reflections. Close-ups of animals, even extraordinarily cute bunnies and kittens, should not be used in healthcare environments. Nothing is as reassuring and comforting to people as images of the sorts of places that provided security for us during the earlier eons of our existence, before we had all of our current defenses against lions and tigers and bears. These are the sorts of meadow, garden, and water scenes described earlier.

Pediatric patients also prefer nature art to abstract art or images from cartoons (child art is popular with children aged 5 to 7). Many children are scared by images of clowns. As with adult patients, children also benefit from art that includes pets or other harmless animals or pleasant and caring faces (if they are viewed from a little distance). Again, close-ups of animal faces should be avoided, even if the animal does not appear dangerous to healthy adults.

Art needs to be placed where patients will be looking if it is to influence their experience. For example, if patients are lying on their backs during a procedure, art should be placed on the ceiling. If they lie for long periods in one position, the art must be easy to see from that position.

If patients will be in a healthcare facility for some time, they should select the art that they see from their bed. This ensures that they have ready access to scenes with personal meaning and gives them an opportunity to control at least part of their in-hospital experience.

Fish tanks reduce patient stress. Even patients waiting for dental surgery experience less stress when they can look into an aquarium. Aquariums fascinate us in the same ways that views out the window do—we can see enough to understand what is happening in the tank, but we can't predict exactly what will occur next, so they can capture our attention and divert us from our current situation.

Sunlight keeps patient and caregiver body (or circadian) rhythms synchronized with those of their neighbors. People whose circadian rhythms are inconsistent with the time zone that they're living in are stressed and tired, become disoriented, and do not sleep well. They lose their mental sharpness and it can be difficult for them to focus. Patients who have had surgery and are placed in sunny rooms require less pain medication than patients assigned less sunny rooms, which reduces the cost of treating them. Patients in sunny rooms also feel less stressed during their in-hospital recovery period. They are released sooner from the hospital than comparable patients who are not in sunny rooms. When people with seasonal affective disorder, depression because of bipolar disorder, general depression, and senile dementia are exposed to morning light, dramatic improvements in their conditions result. Although morning sunlight produces the strongest effects, daylight at other times of the day also significantly reduces depression. Siting buildings and patient rooms within buildings to maximize the exposure of depressed and psychiatric patients to morning light through untinted windows is desirable. Staffs with more access to light are also more satisfied and more comfortable.

Staffs who are trying to assess skin tone will do the best job if they are examining patients in daylight.

The colors used in healthcare environments should be pleasantly relaxing. Chapter 5 details the sorts of colors that produce those effects.

DESIGN IMPLICATION

Nature views and daylight should be creatively integrated into every part of healthcare facilities, using any tools available—including light tubes, backlit simulated windows, and video monitors.

Moderately intense pink, the color of Pepto-Bismol, has been shown to quickly calm individuals, so it can effectively be used in mental health facilities. Skin tones are best checked in day-lit spaces painted in muted, grayish palettes and never in more yellowish spaces (they may make skin tones appear jaundiced). As the complement of red, a muted green is a good choice for spaces where lots of blood may be seen. Color combinations should also be relaxing, without the sharp sorts of contrasts that Chapter 5 details as exciting.

Monochromatic environments are understimulating, so they can be particularly poor choices for healthcare environments where people may already be bored. Monochrome environments are also bad choices for places where people will regain consciousness after surgery. "Waking up" in a space with a darker floor, a lighter ceiling, and walls painted an intermediate color helps patients properly orient themselves on Earth. We are used to a darker ground, lighter sky, and vegetation of intermediate darkness.

Since seeing warmer colors makes people feel warmer, they should be used in spaces where patients are apt to feel cold. A bright color behind a receptionist attracts the attention of people entering waiting areas, which reduces confusion and helps an office to function more effectively.

Visually complex environments are more energizing, so they should be avoided in healthcare facilities. Collections of things (papers, equipment, etc.) should be kept organized behind cabinet doors.

Lighting levels are relevant to hospital design. Since people speak more quietly when lighting levels are lower, keeping lights as low as possible, without compromising staff performance, can be a useful way to cut in-hospital noise levels. Using red lights to guide patients to their bathrooms at night does not disrupt their circadian rhythms as other lights would.

The World Health Organization has recommended that background noise in hospital rooms should be capped at 35 decibels, with the loudest noises at night being below 40 decibels—noise levels in American hospitals are currently generally 45–68 decibels with individual noises occasionally as loud as 85–90 decibels. When noise sensors are placed near a patient's head, they regularly register 70–75 decibels. One study found a noise level of 113 decibels (an important share of which was from staff conversations) as one set of patient caregivers was shifting responsibilities to the next set of caregivers. For comparison, the average alarm clock ring is 80 decibels, a nearby motorcycle generates 90 decibels of noise, and a jackhammer is 110 decibels.

In hospitals, noise from conversations has a more significant influence on stress than other sorts of unwanted sound, just as it does in workplaces. That's because people focus on it and try to understand what is being said. Saying noise from conversations is most stressful does not infer that if it is eliminated, machine noises experienced by patients and caregivers do not need to be minimized. Hospitals need to quash noise from both machines and conversations.

Noise increases the stress levels of patients and nurses, impeding healing among patients and increasing emotional exhaustion and job dissatisfaction among nurses. When patients are stressed, they require more pain medication. High noise levels can also increase staff errors, for example, while they are preparing medications. Patients also associate higher noise levels with lower-quality care.

DESIGN IMPLICATION

Noise levels must be kept as low as possible in healthcare facilities. They can be reduced in hospitals by installing sound insulation in walls and ceilings and ensuring that structural noises, such as those from closing doors, are eliminated. Noise-absorbing materials must extend above dropped ceilings to the true ceilings. Acoustical ceiling tiles should be used even if sound insulation is used in walls because these tiles reduce annoying sound reverberation or echo. Reverberation makes it difficult for patients to relax. Echoing makes it harder to understand speech, so people (including staff) speak more loudly. Staff members participating in one study felt less stressed at work after sound-dampening ceiling tiles were installed.

Softer flooring, such as rubber tiles, also helps to reduce sound levels. Intercom-type communication systems can also be replaced with communication devices carried by each individual healthcare provider, such as a pager. Bedside medical equipment can also be quite noisy, and providing acoustical shielding significantly reduces the level of noise experienced by patients. Single rooms have the same effect.

On surgical hospital floors, closing hospital room doors results in patients experiencing six decibels less noise, but when doors are closed in intensive care units, the noise experienced by patients increases because of the amount of medical equipment in each of the rooms.

Music in medical waiting rooms reduces stress levels. Stress-reducing music is described in Chapter 5. Patients who hear music they enjoy during their hospital stays also seem to experience less pain than patients who do not hear music. Natural sounds, such as ocean waves, reduce patient stress. Pairing natural sounds with natural images, or pairing classical music with the same images, has also been shown to reduce perceived pain to lower levels than when the images are viewed alone.

DESIGN IMPLICATION

Listening to the sorts of smooth, relaxing music described in Chapter 5 and music selected by the patients themselves has been shown to reduce patient stress—make sure patient areas are wired for sound. Many members of the medical community are concerned about using white noise to counter the noise levels in patient care areas because it might muffle patient sounds

they need to hear. Fountains and other similar sorts of white noise generators can be used in more public areas of healthcare facilities. Looking at water in motion is relaxing, as are noises from fountains. If they are properly maintained, in-hospital water features are not a health hazard.

Pleasant smells in waiting rooms also reduce stress in healthcare facilities.

Privacy is important in healthcare facilities, just as it is in other sorts of places. Governments often develop regulatory systems that protect patient privacy. In the United States this system is known as HIPAA. Patient privacy is important even if it is not government mandated; for example, when patients feel that they have privacy, they communicate more freely with healthcare professionals.

Healthcare workers and patients both desperately need private retreats. Both caregivers and patients are in highly stressful situations, and privacy gives them the opportunity to reflect on recent events and integrate them with previous memories. Reflecting and integrating help people cope with complex situations. Providing patients with privacy means allowing them to isolate themselves from society sometimes.

Private patient rooms are one way to prevent the spread of disease from one patient to another while also providing needed seclusion for patients and their family members (Chaudhury, Mahmood, and Valente 2005). Just as patients are more frank and forthcoming in discussing their health with medical professionals when they are in private, as opposed to shared, rooms, emergency room patients separated from other patients by curtains often do not communicate relevant information to people caring for them because they feel that their privacy is compromised. Joseph and Ulrich (2007) suggest private discussion rooms to ensure effective conversations. Nurses also experience less stress when patients are in private rooms. Reducing the movement of noise within healthcare facilities through the use of wall, floor, and ceiling treatments, as described in the last section, increases privacy.

DESIGN IMPLICATION

Provide private retreats for patients, their families, and caregivers.

When patients socialize with family and friends, their health benefits. Patient rooms should have movable chairs that allow people to interact in that space as desired. Family and friends spend more time with patients when they are in single rooms than they do when they are in double rooms. Visits can be encouraged by providing desirable in-room and out-of-room spaces for families, friends, and patients to gather. Carpeting in patient rooms has been linked to longer visits than similar gatherings in spaces without carpeting.

It is important for people to feel that they have control over their own lives, and often patients lose nearly all control over what happens to them. When we lack control, we are stressed, we can become depressed, and our immune systems can be compromised. Control increases the self-esteem and feelings of security among hospitalized patients. Patients (and their supporters) feel as if they have more control when they can modify their environments, such as by turning fans and televisions on and off and opening and closing curtains. People who have control feel that their rooms are more homelike than patients without control over sensory aspects (temperature, light levels, etc.) of their environments. When patients are in private rooms, they feel that they have more freedom to change their room and their visitors feel freer to socialize as they choose, for as long as they choose. People prefer environments that they can control, which is important in situations when patients can choose the hospitals that they use (e.g., when they are giving birth).

People who have control of their environments have the freedom to personalize them, and that personalization has positive psychological ramifications. It makes people feel more comfortable in a space by providing them with some sort of temporary ownership of it. Even people who are only in a hospital briefly, such as to give birth, prefer to personalize their surroundings.

Designing hospital spaces for adolescent patients is particularly challenging because adolescents are in the process of establishing control over their own lives. They want to be distinguished from children, so they dislike the cartoon-like motifs often used in pediatric wards. They also want to be able to entertain friends in their hospital rooms, as they can in their parents' homes, and they want to be able to make easy contact with friends in person or via cell phones. Children and adolescents feel that hospital staff recognize that they "are not babies" when they are allowed to control the lights and heat in their rooms.

Nurses also can feel as if they don't have much control; some feel that their medical knowledge and professional expertise are not appropriately recognized. Providing them with opportunities to control ambient and functional details of their work environments, such the heights of their work surfaces, is therefore desirable. Nurses should be included in the programming and design process, not only because their input is valuable, but also because providing information that is utilized gives them the feeling that they have more control over their professional lives. Nurses also need restorative experiences to reduce stress, and opportunities to interact formally and informally with physicians can diffuse stress levels.

> **DESIGN IMPLICATION**
>
> Provide patients of all ages with the opportunity to control their ambient environments. And don't forget the caregiving staff—make sure that they do not feel that they lack control over their professional environments.

Healthcare facilities must be culturally appropriate for the patients who will use them. A hospital in the Middle East may need to provide different doors for men and women to enter the building, for example. Exam rooms and patient rooms in the Middle East need to be larger to accommodate the larger groups that accompany patients to the facility and through treatment. Corridors in new Middle

> **DESIGN IMPLICATION**
>
> Recognize the cultural traditions of the people who will be patients at healthcare facilities.

Eastern hospitals should be wider than in the United States so large family groups can move through the facility together.

A hospital at the University of New Mexico worked to recognize the three predominant cultures among its patients: European Americans, Native Americans, and Hispanics. Corners have negative spiritual associations for Native Americans, so the hospital chapel is round. It also includes a fireplace where incense important to Native American patients can be burned. Since stone represents healing power to Native Americans, it was incorporated throughout the center. Since more members of Hispanic families attend physical exams and consultations with patients than is the case with European Americans, the hospital at the University of New Mexico has exam and consultation rooms that are large enough to accommodate these groups.

■ COMPLYING

People regularly get lost in healthcare facilities; they don't visit them often, and when they do, they are often distracted by whatever has brought them to the facility in the first place. In hospitals, weak people may be trying to make time-critical trips through a floor plate that has been complicated by additions over the years. People who cannot find their way through a building not only waste their own time and the time of people who must wait for them to arrive, but they also become stressed, and stress erodes health and well-being.

Healthcare environments are stressful for everyone in them—patients are sick and worried, patient supporters are worried, and healthcare professionals are often doing difficult tasks that determine whether people live or die. A thoughtfully designed physical environment can enhance the lives of all of these individuals.

FIGURES 16-4 AND 16-5 ■
Two easy-to-use signs—one in a hospital and one at the entry to a transit line stop. Both make it clear where travelers should go. The subway signs, which are also color coded, are placed so that it is impossible for people not to see them and read them clearly (except during extremely busy travel periods).
Figure 16-4 Copyright © iStock-Photo/Brandon Gunem.
Figure 16-5 Courtesy of Sally Augustin.

DESIGN IMPLICATION

Color-coding sections of buildings or paths through buildings can prevent people from getting lost. Color can be a landmark, just as a sculpture, a distinctive painting, or a change in architectural features can be. Colors used to help people navigate through a space should be readily recognizable with standard names—*teal* is a more confusing term than *green-blue*, which is more confusing than either *green* or *blue* alone.

Signs should be legible to people of all ages who are moving through the space in all sorts of ways (e.g., in wheelchairs and standing on two feet). The words on those signs should match the phrases in patients' heads, not in those of the healthcare professionals treating them, who are familiar with a lot of technical jargon that the general population is not.

Both signs *and* you-are-here maps, where the top of the map is oriented in the direction of forward motion, are useful ways for people to figure out where they are in a space and move toward their destination.

Signs should be located at about every 200 feet. They should be placed at landmarks, such as hallway intersections or patient destinations like public cafeterias, or where design features seem to indicate that some sort of transition is taking place.

When the exterior shape of the building gives people clues about how they should travel through it, they will do so more effectively. For example, if people approaching a hospital can tell that the building is shaped like an X, they will know that inside the building they will find floors with long, crossing corridors. When people can look out windows as they travel through a building and see landmarks outside, it is easier for them to find their way through a structure.

Creating memorable locations within a healthcare environment also aids wayfinding. Landmarks inside the building, such as sculptures, fountains, changing architectural features (if there is a colonnade or a higher ceiling, for example, along one section of a route), or changes in floor coverings make it easier for patients and visitors to avoid getting lost and for other people to give them directions. They help individuals trying to move through a space to remember the spaces that they have been in the past and to understand where they are traveling to. When hallways meet at right angles, people are less likely to get lost than if the hallways meet at other angles.

Men and women use different sorts of tools to navigate through a space—women orient using landmarks that can be seen (or heard or smelled, in some cases) and men prefer to navigate using cardinal directions and named routes, so opportunities to give and follow directions using both sets of tools should be provided.

MAKING PATIENTS AND CAREGIVERS MORE COMFORTABLE

From an interview with George Marmaropoulos,
Design Director, Ambient Experience NA, Philips Design

When George Marmaropoulos and the other members of the team of researchers and designers at Philips Design set out to make people more comfortable, they succeed. Marmaropoulos and his colleagues at Philips watched and listened to people visiting and working in healthcare facilities, stores, offices, and homes. The analyses that these anthropologists, psychologists, human factors experts, designers, engineers, and product interaction specialists completed led to the design of deeply satisfying sensory systems because the systems respond to psychologically significant human needs.

Philips's healthcare multisensory systems provide positive, distracting visual experiences for patients having various sorts of medical procedures, such as a CAT scan. The patients select the sort of audiovisual presentation they experience—and that selection returns some control to them during a situation in which they're often powerless. That sense of control makes patients more comfortable, as do the sorts of soothing images and sounds that they experience. Adults and children can choose to see a light show and animation from among the several options available. Animations related to the requested theme are projected onto the walls and ceiling of the procedure room. These images are coupled with related sounds and music. In the future, associated scents will also be dispensed.

As Marmaropoulos describes, the initial spark for the research that culminated in Philips's sensory systems was a realization that being treated in a healthcare facility and providing that treatment should be pleasant for everyone involved. Initially, Philips focused on improving comfort levels in the CAT scan suite by making patients more relaxed. Having a CAT scan often makes patients anxious, which affects the levels of sedation that they require, and that influences the number of patients that can be examined on a particular day. Patient tension escalates the stress levels of healthcare providers who are doing an exacting job. Reducing stress during procedures has the added benefit of potentially increasing patient referrals and staff retention.

The sorts of light, sound, and scent experiences pioneered in the CAT scan suite will ultimately be available in home, retail, and office applications. They have already moved out of the CAT scan suite to other diagnostic imaging suites such as MRI exam rooms, and also to whole radiology departments, stand-alone imaging centers, hospital emergency departments, oncology centers, and cardiac catheterization laboratories.

Philips does not just provide the hardware to create the sensory experiences; they also make suggestions for the architecture of the room in which they occur. Most of the rooms are rectangular. Philips softens them by introducing round corners where walls meet the floor and ceiling. They also simplify and unclutter the rooms by introducing built-in storage systems so that there are no protruding elements on the walls. Corners on the scanner itself are also rounded.

Philips also recommends that whenever possible, patients gradually begin and end their sensory experiences. They suggest that soothing lights bathe the walls in waiting areas.

The hospital ambient systems also provide something interesting, positive, and nonhealthcare-related for patients and staff members to talk about. When viewing beach images, they can discuss how much they enjoy beach visits, favorite beaches, etc.

Are patients more comfortable in these spaces? Yes. One study of pediatric ambient systems indicates that patients who experienced Philips's ambient system were less anxious and required less sedation than other pediatric patients.

Philips is "turning healthcare into humancare." They expect their current systems to evolve over time, as Philips learns more about human responses to them and they are introduced to additional cultures. Philips's ambient systems for nonhealthcare environments will no doubt also lead to desirable human experiences because the systems satisfy deep-seated human needs for positively distracting, user-controlled sensory experiences.

HOLISTIC HOSPITAL DESIGN:
ENVIRONMENTAL PSYCHOLOGY THAT PROVES DESIGN CARES

From an Interview with Nicholas Watkins, PhD, Director of Research & Innovation, HOK

HOK uses environmental psychology for cutting-edge planning and design of innovative care environments. These environments range from minimally invasive diagnostic and treatment areas to reimagined inpatient units.

That is no small challenge. For instance, there are competing connotations of the term *care* among different consumers of healthcare design. Architects, patients, nurses, physicians, and healthcare administrators in the United States are challenged by a system that vacillates between sanctity of life and monetary cost, social responsibility and capitalist enterprise, and genuine empathy and billable services. The seesaw impacts design. A patient's feelings about her environment can have a strong impact on her happiness and, therefore, her health. However, several recent hospital designs focus on the well-being of a patient while ignoring the other intangible aspects of what it means to "heal" a patient through advances in technology. How can designers create a hospital that satisfies so many competing demands in a single building?

HOK has innovated a research-based design process with tenets of environmental psychology at its cornerstone. Using this approach, HOK comes to understand a healthcare facility as biologists do an organism or ecosystem—never forgetting that a facility is rooted in a relationship among its people and their culture, and that it changes over time. This process ensures sustained clinical, strategic, and business advantages are being realized by improving the quality of care. In turn, the improved quality of care attracts more patients and increases philanthropic support for a hospital from the surrounding community.

Nicholas Watkins, PhD, HOK's Director of Research & Innovation, calls the research-based design approach the comprehensive facility evaluation (CFE) process. Using CFE, Dr. Watkins and his colleagues seamlessly orchestrate the continuum of design services from strategic planning to post-occupancy evaluation. In addition, the CFE process can map the complex interrelationship among design features and hard outcomes for an entire unit or facility. A design or operational change to any one facet of a healthcare organization ricochets throughout the entire organization. For example, by improving the triage process in an emergency department, Dr. Watkins and his colleagues are able to improve operational requirements like bed assignment in intensive care units. Improved operations decrease patient waiting times and improve the patient experience.

Dr. Watkins finds that the CFE approach further enhances the business case for environmental psychology by appealing to multiple consumers of healthcare design. Research-based design recommendations can simultaneously improve the patient experience and staff performance. These outcomes interest healthcare administrators who want to maximize every dollar spent on design features that are intended as long-term investments. During a full CFE, initial costs related to innovative design features are weighed against improved patient experiences, staff retention, and medication errors over several years. Research findings on what design features have traditionally performed the best at other facilities can be used to estimate any extra costs that clients might incur from implementing the same sort of design features at their healthcare facility.

Dr. Watkins is currently applying the CFE process to projects at several hospitals. As an example of his comprehensive approach, Dr. Watkins and his colleagues are leading a study of contemporary advances in diagnosis and treatment (e.g., imaging, genetic medicine, and robotics) and their relationship to the patient experience, staff efficiency,

patient volumes, and square footage. Though labor intensive and long term, the research efforts do have short-term gains. Preliminary research involving facility evaluations and simulations feed directly into programming and design efforts.

Dr. Watkins lives in several worlds. He has one foot in architectural practice and another in intellectual sharing and contributions. Dr. Watkins's work involves frequent participation in environmental psychology-related organizations and initiatives. His participation with Environmental Design Research Association–sponsored publications and conferences provides him with invaluable peer review on his ongoing research efforts within architectural practice. Consequently, Dr. Watkins's research efforts balance rigor and innovation. These research efforts currently include studies measuring the impact of same-handed patient rooms, nursing station configurations, electronic medical records, caregiving models, chemotherapy area design, and commemorative environments on outcomes like patient recovery, patient throughput, hospital-acquired infection rates, staff retention, staff fatigue, group cohesion among staff, and medication errors.

17 PLACE DESIGNERS' VITAL INFLUENCE ON HUMAN WELL-BEING

Places influence people psychologically. That's something that you've seen play out repeatedly in spaces you've designed and used. There are some offices that you walk into and feel comfortable and welcomed, and some that drive you right back to the street as fast as you can get there. Places also have meaning to the people who use them beyond their mere functionality—that's also something you've known for a long time. Why else would we spend so much energy trying to decide which sofa we should select from among all of the equally comfortable seats available? We know that the style of that sofa says something about us to ourselves and to other people—and we want the *right* message broadcast.

Scientists have only recently started to learn the details of how and why spaces matter to us psychologically. The patterns scientists have seen in how humans interact with their physical environments, presented in this book, will help you more thoroughly understand and effectively apply things you have learned through your own design work. What scientists have learned, however, also supplies you with new tools you can use to integrate ambient factors, humans' inherent psychological needs, and cultural proclivities to shape places where people thrive. Humans are not always rational about how they use and respond to space (Vischer 2005). The preceding chapters have outlined some of the reasons why. By thinking about some of the generally unspoken human needs satisfied (or not) through space design, you can create places that superbly satisfy their users.

Using place science when you are designing a space does not constrain your creativity. Instead, it allows you to quickly identify the sorts of design solutions that will work best and then effectively create a place within a framework that you can be confident will be successful. When you determine how saturated and how bright the color should be that will go up onto the walls of a space, you have made an important, but fundamental, decision. Deciding whether red, orange, yellow, green, blue, indigo, or violet paint of the desired saturation and brightness is best is still up to you. There is a version of each of these colors that meets your saturation and brightness specs.

After reading this volume you are also more informed while making decisions regarding visual complexity, ceiling height, window design, materials . . .

Scientists have learned a lot about how humans interact with their physical worlds. It can be challenging to keep the things they have learned in mind as you design, at first. The spaces you create will benefit from your efforts to do just that.

I look forward to discussing applying environmental psychology to place design with you. I can be reached at sallyaugustin@yahoo.com.

IMPORTANT SOURCES/RELATED READINGS

S = *Suggested Reading*

Aarts, H., and Dijksterhuis, A. (2003). "The Silence of the Library: Environment, Situational Norm, and Social Behavior." *Journal of Personality and Social Psychology* 84(1): 18–28.

Adams, F., and Osgood, C. (1973). "A Cross-Cultural Study of the Affective Meaning of Color." *Journal of Cross-Cultural Psychology* 28(4): 352–355.

Adams, L., and Zuckerman, D. (1991). "The Effect of Lighting Conditions on Personal Space Requirements." *Journal of General Psychology* 118(4): 335–540.

Adler, A. (1968). *Understanding Human Nature.* Greenwich, CT: Fawcett.

Aiello, J. (1987). "Human Spatial Behavior." In D. Stokols and I. Altman (eds.), *Handbook of Environmental Psychology, Volume 1.* New York: John Wiley & Sons, 389–504.

Aiello, J., and Doulhitt, E. (2001). "Social Facilitation from Triplette to Electronic Performance Monitoring." *Group Dynamics: Theory and Practice* 5(3): 163–180.

Alexander, C., Ishikowa, S., Silverstein, M., Jacobson, M., King, I., and Angle, S. (1977). *A Pattern Language.* New York: Oxford University Press.

Allan, D. (2008). "Sound Retailing: A Review of Experimental Evidence on the Effects of Music on Shopping Behavior." In T. Lowrey (ed.), *Bricks and Mortar: Shopping in the 21st Century.* New York: Taylor and Francis, 33–53. (S)

Allen, T. (1984). *Managing the Flow of Technology.* Cambridge, MA: MIT Press.

Allen, T. (2007). "Architecture and Communication Among Product Development Engineers." *California Management Review* 49(2): 23–41.

Allen, T., and Henn, G. (2007). *The Organization and Architecture of Innovation: Managing the Flow of Technology.* New York: Elsevier. (S)

Altman, I. (1975). *The Environment and Social Behavior*. Monterey, CA: Brooks/Cole.

Altman, I., and Chemers, M. (1980). *Culture and Environment*. New York: Cambridge University Press.

Altman, I., and Gauvain, M. (1981). "A Cross-Cultural and Dialectic Analysis of Homes." In L. Liben, A. Patterson, and N. Newcombe (eds.), *Spatial Representation and Behavior Across the Life Span*. New York: Academic Press, 283–320.

Amabile, T. (1986). *Creativity in Context*. New York: Westview Press. (S)

Amadeo, D., and Dyck, J. (2003). "Activity-Enhancing Arenas of Designs: A Case Study of the Classroom Layout." *Journal of Architectural and Planning Research* 20(4): 323–343.

American Society of Interior Designers. (1999). *Recruiting and Retaining Qualified Employees—By Design*. Washington, DC: American Society of Interior Designers.

Andreu, L., Bigne, E., Chumpitaz, R., and Swaen, V. (2006). "How Does the Perceived Retail Environment Influence Consumers' Emotional Experience? Evidence from Two Retail Settings." *International Review of Retail, Distribution and Consumer Research* 16(5): 559–578.

Appleton, J. (1975). *The Experience of Landscape*. London: Wiley. (S)

Archea, J. (1977). "Privacy as a Behavioral Phenomenon." *Journal of Social Issues* 33(3): 116–138.

Areni, C., and Kim, D. (1993). "The Influence of Background Music on Shopping Behavior." *Advances in Consumer Research* 20: 336–340.

Argyle, M., and Dean, J. (1965). "Eye Contact, Distance, and Affiliation." *Sociometry* 28: 289–304.

Arneill, A., and Devlin, A. (2002). "Perceived Quality of Care: The Influence of the Waiting Room Environment." *Journal of Environmental Psychology* 22(4): 345–360.

Arnold, M., and Reynolds, K. (2003). Hedonic Shopping Motivations." *Journal of Retailing* 79(2): 77–95.

Aslam, M. (2006). "Are You Selling the Right Colour? A Cross-Cultural Review of Colour as a Marketing Cue." *Journal of Marketing Communications* 12(1): 15–30. (S)

Ayoko, O., and Hartel, C. (2003). "The Role of Space as Both a Conflict Trigger and a Conflict Control Mechanism in Culturally Heterogeneous Workgroups." *Applied Psychology* 52(3): 383–412.

Babin, B., and Attaway, J. (2000). "Atmospheric Affect as a Tool for Creating Value and Gaining Share of Customer." *Journal of Business Research* 49(2): 91–99.

Babin, B., and Babin, L. (2001). "Seeking Something Different? A Model of Schema Typicality, Consumer Affect, Purchase Intentions and Perceived Shopping Value." *Journal of Business Research* 54(2): 89–96.

Baird, J., Cassidy, B., and Kurr, J. (1978). "Room Preference as a Function of Architectural Features and User Activities." *Journal of Applied Psychology* 63(6): 719–727.

Baker, J., Parasuraman, A., Crewal, D., and Voss, G. (2002). "The Influence of Multiple Store Environment Cues on Perceived Merchandise Value and Patronage Intentions." *Journal of Marketing* 66: 120–141.

Balcetis, E., and Dunning, D. (2007). "Cognitive Dissonance and the Perception of Natural Environments." *Psychological Science* 18(10): 917–921.

Banbury, S., and Berry, D. (2005). "Office Noise and Employee Concentration: Identifying Causes of Disruption and Potential Improvements." *Ergonomics* 48: 25–37.

Bar, M., and Neta, M. (2006). "Humans Prefer Curved Visual Objects." *Psychological Science* 17(8): 645–648.

Barker, R. (1968). *Ecological Psychology: Concepts and Methods for Studying the Environment of Human Behavior.* Stanford, CA: Stanford University Press.

Barker, S., Grayhem, P., Koon, J., Perkins, J., Whalen, A., and Raudenbush, B.(2003). "Improved Performance on Clerical Tasks Associated with Administration of Peppermint Odor." *Perceptual and Motor Skills* 97(3): 1007–1010.

Baron, R. (1990a). "Environmentally Induced Positive Affect: Its Impact on Self-Efficacy, Task Performance, Negotiation, and Conflict." *Journal of Applied Social Psychology* 20(5): 368–384.

Baron, R. (1990b). "Lighting as a Source of Positive Affect." *Progressive Architecture* 11: 123–124.

Baron, R. (1997). "The Sweet Smell of . . . Helping." *Personality and Social Psychology Bulletin* 23: 498–503.

Baron, R., Rea, M., and Daniels, S. (1992). "Effects of Indoor Lighting (Illuminance and Spectral Distribution) on the Performance of Cognitive

Tasks and Interpersonal Behaviors." *Motivation and Emotion* 116 (1): 1–33.

Basso, M. (2001). "Neurobiological Relationships Between Ambient Lighting and the Startle Response to Acoustic Stress in Humans." *International Journal of Neuroscience* 110(3/4): 147–157.

Baum, A., and Paulus, P. (1987). "Crowding." In D. Stokols and I. Altman (eds.), *Handbook of Environmental Psychology, Volume 1*. New York: John Wiley & Sons, 533–570.

Beaulieu, C. (2004). "Intercultural Study of Personal Space: A Case Study." *Journal of Applied Social Psychology* 34(4): 794–805.

Becker, F. (1991). "Workplace Planning, Design and Management." In E. Zube and G. Moore (eds.), *Advances in Environmental Behavior and Design, Volume 3*, New York: Plenum Press, 115–151.

Becker, F. (2007). "Organizational Ecology and Knowledge Networks." *California Management Review* 49(2): 42–61.

Becker, F., and Douglass, S. (2006). "The Ecology of the Patient Visit: Attractiveness, Waiting Times, and Perceived Quality of Care." *Healthcare Design* 11: 12–19.

Becker, F., Sims, W., and Schoss, J. (2002). *Interaction, Identity and Collocation: What Value Is a Corporate Campus?* Ithaca, NY: Cornell University, International Workplace Studies Program.

Becker, F., and Steele, F. (1995). *Workplace by Design*. San Francisco: Jossey-Bass. (S)

Belojevic, G., Slepcevic, V., and Jakovljevic, B. (2001). "Mental Performance in Noise: The Role of Introversion." *Journal of Environmental Psychology* 21(2): 209–213.

Belk, R. W. (1988). "Possessions and the Extended Self." *Journal of Consumer Research* 15(2): 139–168.

Bellizzi, J., Crowley, A., and Hasty, R. (1983). "The Effects of Color in Store Design." *Journal of Retailing* 59(1): 21–45.

Bellizzi, J., and Hite, R. (1992). "Environmental Color, Consumer Feelings, and Purchase Likelihood." *Psychology and Marketing* 9(5): 347–363.

Bencivenga, P. (1998). "A Humanistic Approach to Space." *HR Magazine*, March: 68–78.

Berg, B. (2004). *Quantitative Research Methods for the Social Sciences*. 5th ed. New York: Pearson.

Berger, P., and Luckmann, T. (1967). *The Social Construction of Reality: A Treatise in the Sociology of Knowledge.* New York: Penguin.

Berry, L., and Bendapudi, N. (2003). "Cluing in Customers." *Harvard Business Review* 81(2): 100–106.

Berto, R. (2005). "Exposure to Restorative Environments Helps Restore Attentional Capacity." *Journal of Environmental Psychology* 25(3): 249–259.

Bille, M., and Sorensen, T. (2007). "An Anthropology of Luminosity: The Agency of Light." *Journal of Material Culture* 12(3): 263–284.

Biner, P., Butler, D., and Winstead, D. (1991). "Inside Windows: An Alternative to Conventional Windows in Offices and Other Settings." *Environment and Behavior* 23(3): 359–382.

Birch, J., Curtis, P., and James, A. (2007). "Sense and Sensibilities: In Search of the Child-Friendly Hospital." *Built Environment* 33(4): 405–416.

Bitgood, S., and Dukes, S. (2006). "Not Another Step! Economy of Movement and Pedestrian Choice Point Behavior in Shopping Malls." *Environment and Behavior* 38(3): 394–405.

Bitner, M. (1992). "Servicesscapes: The Impact of Physical Surroundings on Customers and Employees." *Journal of Marketing* 56(1): 57–71.

Bloomer, K. (2008). "The Picture Window: The Problem of Viewing Nature Through Glass." In S. Kellert, J. Heerwagen, and M. Mador (eds.), *Biophilic Design*. Hoboken, NJ: John Wiley & Sons, 253–261.

Bluedown, A., Turban, D., and Love, M. (1999). "The Effects of Stand-Up and Sit-Down Meeting Formats on Meeting Outcomes." *Journal of Applied Psychology* 84: 277–285.

Blumberg, R., and Devlin, A. (2006). "Design Issues in Hospitals: The Adolescent Client." *Environment and Behavior* 38(3): 293–317.

Blumer, H. (1969). *Symbolic Interactionism: Perspective and Method.* Englewood Cliffs, NJ: Prentice-Hall.

Bone, P., and Ellen, P. (1999). "Scents in the Marketplace: Explaining a Fraction of Olfaction." *Journal of Retailing* 75(2): 243–262.

Bosmans, A. (2006). "Scents and Sensibility: When Do (In)Congruent Ambient Scents Influence Product Evaluations?" *Journal of Marketing* 70(1):32–43.

BOSTI. (1984). *The Impact of Office Environment on Productivity and Quality of Working Life*. Buffalo, NY: Buffalo Organization for Social and Technological Innovation.

Boutelle, K., Jeffrey, R., Murray, D., and Schmitz, M. (2001). "Using Signs, Artwork, and Music to Promote Stair Use in a Public Building." *American Journal of Public Health* 91(12): 2004–2006.

Boyatzis, C., and Varghese, R. (1994) "Children's Emotional Associations with Colors." *Journal of Genetic Psychology* 155(1): 77–85.

Brager, G., Heerwagen, J., Bauman, F., Huizenga, C., Powell, K., Ruland, A., and Ring, E. (2000). "Team Spaces and Collaboration: Link to the Physical Environment." Final Draft Internal Report. University of California, Berkeley: Center for the Built Environment.

Brand, S. (1994). *How Buildings Learn*. New York: Penguin Books. (S)

Brennan, A., Chugh, J., and Kline, T. (2002). "Traditional Versus Open Office Design: A Longitudinal Field Study." *Environment and Behavior* 34(3): 279–299. (S)

Bridges, W. (2000). *The Character of Organizations: Using Personality Type in Organization Development*. Palo Alto, CA: Davies-Black. (S)

Brief, A., and Weiss, H. (2002). "Organizational Behavior: Affect in the Workplace." In S. Fiske, D. Schacter, and C. Zahn-Waxler (eds.), *Annual Review of Psychology, Volume 53*. Palo Alto, CA: Annual Reviews, 279–307.

Brill, M., Weidemann, S., and the BOSTI Associates. (2001). *Disproving Widespread Myths About Workplace Design*. Jasper, IN: Kimball International. (S)

Brown, B. (1987). "Territoriality." In D. Stokols and I. Altman (eds.), *Handbook of Environmental Psychology, Volume 1*. New York: John Wiley & Sons, 505–532.

Brown, G., Lawrence, T., and Robinson, S. (2005). "Territoriality in Organizations." *Academy of Management Review* 30(3): 577–594.

Bruner, G. (1990). "Music, Mood and Marketing." *Journal of Marketing* 54(4): 94–104.

Butler, D., and Steuerwald, B. (1991). "Effects of View and Room Size on Window Size Preference in Models." *Environment and Behavior* 23(3): 334–358.

Cameron, K., and Quinn, R. (1999). *Diagnosing and Changing Organizational Culture: Based on the Competing Values Framework*. New York: Addison-Wesley.

Case, F., and Matthews, C. (2002). "Home Design and Personality Type." Annual Meeting of the Environmental Design Research Association.

Cassidy, G., and MacDonald, R. (2007). "The Effect of Background Music and Background Noise on the Task Performance of Introverts and Extraverts." *Psychology of Music* 35(3): 517–537.

Chang, C., and Chen, P. (2005). "Human Response to Window Views and Indoor Plants in the Workplace." *HortScience* 40(5): 1354–1359.

Chaudhury, H., Mahmood, A., and Valente, M. (2005). "Advantages and Disadvantages of the Singe- Versus Multiple-Occupancy Rooms in Acute Care Environments: A Review and Analysis of the Literature." *Environment and Behavior* 37(6): 760–786.

Chebat, J., Chebat, C., and Vaillant, D. (2001). "Environmental Background Music and In-Store Selling." *Journal of Business Research* 54: 115–123.

Chebat, J., and Michon, R. (2003). "Impact of Ambient Odors on Mall Shoppers' Emotions, Cognition, and Spending." *Journal of Business Research* 56: 529–539.

Christie, D., and Glickman, C. (1980). "The Effects of Classroom Noise on Children: Evidence for Sex Differences." *Psychology in the Schools* 17: 405–408.

Cohen, S., and Trostle, S. (1990). "Young Children's Preferences for School-Related Physical-Environmental Setting Characteristics." *Environment and Behavior* 22(6): 753–766.

Collins, K., Dansereau, D., Brooks, L., and Holley, C. (1986). "Effect of Conversational Noise, Locus of Control, and Field Dependence/ Independence on the Performance of Academic Tasks." *Contemporary Educational Psychology* 11: 139–149.

Commission for Architecture and the Built Environment. (2008). "SureStart: Every Building Matters." http://www.cabe.org.uk.

Commission for Architecture and the Built Environment and the British Council for Offices. (2006). "The Impact of Office Design on Business Performance." http://www.cabe.org.uk.

Cook, N., and Hayashi, T. (2008). "The Psychoacoustics of Harmony Perception." *American Scientist* 96: 311–319.

Cote, S. (1999). "Affect and Performance in Organizational Settings." *Current Directions in Psychological Science* 8(2): 65–68.

Crader, S., and Zaichkowsky, J. (2008). "The Art of Marketing." In T. Lowrey (ed.), *Bricks and Mortar: Shopping in the 21st Century.* New York: Taylor and Francis, 87–106. (S)

Crompton, A. (2001). "The Fractal Nature of the Everyday Environment." *Environment and Planning B: Planning and Design* 28: 243–254.

Csikszentmihalyi, M. (1993). *The Evolving Self: A Psychology for the Third Millennium.* New York: HarperCollins.

Csikszentmihalyi, M., and Rochberg-Halton, E. (1981). *The Meaning of Things: Domestic Symbols and the Self.* New York: Cambridge University Press.

Cunningham, M. (1977). "Notes on the Psychological Basis of Environmental Design: The Right-Left Dimension in Apartment Floor Plans." *Environment and Behavior* 9(1): 125–136.

Cupchik, G., Ritterfeld, U., and Levin, J. (2003). "Incidental Learning of Features from Interior Living Spaces." *Journal of Environmental Psychology* 23(2): 189–197.

Dalke, H., Little, J., Niemann, E., Camgoz, N., Steadman, G., Hill, S., and Stott, L. (2006). "Colour and Lighting in Hospital Design." *Optics and Laser Technology* 38: 343–365.

Danielsson, C., and Bodin, L. (2008). "Office Type in Relation to Health, Well-Being, and Job Satisfaction Among Employees." *Environment and Behavior* 40(5): 636–668.

De Croon, E., Sluiter, J., Kuiger, P., and Frings-Dresen, M. (2005). "The Effect of Office Concepts on Worker Health and Performance: A Systematic Review of the Literature." *Ergonomics* 48: 119–134.

Denison, D., Haaland, S., and Goelzer, P. (2003). "Corporate Culture and Organizational Effectiveness: Is There a Similar Pattern Around the World?" *Advances in Global Leadership* 3: 205–227.

Despres, C. (1991). "The Meaning of Home: Literature Review and Directions for Future Research and Theoretical Development." *The Journal of Architectural and Planning Research* 8(2): 96–115.

Devereux, J. (2004). "Rhythm and Blues." *Metropolis* 23(9): 30–34.

Devlin, A., and Arneill, A. (2003). "Health Care Environments and Patient Outcomes: A Review of the Literature." *Environment and Behavior* 35(5): 665–694.

Dittmar, H. (1989). "Gender Identity-Related Meanings of Personal Possessions." *British Journal of Social Psychology* 28(6): 159–171.

Dittmar, H. (1992). *The Social Psychology of Material Possessions: To Have Is to Be*. New York: St. Martin's Press. (S)

Donovan, R., and Rossiter, J. (1982). "Store Atmosphere: An Environmental Psychology Approach." *Journal of Retailing* 58(1): 34–57.

Donovan, R., Rossiter, J., Marcoolyn, G., and Nesdale, A. (1994). "Store Atmosphere and Purchasing Behavior." *Journal of Retailing* 70(3): 283–294. (S)

Dravigne, A., Waliczek, T., Lineberger, R., and Zajícek, J. (2008). "The Effect of Live Plants and Window Views of Green Spaces on Employee Perceptions of Job Satisfaction." *HortScience* 43(1): 183–187.

Dube, L., Chebat, J., and Morin, S. (1995). "The Effects of Background Music on Consumers' Desire to Affiliate in Buyer-Seller Interactions." *Psychology and Marketing* 12: 305–319.

Dube, L., and Morin, S. (2001). "Background Music Pleasure and Store Evaluation: Intensity Effects and Psychological Mechanisms." *Journal of Business Research* 54: 107–113.

Duffy, F. (1997). *The New Offices*. London: Conran.

Durao, M. (2007). "Colour." Senses, Brain and Spaces Workshop, University of Salford.

Duvall-Early, K., and Benedict, J. (1992). "The Relationship Between Privacy and Different Components of Job Satisfaction." *Environment and Behavior* 24(5): 670–679.

Edwards, B., Bell, S., Arthur, W., and Decuir, A. (2008). "Relationships Between Facets of Job Satisfaction and Task and Contextual Performance." *Applied Psychology* 57(3): 441–465.

Eggen, B., Hollemans, G., and van de Sluis, R. (2003). "Exploring and Enhancing the Home Experience." *Cognition, Technology and Work* 5(1): 44–54. (S)

Ehrlichman, H., and Halpern, J. (1988). "Affect and Memory: Effects of Pleasant and Unpleasant Odors on Retrieval of Happy and Unhappy Memories." *Journal of Personality and Social Psychology* 55(5): 769–779.

Eich, E. (1995). "Mood as a Mediator of Place Dependent Memory." *Journal of Experimental Psychology: General* 124(3): 293–308.

Elliot, A., Maier, M., Moller, A., Friedman, R., and Meinhardt, J. (2007). "Color and Psychological Functioning: The Effect of Red on Performance Attainment." *Journal of Experimental Psychology: General* 136(1): 154–168.

Elsbach, K. (2003). "Relating Physical Environment to Self-Categorizations: Identity Threat and Affirmation in a Non-Territorial Office Space." *Administrative Science Quarterly* 48: 622–654.

Elsbach, K. (2006). *Organizational Perception Management*. Mahwah, NJ: Lawrence Earlbaum Associates. (S)

Elsbach, K., and Bechky, B. (2007). "It's More Than a Desk: Working Smarter Through Leveraged Office Design." *California Management Review* 49(2): 80–101.

Erez, M., and Earley, P. C. (1993). *Culture, Self-Identity, and Work*. New York: Oxford University Press.

Eroglu, S., and Machleit, K. (1990). "An Empirical Study of Retail Crowding." *Journal of Retailing* 66: 201–221.

Eroglu, S., and Machleit, K. (2008). "Theory in Consumer-Environment Research: Diagnosis and Prognosis." In C. Haugtvedt, P. Herr, and F. Kardes (eds.), *Handbook of Consumer Psychology*. New York: Lawrence Erlbaum Associates, 823–835.

Eroglu, S., Machleit, K., and Chebat, J. (2005). "The Interaction of Retail Density and Music Tempo: Effects on Shopper Responses." *Psychology and Marketing* 22(7): 577–589.

Evans, G. (2006). "Child Development and the Physical Environment." *Annual Review of Psychology* 57: 425–451.

Evans, G., and Cohen, S. (1987). "Environmental Stress." In D. Stokols and I. Altman (eds.), *Handbook of Environmental Psychology, Volume 1*. New York: John Wiley & Sons, 571–610.

Evans, G., and Johnson, D. (2000). "Stress and Open-Office Noise." *Journal of Applied Psychology* 85(5): 779–783.

Evans, G., Lepore, S., and Allen, K. (2000). "Cross-Cultural Differences in Tolerance for Crowding: Fact or Fiction?" *Journal of Personality and Social Psychology* 79(2): 204–210.

Evans, G., and McCoy, J. (1998). "When Buildings Don't Work: The Role of Architecture in Human Health." *Journal of Environmental Psychology* 18(1): 85–94. (S)

Fehrman, K., and Fehrman, C. (2000). *Color: The Secret Influence*. Upper Saddle River, NJ: Prentice Hall.

Feria, C., Braunstein, M., and Anderson, G. (2003). "Judging Distance Across Texture Discontinuities." *Perception* 32: 1423–1440.

Fischer, G. (1997). *Individuals and Environment*. New York: Walter de Gruyter.

Fischer, G., Tarquinio, C., and Vischer, J. (2004). "Effects of the Self-Schema on Perception of Space at Work." *Journal of Environmental Psychology* 24(2): 131–140.

Fjeld, T., Veiersted, B., Sandvik, L., Riise, G., and Levy, P. (1998). "The Effect of Indoor Foliage Plants on Health and Discomfort Symptoms Among Office Workers." *Indoor and Built Environment* 7: 204–209.

Fletcher, J. (2004). "New Floor Plans Provide Peace, Quiet, and Privacy." *Wall Street Journal* Online, April 7, http://www.wsj.com.

Fowler, F. (1995). *Improving Survey Questions.* Thousand Oaks, CA: Sage.

Francse, P. (2003). "Well Enough Alone." *American Demographics* 25(9): 32–33.

Fredrickson, B. (2001). "The Role of Positive Emotions in Positive Psychology." *American Psychologist* 56(3): 218–226.

Fredrickson, B., and Branigan, C. (2005). "Positive Emotions Broaden the Scope of Attention and Thought-Action Repertoires." *Cognition and Emotion* 19(3): 313–332.

Freedman, J. (1975). *Crowding and Behavior.* San Francisco: Freeman.

Furham, A., and Strbac, L. (2002). "Music Is as Distracting as Noise: The Differential Distraction of Background Music and Noise on the Cognitive Test Performance of Introverts and Extraverts." *Ergonomics* 45(3): 203–217.

Gable, P., and Hermon-Jones, E. (n.d.). "Approach-Motivated Positive Affect Reduces Breadth of Attention." *Psychological Science*, in press.

Gagliardi, P. (1996). "Exploring the Aesthetic Side of Organizational Life." In S. Clegg, C. Hardy, and W. Nord (eds.), *Handbook of Organization Studies.* Thousand Oaks, CA: Sage, 565–580.

Gardin, H., Kaplan, C., Firestone, I., and Cowan, G. (1973). "Proxemic Effects on Cooperation, Attitude and Approach-Avoidance in Prisoners' Dilemma Game." *Journal of Personality and Social Psychology* 34: 47–53.

Gardyn, R. (2003). "Trend Central: What's Hot in the Living Spaces of Young Adults" *American Demographics*, http://www.americandemo-graphics.com.

George, J., and Brief, A. (1992). "Feeling Good—Doing Good: A Conceptual Analysis of the Mood at Work—Organizational Spontaneity Relationship." *Psychological Bulletin* 112(2): 310–329.

George, J., and Zhou, J. (2002). "Understanding When Bad Moods Foster Creativity and Good Ones Don't." *Journal of Applied Psychology* 87: 687–697.

Gierwyn, T. (2002). "What Buildings Do." *Theory and Society* 31: 35–74. (S)

Gifford, R. (2007). *Environmental Psychology: Principles and Practice.* 4th ed. Colville, WA: Optimal Books.

Gilbert, A. (2008). *What the Nose Knows.* New York: Crown. (S)

Gilboa, S., and Rafeli, A. (2003). "Store Environment, Emotions and Approach Behavior: Applying Environmental Aesthetics to Retailing." *International Review of Retail Distribution and Consumer Research* 33(2): 195–211.

Goatman, M. (2004). "Can Personality Categorizations Inform the Design of Products and Interfaces." In D. McDonagh, P. Hekkert, J. van Erp, and D. Gyi (eds.), *Design and Emotion.* New York: Taylor and Francis, 82–86.

Goffman, E. (1959). *The Presentation of Self in Everyday Life.* Garden City, NY: Doubleday.

Goodrich, R. (1982). "Seven Office Evaluations." *Environment and Behavior* 14(3): 353–378.

Gorman, N., Lackney, J., Rollings, K., and Hwang, T. (2007). "Designer Schools: The Role of School Space and Architecture in Obesity Prevention." *Obesity* 15(11): 2521–2530.

Gosling, S., Ko, S., Mannarelli, T., and Morris, M. (2002). "A Room with a Cue: Personality Judgments Based on Offices and Bedrooms." *Journal of Personality and Social Psychology* 82(3): 379–398. (S)

Government Services Administration. (1999). *The Integrated Workplace.* Washington, DC.

Grawitch, M., Munz, D., and Kramer, T. (2003). "Effects of Member Mood States on Creative Performance in Temporary Work Groups." *Group Dynamics: Theory, Research, and Practice* 7: 41–54.

Grinfeld, M., and Grinfeld, A. (2002a). "Let the Sun Shine In." *RIBA Journal* 109(6): 90–91.

Grinfeld, M., and Grinfeld, A. (2002b). "Lighting the Way Ahead." *RIBA Journal* 109(10): 68–69.

Groat, L., and Wang, D. (2002). *Architectural Research Methods.* New York: John Wiley & Sons. (S)

Grosskopf, K. (2006). "Evaluating the Societal Response to Antiterrorism Measures." *Journal of Homeland Security and Emergency Management* 3(2): 1–9.

Gulwadi, G. (2006). "Seeking Restorative Experiences: Elementary School Teachers' Choices for Places That Enable Coping with Stress." *Environment and Behavior* 38(4): 503–520.

Gump, P. (1987). "School and Classroom Environments." In D. Stokols and I. Altman (eds.), *Handbook of Environmental Psychology, Volume 1*. New York: John Wiley & Sons, 691–732.

Hagerhall, C., Purcell, T., and Taylor, R. (2004) "Fractal Dimension of Landscape Silhouette Outlines as a Predictor of Landscape Preference." *Journal of Environmental Psychology* 24: 247–255.

Hall, E. (1982). *The Hidden Dimension*. New York: Anchor Books.

Hallowell, E. (1999). "The Human Moment at Work." *Harvard Business Review* 7: 58–66.

Han, K. (n.d.). "Influence of Limitedly Visible Leafy Indoor Plants on the Psychology, Behavior, and Health of Students at a Junior High School in Taiwan." *Environment and Behavior,* in press.

Hansen, W. B., and Altman, I. (1976). "Decorating Personal Places: A Descriptive Analysis." *Environment and Behavior* 8(4): 491–505.

Harleman, M., Werner, I., and Millger, M. (2006). "Significance of Colour on Room Character: Study on Predominantly Reddish and Greenish Colours in North-Respective South-Facing Rooms." Design and Emotion Conference.

Harrell, G., Hutt, M., and Anderson, J. (1990). "Path Analysis of Buyer Behavior Under Conditions of Crowding." *Journal of Marketing Research* 17: 45–51.

Harris, P., McBride, G., Ross, C., and Curtis, L. (2002). "A Place to Heal: Environmental Sources of Satisfaction Among Hospital Patients." *Journal of Applied Social Psychology* 32(6): 1276–1299. (S)

Hartig, T., Bringslimark, T., and Patil, G. (2008). "Restorative Environment Design: What, When, Where, and for Whom?" In S. Kellert, J. Heerwagen,and M. Mador (eds.), *Biophilic Design*. Hoboken, NJ: John Wiley & Sons, 133–151.

Hasell, M., and Peatross, F. (1990). "Exploring Connections Between Women's Changing Roles and House Forms." *Environment and Behavior* 22(1): 3–26.

Hatch, M., and Cunliffe, A. (2006). *Organizational Theory*. 2nd ed. New York: Oxford University Press.

Hathorn, K., and Nanda, U. (2008). "A Guide to Evidence-Based Art." Center for Health Design, http://www.healthdesign.org. (S)

Hedge, A. (2000). "Where Are We in Understanding the Effects of Where We Are." *Ergonomics* 43(7): 1019–1029.

Heerwagen, J., and Gregory, B. (2008). "Biophilia and Sensory Aesthetics." In S. Kellert, J. Heerwagen, and M. Mador (eds.), *Biophilic Design*. Hoboken, NJ: John Wiley & Sons, 227–241. (S)

Heerwagen, J., Kampshroer, K., Powell, K., and Loftness, V. (2004). "Collaborative Knowledge Work Environments." *Building Research and Information* 36(6): 510–528.

Heft, H., and Wohlwill, J. (1987). "Environmental Cognition in Children." In D. Stokols and I. Altman (eds.), *Handbook of Environmental Psychology, Volume 1*. New York: John Wiley & Sons, 175–204.

Herrington, J., and Capella, L. (1996). "Effects of Music in Service Environments: A Field Study." *Journal of Services Marketing* 10(2): 26–41.

Herrington, L. (1952). "Effects of Thermal Environment on Human Action." *American School and University* 24: 367–376.

Herzog, T., and Stark, J. (2004). "Typicality and Preference for Positively and Negatively Valued Environmental Settings." *Journal of Environmental Psychology* 24: 85–92.

Heschong, L. (2002). "Daylighting and Human Performance." *ASHRAE Journal* 44(6): 65–67.

Heschong, L., Wright, R., and Okuta, S. (2002a). "Daylighting Impacts on Human Performance in Schools." *Journal of the Illuminating Engineering Society* 31: 101–114.

Heschong, L., Wright, R., and Okuta, S. (2002b). "Daylighting Impacts on Retail Sales Performance." *Journal of the Illuminating Engineering Society* 31: 21–25.

Hildebrand, G. (1999). *Origins of Architectural Pleasure*. Berkeley: University of California Press. (S)

Hildebrand, G. (2008). "Biophilic Architectural Space." In S. Kellert, J. Heerwagen, and M. Mador (eds.), *Biophilic Design*. Hoboken, NJ: John Wiley & Sons, 263–275.

Hill, N., Brierley, J., and MacDougall, R. (2003). *How to Measure Customer Satisfaction*. 2nd ed. Aldershot, Hampshire, England: Gower. (S)

Hirsch, A. (1995). "Effects of Ambient Odors on Slot Machine Usage in a Las Vegas Casino." *Psychology and Marketing* 12(7): 585–594.

Hirsch, A. (2003) *Life's a Smelling Success*. New York: Authors of Unity Publishing.

Hoegg, J., and Alba, J. (2008). "A Role for Aesthetics in Consumer Psychology." In C. Haugtvedt, P. Herr, and F. Kardes (eds.), *Handbook of Consumer Psychology*. New York: Lawrence Erlbaum Associates, 733–754. (S)

Hofstede, G., and Hofstede, G. (2005). *Cultures and Organizations: Software of the Mind*. New York: McGraw-Hill. (S)

Holscher, C., Meilinger, T., Vrachiliotis, G., Brosamle, M., and Knauff, M. (2006). "Up the Down Staircase: Wayfinding Strategies in Multi-Level Buildings." *Journal of Environmental Psychology* 26(3): 284–299.

Horne, S. C. (1997). "The Classroom Environment and the Effects on the Practice of Teachers." Unpublished paper, personal communication.

"Hot Design May Burn Knowledge Sharing Effectiveness." (2008). Press Release, British Psychological Society, http://www.bps.org.uk.

Hui, M., and Bateson, J. (1991). "Perceived Control and the Effects of Crowding and Consumer Choice on the Service Experience." *Journal of Consumer Research* 18: 174–184.

Hurlbert, A., and Ling, Y. (2007). "Biological Components of Sex Differences in Color Preferences." *Current Biology* 17 (16): R623–R625.

Hygge, S., Evans, G., and Bullinger, M. (2002). "A Prospective Study of Some Effects of Aircraft Noise on Cognitive Performance in Schoolchildren." *Psychological Science* 13: 469–474.

Hygge, S., and Knez, I. (2001). "Effects of Noise, Heat and Indoor Lighting on Cognitive Performance and Self-Reported Affect." *Journal of Environmental Psychology* 21: 291–299.

IIjima, M., Arisaka, O., Minamoto, F., and Arai, Y. (2001). "Sex Differences in Children's Free Drawings." *Hormones and Behavior* 40: 99–104.

"Incense Is Psychoactive." (2008). Press Release, *The FASEB Journal*, http://www.fasebj.org.

Iqbal, S., and Horvitz, E. (2007). "Disruption and Recovery of Computing Tasks." Proceedings of CHI.

Isen, A. (2001). "An Influence of Positive Affect on Decision Making in Complex Situations: Theoretical Issues with Practical Implications." *Journal of Consumer Psychology* 11(2): 75–85. (S)

Isen, A., and Baron, R. (1991). "Positive Affect as a Factor in Organizational Behavior." In B. Staw and L. Cummings (eds.), *Research in Organizational Behavior,* Volume 13. Greenwich, CT: JAI Press, 1–53.

Isen, A., Johnson, M., Mertz, E., and Robinson, G. (1985). "The Influence of Positive Affect on the Usualness of Word Associations." *Journal of Personality and Social Psychology* 48(6): 1413–1426.

Israel, T. (2003). *Some Place Like Home.* Chichester, West Sussex, England: John Wiley & Sons.

James, K., Brodersen, M., and Eisenberg, J. (2004). "Workplace Affect and Workplace Creativity: A Review and Preliminary Model." *Human Performance* 17(2): 169–194.

Johns, G. (1996). *Organizational Behavior: Understanding and Managing Life at Work.* New York: Harper Collins.

Johns, N., and Kivela, J. (2001). "Perceptions of the First Time Restaurant Customer." *Food Service Technology* 1: 5–11.

Johnson, K. (2007). "Natural Light." Senses, Brain and Spaces Workshop, University of Salford.

Jones, M. (1996). *Studying Organizational Symbolism.* Thousand Oaks, CA: Sage.

Joseph, A., and Ulrich, R. (2007). "Sound Control for Improved Outcomes in Healthcare Settings." The Center for Health Design, http://www.healthdesign.org.

Joye, Y. (2007). "Architectural Lessons from Environmental Psychology: The Case of Biophilic Architecture." *Review of General Psychology* 11 (4): 305–328.

Juhasz, J., and Paxson, L. (1978). "Personality and Preference for Architectural Style." *Perceptual and Motor Skills* 47: 241–242.

Kaltcheva, V., and Weitz, B. (2006). "When Should a Retailer Create an Exciting Store Environment." *Journal of Marketing* 70: 107–118.

Kampschroer, K., Heerwagen, J., and Powell, K. (2007). "Creating and Testing Workplace Strategy." *California Management Review* 49(2): 119–137.

Kamptner, N. L. (1991). "Personal Possessions and Their Meanings: A Life-Span Perspective." *Journal of Social Behavior and Personality* 6(6): 209–228.

Kaplan, R. (1977). "Patterns of Environmental Preference." *Environment and Behavior* 9(2): 195–216.

Kaplan, R. (1993). "The Role of Nature in the Context of the Workplace." *Landscape and Urban Planning* 26: 193–201.

Kaplan, R. (2001). "The Nature of the View from Home." *Environment and Behavior* 33(4): 507–542.

Kaplan, S. (1983). "A Model of Person-Environment Compatibility." *Environment and Behavior* 15(3): 311–332.

Kaplan, S. (1987). "Aesthetics, Affect, and Cognition: Environmental Preference from an Evolutionary Perspective." *Environment and Behavior* 19(1): 3–32.

Kaplan, S. (1995). "The Restorative Benefits of Nature: Toward an Integrative Framework." *Journal of Environmental Psychology* 15: 169–182.

Kaplan, S. (2001). "Meditation, Restoration, and the Management of Mental Fatigue." *Environment and Behavior* 33(4): 480–506.

Kaplan, S., Bardwell, L., and Slakter, D. (1993). "The Museum as a Restorative Environment." *Environment and Behavior* 25(6): 725–742.

Katcher, A., Segal, H., and Beck, A. (1984). "Comparison of Contemplation and Hypnosis for the Reduction of Anxiety and Discomfort During Dental Surgery." *American Journal of Clinical Hypnosis* 27: 14–21.

Kats, G. (2006). *Greening America's Schools.* Retrieved from the Web site of the United States Green Building Council (12/3/08), http://www. usgbc.org.

Kay, A., Wheeler, S., Bargh, J., and Ross, L. (2004). "Material Priming: The Influence of Mundane Physical Objects on Situational Construal and Competitive Behavioral Choice." *Organizational Behavior and Human Decision Processes* 95: 83–96.

Kaya, N., and Burgess, B. (2007). "Territoriality: Seat Preferences in Different Types of Classroom Arrangements." *Environment and Behavior* 39(6): 859–876.

Keeley, R., and Edney, J. (1983). "Model Home Designs for Privacy, Security and Social Interaction." *The Journal of Social Psychology* 119: 219–228.

Kellaris, J. (2008). "Music and Consumers." In C. Haugtvedt, P. Herr, and F. Kardes (eds.), *Handbook of Consumer Psychology.* New York: Lawrence Erlbaum Associates, 837–856.

Kellert, S. (2005). *Building for Life: Designing and Understanding the Human-Nature Connection.* Washington, DC: Island Press. (S)

Kellert, S. (2008). "Dimensions, Elements, and Attributes of Biophilic Design." In S. Kellert, J. Heerwagen, and M. Mador (eds.), *Biophilic Design*. Hoboken, NJ: John Wiley & Sons, 3–19.

Kelly, J., Avaamides, M., and Loomis, J. (2007). "Sensorimotor Alignment Effects in the Learning Environment and Novel Environments." *Journal of Experimental Psychology—Learning, Memory, and Cognition* 33(6): 1092–1107.

Kennedy, J. (2006). "How the Blind Draw." Special issue, *Scientific American: Secrets of the Sense* 16(3): 44–51.

Kent, S. (1991). "Partitioning Space: Cross-Cultural Factors Influencing Domestic Spatial Segmentation." *Environment and Behavior* 23(4): 438–473.

Kingmann, A. (2007). *Brandscapes: Architecture in the Experience Economy*. Cambridge, MA: MIT Press.

Kluckhohn, F. (1953). "Dominant and Variant Value Orientations." In C. Kluckhohn, H. Murray, and D. Schneider (eds.), *Personality in Nature, Society, and Culture*. New York: Knopf, 342–357.

Knez, I. (1995). "Effects of Indoor Lighting on Mood and Cognition." *Journal of Environmental Psychology* 15(1): 39–51.

Knez, I. (2001). "Effects of Colour of Light on Nonvisual Psychological Processes." *Journal of Environmental Psychology* 21(2): 201–208.

Knez, I., and Ernmarker, I. (1998). "Effects of Office Lighting on Mood and Cognitive Performance and a Gender Effect in Work-Related Judgment." *Environment and Behavior* 30(4): 553–567.

Knez, I., and Hygge, S. (2002). "Irrelevant Speech and Indoor Lighting: Effects on Cognitive Performance and Self-Reported Affect." *Applied Cognitive Psychology* 16(6): 709–718.

Knoop, M. (2007). "Artificial Light." Sense, Brain and Spaces Workshop, University of Salford.

Koelsch, S., Kilches, S., Steinbeis, N., and Schelinski, S. (2008). "Effects of Unexpected Chores and of Performers' Expression on Brain Responses and Electrodermal Activity." *PLoS One* 3(7) http://www.plosone.org.

Korpela, K., Hartig, T., Kaiser, F., and Fuhrer, U. (2001). "Restorative Experience and Self-Regulation in Favorite Places." *Environment and Behavior* 33(4): 572–589.

Kotler, P. (1973–1974). "Atmospherics as a Marketing Tool." *Journal of Retailing* 49(4): 48–64.

Kuller, R., Ballal, S., Laike, T., Mikellides, B., and Tonell, G. (2006). "The Impact of Light and Color on Psychological Mood: A Cross-Cultural Study of Indoor Work Environments." *Ergonomics* 49(14): 1496–1507.

Kuller, R., and Lindsten, C. (1992). "Health and Behavior of Children in Classrooms with and without Windows." *Journal of Environmental Psychology* 12(4): 305–317.

Kumar, R., O'Malley, P., and Johnston, L. (2008). "Association Between Physical Environment of Secondary School and Student Problem Behavior." *Environment and Behavior* 40(4): 455–486.

Kuna, D., Ringberg, T., and Peracchio, L. (n.d.). "One Individual, Two Identities: Fame-Switching Among Biculturals." *Journal of Consumer Research,* in press.

Kupritz, V. (2003) "Accomodating Privacy to Facilitate New Ways of Working." *Journal of Architectural and Planning Research* 20(2): 122–135.

Lang, D. (1996). "Essential Criteria for an Ideal Learning Environment." http://www.newhorizons.org/strategies/learning_environments/lang.htm.

Lang, J. (1987). *Creating Architectural Theory.* New York: Van Nostrand Reinhold.

Laresn, L., Adams, J., Deal, B., Kweon, B., and Tyler, E. (1998). "Plants in the Workplace: The Effects of Plant Density on Productivity, Attitudes and Perceptions." *Environment and Behavior* 30(3): 261–281.

Larson, B. (2002). "Healing Architecture." *The Architectural Review* 210(1261): 72–75.

Larson, C., Aronoff, J., and Stearns, J. (2007). "The Shape of Threat: Simple Geometric Forms Evoke Rapid and Sustained Capture of Attention." *Emotion* 7(3): 526–534.

Larson, J., Bradlow, E., and Fader, P. (2005). "An Exploratory Look at Supermarket Shopping Paths." *International Journal of Research in Marketing,* 22(4): 395–414.

Lawrence, D., and Low, S. (1990). "The Built Environment and Spatial Form." *Annual Review of Anthropology* 19: 453–505.

Lawrence, P., and Nohria, N. (2002). *Driven.* San Francisco: Jossey-Bass.

Lawrence, R. (1987). "What Makes a House a Home?" *Environment and Behavior* 19(2): 154–179.

Leaman, A., and Bordass, B. (2007). "Are Users More Tolerant of 'Green' Buildings." *Building Research and Information* 35(6): 662–673.

Leather, P., Beale, D., Santos, A., Watts, J., and Lee, L. (2003). "Outcomes of Environmental Appraisal of Different Hospital Waiting Areas." *Environment and Behavior* 35(6): 842–869.

Leather, P., Pyrgas, M., Beale, D., and Lawrence, C. (1998). "Windows in the Workplace." *Environment and Behavior* 30(6): 739–762.

Lee, S., and Brand, J. (2005). "Effects of Control Over Office Workspace on Perceptions of the Work Environment and Work Outcomes." *Journal of Environmental Psychology* 25: 323–333.

Leeds, J. (2001) *The Power of Sound.* Rochester, VT: Healing Arts Press.

Legendre, A. (2003). "Environmental Features Influencing Toddlers' Bioemotional Reactions in Day Care Centers." *Environment and Behavior* 35(4): 523–549.

Legendre, A., and Fontaine, A. (1991). "The Effects of Visual Boundaries in Two-Year-Olds' Playrooms." *Children's Environments Quarterly* 8: 2–16.

Leslie, R. (2003). "Capturing the Daylight Dividend in Buildings." *Buildings and Environment* 38 (2): 381–385.

Li, W., Howard, J., Parrish, T., and Gottfried, J. (2008). "Aversive Learning Enhances Perceptual and Cortical Discrimination of Indiscriminable Odor Cues." *Science* 319 (5871): 1842–1845.

Li, W., Moallem, I., Paller, K., and Gottfried, J. (2007). "Subliminal Smells Can Guide Social Preference." 18(12): 1043–1047.

Li, X. (2008). "The Effects of Appetite Stimuli on Out-of-Domain Consumption Impatience." *Journal of Consumer Research* 34(5): 649–656.

Little, B. (1987). "Personality and the Environment." In D. Stokols and I. Altman (eds.), *Handbook of Environmental Psychology, Volume 1.* New York: John Wiley & Sons, 205–244.

Locher, P., Frens, J., and Overbeeke, K. (2008). "The Influence of Induced Positive Affect and Design Experience on Aesthetic Responses to New Product Designs." *Psychology of Aesthetics, Creativity, and the Arts* 2(1): 1–7.

Loewen, L., and Suedfeld, P. (1992). "Cognitive and Arousal Effects of Masking Office Noise." *Environment and Behavior* 24(3): 381–395.

Loftness, V., and Snyder, M. (2008). "Where Windows Become Doors." In S. Kellert, J. Heerwagen, and M. Mador (eds.), *Biophilic Design*. Hoboken, NJ: John Wiley & Sons, 119–131.

Lohr, V., Pearson-Mims, C., and Goodwin, G. (1996). "Interior Plants May Improve Worker Productivity and Reduce Stress in a Windowless Room." *Journal of Environmental Horticulture* 14(2): 97–100.

Loken, B. (2006). "Consumer Psychology: Categorization, Inferences, Affect, and Persuasion." In S. Fiske, D. Schacter, and C. Zahn-Waxler (eds.), *Annual Review of Psychology, Volume 57*. Palo Alto, CA: Annual Reviews, 453–485.

Machleit, K., Eroglu, S., and Mantel, S. (2000). "Retail Crowding and Shopping Satisfaction." *Journal of Consumer Psychology* 9: 29–42.

Maher, A., and von Hippel, C. (2005). "Individual Differences in Employee Reactions to Open-Plan Offices." *Journal of Environmental Psychology* 25: 219–229. (S)

Mahnke, F. (1996). *Color, Environment and Human Response*. New York: Van Nostrand Reinhold.

Malnar, J., and Vodvarka, F. (2004). *Sensory Design*. Minneapolis, MN: University of Minnesota Press.

Manav, B. (2007). "An Experimental Study on the Appraisal of the Visual Environment at Offices in Relation to Color Temperature and Illuminance." *Building and Environment* 42: 979–983.

Marcus, C. C. (1995). *House as a Mirror of Self: Exploring the Deeper Meaning of Home*. Berkeley, CA: Conari.

Mark, G., Gonzalez, V., and Harris, J. (2005). "No Task Left Behind? Examining the Nature of Fragmented Work." *Proceedings of the Conference on Human Factors in Computer Systems*, 321–330.

Martin, G., and Cooper, J. (2007). "Adding Zest to Difficult Journeys: Odour Effects on Simulated Driving Performance." Proceedings of the 2007 Annual Conference of the British Psychological Society, http://www.bps.org.uk/publications/proceedings.

Martindale, C., and Moore, K. (1988). "Priming, Prototypicality, and Preference." *Journal of Experimental Psychology: Human Perception and Performance* 14: 661–670.

Matsumoto, D., and LeRoux, J. (1994). "Perception." In M. Matsumoto (ed.), *Psychology from a Cultural Perspective*. Pacific Grove, CA: Brooks/Cole, 39–50.

Mattila, A., and Wirtz, J. (2001). "Congruency of Scent and Music as a Driver of In-Store Evaluations and Behavior." *Journal of Retailing* 77: 273–289.

Maxwell, L. (2007). "Competency in Child Care Settings: The Role of the Physical Environment." *Environment and Behavior* 20(2): 229–245.

Maxwell, L., and Chmielewski, E. (2008). "Environmental Personalization and Elementary School Children's Self-Esteem." *Journal of Environmental Psychology* 28: 143–253.

McCarthy, E. D. (1984). "Toward a Sociology of the Physical World: George Herbert Mead on Physical Objects." In N. Denzin (ed.), *Studies in Symbolic Interaction, Volume 5.* Greenwich, CT: JAI Press, 105–121.

McColl, S., and Veitch, J. (2001). "Full Spectrum Fluorescent Lighting." *Psychological Medicine* 31(6): 949–964.

McCoy, J. (2002). "Work Environments." In B. Bechtel and A. Churchman (eds.), *Handbook of Environmental Psychology.* New York: John Wiley & Sons, 443–460.

McCoy, J. (2005). "Linking the Physical Work Environment to Creative Context." *Journal of Creative Behavior* 39(3): 169–191.

McCoy, J., and Evans, G. (2002). "The Potential Role of the Physical Environment in Fostering Creativity." *Creativity Research Journal* 14(3–4): 409–426.

McCoy, J., and Evans, G. (2005). "Physical Work Environment." In J. Barling, K. Kelloway, and M. Frone (eds.), *Handbook of Work and Stress.* Thousand Oaks, CA: Sage, 219–246.

McElry, J., Morrow, P., and Ackerman, R. (1983). "Personality and Interior Office Design: Exploring the Accuracy of Visitor Attributions." *Journal of Applied Psychology* 68(3): 541–544.

McKechnie, G. (1974). *ERI Manual.* Berkeley, CA: Consulting Psychologists Press.

McManus, C., Jones, A., and Cottrell, J. (1981). "The Aesthetics of Colour." *Perception* 10: 651–666.

Mednick, S., Nakayama, K., Cantero, J., Tienza, M., Levin, A., Pathaik, N., and Strickgad, R. (2002). "The Restorative Effect of Naps on Perceptual Deterioration." *Nature Neuroscience* 5, http://www.nature-neuroscience.com.

Mehrabian, A. (1977). "Individual Differences in Stimulus Screening and Arousability." *Journal of Personality* 45(2): 237–250.

Mehrabian, A., and Diamond, S. (1971). "Effects of Furniture Arrangement, Props, and Personality on Social Interaction." *Journal of Personality and Social Psychology* 20(1): 18–30.

Mehrabian, A., and Russell, J. (1974). *An Approach to Environmental Psychology.* Cambridge, MA: MIT Press.

Meiselman, H., Johnson, J., and Reeve, W. (2000). "Demonstrations of the Influence of the Eating Environment on Food Acceptance." *Appetite* 35(3): 231–237.

Melcher, A. (1976). *Structure and Process of Organizations.* Englewood Cliffs, NJ: Prentice Hall.

Metzger, R., Boschee, P., Haugen, T., and Schnobrich, B. (1979). "The Classroom as Learning Context." *Journal of Educational Psychology* 71(4): 440–442.

Meyers-Levy, J., and Zhu, R. (2007). "The Influence of Ceiling Height: The Effect of Priming on the Type of Processing That People Use." *Journal of Consumer Research* 34(2): 174–186.

Michon, R., Chebat, J., and Turley, L. (2005). "Mall Atmospherics: The Interaction Effects of the Mall Environment on Shopping Behavior." *Journal of Business Research* 58: 576–583.

Miller, A., and Maxwell, L. (2003). "Exploring the Role of Home Design in Fostering Family Interaction: The Use of Programming Methods in Research." *Journal of Interior Design* 29(1–2): 50–65.

Milliman, R. (1982). "Using Background Music to Affect the Behavior of Supermarket Shoppers." *Journal of Marketing* 46: 86–91.

Milliman, R. (1986). "The Influence of Background Music on the Behavior of Restaurant Patrons." *Journal of Consumer Research* 13: 286–289.

Mittleman, D., Wener, R., Zamani, P., and Zimring, C. (2003). "The Smart Classroom: Investigation in Aligning Pedagogy, Technology, and the Built Environment to Enhance Learning." Environmental Design Research Association Annual Meeting.

Miwa, Y., and Hanyu, K. (2006). "The Effects of Interior Design on Communication and Impressions of a Counselor in a Counseling Room." *Environment and Behavior* 38(4): 484–502.

Miyake, S. (2001). "Foliage Plants at the Workplace." *Proceedings of the Human Factors and Ergonomics Society, 45th Annual Meeting,* 813–817.

Miyamoto, Y., Nisbett, R., and Masuda, T. (2006). "Culture and the Physical Environment: Holistic Versus Analytic Perceptual Affordances." *Psychological Science* 17(2): 113–119.

Morrin, M., and Chebat, J. (2005). "Person-Place Congruency: The Interactive Effects of Shopper Style and Atmospherics on Consumer Expenditures." *Journal of Service Research,* 8(2): 181–191.

Morrin, M., and Ratneshwar, S. (2000). "The Impact of Ambient Scent on Evaluation, Attention, and Memory for Familiar and Unfamiliar Brands." *Journal of Business Research* 9: 157–165.

Moss, M. (2002). "Smell of Rosemary Improves Memory, Lavender Is Calming." British Psychological Society Conference.

Moss, M., Hewitt, S., Moss, L., and Wesnes, K. (2008). "Modulation of Cognitive Performance and Mood by Aromas of Peppermint and Ylang-Ylang." *International Journal of Neuroscience* 118(1): 59–77.

Mostafa, M. (2007). "An Architecture for Autism: Concepts of Design Intervention for the Autistic User." *International Journal of Architectural Research* 2(1): 189–211.

Myers, D. (1996). *Social Psychology.* 5th ed. New York: McGraw-Hill.

Myers, I., McCaulley, M., Quenk, N., and Hammer, A. (2003). *MBTI Manual.* Mountain View, CA: CPP.

Nanda, U., Eisen, S., and Baladandayuthapani, V. (2008). "Undertaking an Art Survey to Compare Patient Versus Student Art Preferences." *Environment and Behavior* 40(2): 269–301.

Nasar, J. (1994). "Urban Design Aesthetics." *Environment and Behavior* 26(3):377–401.

Nasar, J. (2000). "The Evaluative Image of Places." In W. Walsh, K. Craik, and R. Price (eds.), *Person-Environment Psychology: New Directions and Perspectives.* 2nd ed. Mahwah, NJ: Lawrence Erlbaum Associates, 117–168. (S)

Nasar, J. (2008). *Visual Quality by Design.* Holland, MI: Haworth.

National Research Council of Canada. (2004). "Workstation Design for Organizational Productivity." http://irc.nrc-cnrc.gc.ca/ie/cope/index.html.

Nelson, P., and Soli, S. (2000). "Acoustical Barriers to Learning." *Language, Speech and Hearing Services in Schools* 31: 356–361.

Newsham, G., and Brand, J. (2007). "Linking the Physical Environment and Organizational Productivity in Offices." NeoCon Chicago (June 13).

Ng, C. (2003). "Satisfying Shoppers' Psychological Needs: From Public Market to Cyber-Mall." *Journal of Environmental Psychology* 23(4): 439–455.

Nippert-Eng, C. (1996). *Home and Work*. Chicago: University of Chicago Press.

Nippert-Eng, C. (2007). "Privacy in the United States: Some Implications for Design." *International Journal of Design* 1(3): 1–10.

Nisbett, R. (2003). *The Geography of Thought*. New York: Free Press.

Norman, D. (2004). *Emotional Design*. New York: Basic Books.

North, A., and Hargreaves, D. (1999). "Can Music Move People? The Effects of Musical Complexity and Silence on Waiting Time." *Environment and Behavior* 31(1): 136–149.

North, A., Hargreaves, D., and McKendrick, J. (1999). "The Influence of In-Store Music on Wine Selections." *Journal of Applied Psychology* 84(2): 271–276.

North, A., Shilcock, A., Hargreaves, D. (2003). "The Effect of Musical Style on Restaurant Customers' Spending." *Environment and Behavior* 35(5): 712–718.

North, A., Tarrant, M., Hargreaves, D. (2004). "The Effects of Music on Helping Behavior: A Field Study." *Environment and Behavior* 36(2): 266–275.

Oakes, S. (2003). "Musical Tempo and Waiting Perceptions." *Psychology and Marketing* 20: 685–705.

Ogle, J., Hyllegard, K., and Dunbar, B. (2004). "Predicting Patronage Behaviors in a Sustainable Retail Environment." *Environment and Behavior* 36(5): 717–741.

Ornstein, R., and Sobel, D. (1989). "Coming to Our Senses." *Advances* 6 (3):49–56.

Ornstein, S. (1986). "Organizational Symbols: A Study of Their Meanings and Influence on Perceived Psychological Climate." *Organizational Behavior and Human Decision Processes* 38: 207–229.

Ornstein, S. (1992). "First Impressions of the Symbolic Meanings Connoted by Reception Area Design." *Environment and Behavior* 24: 85–110.

Osborn, D. (1988). "Personality Traits Expressed: Interior Design as Behavior-Setting Plan." *Personality and Social Psychology Bulletin* 14(2): 368–373.

Ou, L., and Luo, M. (2004). "Colour Preference and Colour Emotion." In D. McDonagh, P. Hekkert, J. van Erp, and D. Gyi (eds.), *Design and Emotion*. New York: Taylor and Francis, 185–189.

Park, Y., and Guerin, D. (2002). "Meaning and Preference of Interior Color Palettes Among Four Cultures." *Journal of Interior Design* 38(1): 27–39.

Paul, P. (2002). "Color by Numbers." *American Demographics* XX: 30–35.

Peck, J., and Childers, T. (2005). "Individual Differences in Haptic Information Processing: The Need for Touch Scale." *Journal of Consumer Research* 30: 430–442.

Peck, J., and Childers, T. (2008). "Effects of Sensory Factors on Consumer Behavior." In C. Haugtvedt, P. Herr, and F. Kardes (eds.), *Handbook of Consumer Psychology*. New York: Lawrence Erlbaum Associates, 193–219.

Penn, M. (2007). *Micro Trends: The Small Forces Behind Tomorrow's Big Changes*. New York: Twelve Press.

Peponis, J., Bafna, S., Bajaj, R., Bromberg, J., Congdon, C., Rashid, M., Warmels, S., Zhang, Y., and Zimring, C. (2007). "Designing Spaces to Support Knowledge Work." *Environment and Behavior* 39(6): 815–840. (S)

Perunovic, W., Heller, D., and Rafaeli, E. (2007). "Within-Person Changes in the Structure of Emotion." *Psychological Science* 18(7): 607–613.

Platten, J., Evans, G., and Danko, S. (2003). "The Role of Permanent Student Artwork in Students' Sense of Ownership in an Elementary School." *Environment and Behavior* 35(2): 250–263.

Posavac, S., Brakus, J., Jain, S., and Cronley, M. (2007). "Selective Assessment and Positivity Bias in Environmental Valuation." *Journal of Experimental Psychology: Applied* 12(1): 43–49.

"Pumas, Planets, and Pens: How Cues in the Environment Influence Consumer Choice." (2008). Knowledge @ Wharton, http://knowledge.wharton.upenn.edu.

Rafaeli, A. and Pratt, M. (Eds.) (2006) *Artifacts and Orgnizations: Beyond Mere Symbolism*. Mahwah, NJ: Lawrence Earlbarm Associates, Publishers.

Raffaello, M., and Maass, A. (2002). "Chronic Exposure to Noise in Industry: The Effects on Satisfaction, Stress Symptoms, and Company Attachment." *Environment and Behavior* 34(5): 651–671.

Rapoport, A. (2005). *Culture, Architecture, and Design*. Chicago, IL: Locke Science Publishing.

Rapoport, A. (2007). "Some Further Thoughts on Culture and Environment." *Archnet-IJAR* 2(1): 16–39.

Rashid, M., Kampschroer, K., Wineman, J., and Zimring, C. "Face-to-Face Interaction in Office Settings: What You Know About It May Not Always Be True." http://www.arch.gatech.edu.

Rashid, M., and Zimring, C. (2008). "A Review of the Empirical Literature on the Relationship Between Indoor Environment and Stress in Health Care and Office Settings: Problems and Prospects of Sharing Evidence." *Environment and Behavior* 40(2): 151–190. (S)

Read, M., Sugawara, A., and Brandt, J. (1999). "Impact of Space and Color in the Physical Environment on Preschool Children's Cooperative Behavior." *Environment and Behavior* 31(3): 413–428.

Reiss, S. (2004). "Multifaceted Nature of Intrinsic Motivation: The Theory of 16 Basic Drives." *Review of General Psychology* 8(3): 179–193.

Richardson, J., and Zucco, G. (1989). "Cognition and Olfaction." *Psychological Bulletin* 105(3): 352–360.

Richins, M. L. (1994). "Valuing Things: The Public and Private Meanings of Possessions." *Journal of Consumer Research* 21(3): 504–521.

Robson, S. (1999). "The Psychology of Design for High-Volume Restaurants." *Cornell Hotel and Restaurant Administration Quarterly* 40(3): 56–63.

Rodemann, P. (1999). *Patterns in Interior Environments*. New York: John Wiley & Sons.

Rosenbaum, M. (2008). "Restorative Servicescapes: Restoring Directed Attention in Third Places." American Psychological Association Annual Meeting.

Rosenberg, M. (1986). *Conceiving the Self*. Malabar, FL: Krieger

Rubenstein, J., Meyer, D., and Evans, J. (2001). "Executive Control of Cognitive Processes in Task Switching." *Journal of Experimental Psychology: Human Perception and Performance* 27(4): 763–797.

Russell, J., and Mehrabian, A. (1978). "Approach-Avoidance and Affiliation as Functions of the Emotion-Eliciting Quality of an Environment." *Environment and Behavior* 10(3): 355–387.

Russell, J., and Snodgrass, J. (1987). "Emotion and the Environment." In D. Stokols, and I. Altman (eds.), *Handbook of Environmental Psychology, Volume 1*. New York: John Wiley & Sons, 245–281.

Russell, J., Ward, L., and Pratt, G. (1981). "Affective Quality Attributed to Environments: A Factor Analytic Study." *Environment and Behavior* 13(3): 259–288.

Russell, P. (2003). "Efforts After Meaning and the Hedonistic Value of Paintings." *British Journal of Psychology* 94(1): 99–110.

Sadalla, E., and Oxley, D. (1984). "The Perception of Room Size." *Environment and Behavior* 16(3): 394–405.

Sadalla, E., and Sheets, V. (1993). "Symbolism in Building Materials." *Environment and Behavior* 25(2): 155–180.

Samuelson, D., and Lindauer, M. (1976). "Perception, Evaluation, and Performance in a Neat and Messy Room by High and Low Sensation Seekers." *Environment and Behavior* 8(2): 291–306.

Saucier, R. (2001). *Influencing Sales Through Store Design.* Lewiston, NY: Mellon Press.

Sax, L. (2005). *Why Gender Matters.* New York: Broadway Books.

Schab, F. (1990). "Odor and the Remembrance of Things Past." *Journal of Experimental Psychology* 16(4): 648–655.

Scharine, A., and McBeath, M. (2002). "Right-Handers and Americans Favor Turning to the Right." *Human Factors* 44(1): 248–256.

Scheiberg, S. L. (1990). "Emotions on Display: The Personal Decoration of Work Spaces." *American Behavioral Scientist* 33(3): 330–338.

Schein, E. (1992). *Organizational Culture and Leadership.* San Francisco: Jossey-Bass. (S)

Schifferstein, H., and Spence, C. (2008). "Multi-Sensory Product Experience." In H. Schifferstein and P. Hekkert (eds.), *Product Experience.* New York: Elsevier, 133–161.

Schimmel, K., and Forster, J. (2008). "How Temporal Distance Changes Novices' Attitudes Towards Unconventional Arts." *Psychology of Aesthetics, Creativity, and the Arts* 2(1): 53–60.

Schneider, M. (2002). "Do School Facilities Affect Academic Outcomes." National Clearinghouse for Educational Facilities, http://www.edfacilities.org.

Schubert, T. (2005). "Your Highness: Vertical Positions as Perceptual Symbols of Power." *Journal of Personality and Social Psychology* 89(1): 1–21.

Schwartz, B. (2004). *The Paradox of Choice: Why More is Less.* New York: HarperCollins.

Schweitzer, M., Gilpin, L., and Frampton, S. (2004). "Healing Spaces: Elements of Environmental Design That Make an Impact on Health." *The Journal of Alternative and Complementary Medicine* 10: a71–a83.

Seo, H., Hirano, M., Shibato, J., Rakwal, R., Hwang, I., and Masuo, T. (2008). "Effects of Coffee Bean Aroma on the Rat Brain Stressed by Sleep Deprivation." *Journal of Agricultural and Food Chemistry* 56(12): 4665–4673.

Sharma, A., and Stafford, T. (2000). "The Effect of Retail Atmospherics on Customers' Perceptions of Salespeople and Customer Persuasion." *Journal of Business Research* 49(2): 183–191.

Sherman, E., Mathur, A., and Smith, R. (1997). "Store Environment and Consumer Purchase Behavior: Mediating Role of Consumer Emotions." *Psychology and Marketing* 14(4): 361–378.

Shibata, S., and Suzuki, N. (2002). "Effects of the Foliage Plant on Task Performance and Mood." *Journal of Environmental Psychology* 22(3): 265–272.

Shim, J., Maxwell, L. L., and Eshelman, P. (2004). "Hospital Birthing Room Design: A Study of Mother's Perception of Hominess." *Journal of Interior Design* 30(2): 23–36.

Shiraev, E., and Levy, D. (2007). *Cross-Cultural Psychology*. 3rd ed. New York: Pearson.

Shizura, L., and Marsella, A. (1981). "The Sensory Processes of Japanese-American and Caucasian-American Students." *The Journal of Social Psychology* 114: 147–158.

Sikstron, S. and Soderlund, G. (2007). "Stimulus Dependent Dopamine Release in Attention-Deficit/Hyperactivity Disorder." *Psychology Review* 114(4): 1047–1075.

Smail, D. (2008). *On Deep History and the Brain*. Berkeley: University of California Press.

Smith, K. (2008). "Perception Colored by Language." Nature News, http://www.nature.com/news/2008/080303/full/news.2008.638.html.

Smith, P., and Curnow, R. (1966). "Arousal Hypothesis and the Effects of Music on Purchasing Behavior." *Journal of Applied Psychology* 50: 255–256.

Smith, S. (1994). "The Essential Qualities of a Home." *Journal of Environmental Psychology* 14: 31–46.

Sommer, R. (1959). "Studies in Personal Space." *Sociometry* 22: 247–260.

Sommer, R. (1967). "Small Group Ecology." *Psychological Bulletin* 67: 145–152.

Sommer, R. (1969). *Personal Space: The Behavioral Basis of Design*. Englewood Cliffs, NJ: Prentice Hall.

Sommer, R. (1974). *Tight Spaces: Hard Architecture and How to Humanize It*. Englewood Cliffs, NJ: Prentice Hall.

Sommer, R. (1983). *Social Design: Creating Buildings with People in Mind*. New York: Prentice-Hall.

Sommer, R., Wynes, M., and Brinkley, G. (1992). "Social Facilitation Effects in Shopping Behavior." *Environment and Behavior* 24(3): 285–297.

Spangenberg, E. (2006). "Gender-Congruent Ambient Scent Influences on Approach and Avoidance Behaviors in a Retail Store." *Journal of Business Research* 59: 1281–1287.

Spangenberg, E., Crowley, A., and Henderson, P. (1996). "Improving the Store Environment: Do Olfactory Cues Affect Evaluations and Behaviors?" *Journal of Marketing* 60: 67–80.

Spangenberg, E., Grohmann, B., and Sprott, D. (2005). "It's Beginning to Smell (and Sound) a Lot Like Christmas: The Interactive Effects of Ambient Scent and Music in a Retail Setting." *Journal of Business Research* 58(11): 2583–1589.

Spaulding, W. (1978). "Underdiscovered Values in Meetings." *Journal of Systems Management* 29: 24–27.

Spreckelmeyer, K. (1993). "Office Relocation and Change." *Environment and Behavior* 25(2): 181–204.

Stamps, A., and Krishnan, V. (2006). "Spaciousness and Boundary Roughness." *Environment and Behavior* 38(6): 841–872.

Steele, F. (1973). *Physical Settings and Organizational Development*. Reading, MA: Addison-Wesley.

Stone, N. (2001). "Designing Effective Study Environments." *Journal of Environmental Psychology* 21(2): 179–190.

Stone, N. (2003). "Environmental View and Color for a Simulated Telemarketing Task." *Journal of Environmental Psychology* 23(1): 63–78.

Stone, N., and English, A. (1998). "Task Type, Posters, and Workspace Color on Mood, Satisfaction, and Performance." *Journal of Environmental Psychology* 18(2): 174–185.

Strodtbeck, F., and Hook, H. (1961). "The Social Dimensions of a 12-Man Jury Table." *Sociometry* 24: 397–415.

Sundstrom, E. (1986). *Work Places: The Psychology of the Physical Environment in Offices and Factories.* New York: Cambridge University Press.

Sundstrom, E. (1987). "Work Environments: Offices and Factories." In D. Stokols and I. Altman (eds.), *Handbook of Environmental Psychology, Volume 1.* New York: John Wiley & Sons, 733–782.

Sundstrom, E., and Altman, I. (1989). "Physical Environments and Work-Group Effectiveness. In L. Cummings and B. Staw (eds.), *Research in Organizational Behavior, Volume 11.* Greenwich, CT: JAI Press.

Sundstrom, E. and Associates (1999) *Supporting Work Team Effectiveness.* San Francisco, CA: Jossey-Bass Inc., Publishers.

Sundstrom, E., Demuse, K., and Futrell, D. (1990). "Work Teams." *American Psychologist* 45: 120–133.

Sundstrom, E., Town, J., Rice, R., Osborn, D., and Brill, M. (1994). "Office Noise, Satisfaction and Performance." *Environment and Behavior* 26(2): 195–222.

Susanka, S. (1998). *The Not So Big House.* Newtown, CT: Taunton Press.

Sussman, N., and Rosenfeld, H. (1982). "Influence of Culture, Language, and Sex on Conversation Distance." *Journal of Personality and Social Psychology* 42(1): 66–74.

Tan, L., Chan, A., Kay, P., Khong, P., Yip, L., and Luke, K. (2008). "Language Affects Patterns of Brain Activation Associated with Perceptual Decision." Proceedings of the National Academy of Sciences of the United States of America 105(10), http://www.pnas.org.

Tanner, C., and Lackney, J. (2006). *Educational Facilities Planning.* New York: Allyn and Bacon.

Taylor, R., and Lanni, J. (1981). "Territorial People's Dominance." *Journal of Personality and Social Psychology* 41: 909–915.

Tenner, E. (2003). *Our Own Devices: How Technology Remakes Humanity.* New York: Vintage Books.

Tennessen, C., and Cimprich, B. (1995). "Views to Nature: Effects on Attention." *Journal of Environmental Psychology* 15(1): 77–85.

Thoresen, C., Kaplan, S., Barsky, A., Waren, C., and Chemont, K. (2003). "The Affective Underpinnings of Job Perceptions and Attitudes: A Meta-Analytic Review and Integration." *Psychological Bulletin* 129(6): 914–945.

Tieger, P., and Barron, B. (2007). *Do What You Are*. 4th ed. New York: Little, Brown and Company.

Tognoli, J. (1987). "Residential Environments." In D. Stokols and I. Altman (eds.), *Handbook of Environmental Psychology, Volume 1*. New York: John Wiley & Sons, 2655–2690.

Toner, R. (2008). "Attentional Bias as Trait: Correlations with Novelty Seeking." *Neuropsychologia* 46(7): 2064–2070.

"Too Many Office Trinkets? Professional Image May Suffer." 2007. University of Michigan News Service.

Tovorsak, T., Britto, M., Klostermann, B., Nebrig, D., and Slap, G. (2004). "Are Pediatric Practice Settings Adolescent Friendly? An Exploration of Attitudes and Preferences." *Clinical Pediatrics* 43(1): 55–62.

Trice, H., and Beyer, J. (1983). *The Cultures of Work Organizations*. Englewood Cliffs, NJ: Prentice Hall.

Tsai, J. (2007). "Ideal Affect: Cultural Causes and Behavioral Consequences." *Perspectives on Psychological Science* 2(3): 242–259.

Tsunetsuga, Y., Miyazaki, Y., and Sato, H. (2003). "Visual Effects of Interior Design in Actual-Size Living Rooms on Physiological Responses." *Building and Environment* 40(10): 1341–1346.

Tucci, L., and Talaga, J. (2000). "Determinants of Consumer Perceptions of Service Utility in Restaurants." *Journal of Food Products Marketing* 6(2): 3–13.

Turley, L., and Milliman, R. (2000). "Atmospheric Effects on Shopping Behavior: A Review of the Experimental Evidence." *Journal of Business Research* 49: 193–211.

Twenge, J., Konrath, S., Foster, J., Campbell, W., and Bushman, B. (2008). "Egos Inflating Over Time: A Cross-Temporal Meta-Analysis of the Narcissistic Personality Inventory." *Journal of Personality* 76(4): 875–902.

Ulrich, R. (1984). "View Through a Window May Influence Recovery from Surgery." *Science* 224: 420–421.

Ulrich, R. (2008). "Biophilic Theory and Research for Healthcare Design." In S. Kellert, J. Heerwagen, and M. Mador (eds.), *Biophilic Design*. Hoboken, NJ: John Wiley & Sons, 87–106. (S)

Ulrich, R., and Gilpin, L. (2003). "Healing Arts." In S. Frampton, L. Gilpin, and P. Charmel (eds.), *Putting Patients First*. San Francisco: Jossey-Bass, 117–146.

Ulrich, R., Simons, R., Lusito, B., Fiorito, E., Miles, M., and Zelson, M. (1991). "Stress Recovery During Exposure to Natural and Urban Environments." *Journal of Environmental Psychology* 11: 201–230.

Ulrich, R., Simons, R., and Mills, M. (2003). "Effects of Environmental Simulations and Television on Blood Donor Stress." *Journal of Architectural and Planning Research* 20(1): 38–47.

Ulrich, R., and Zimring, C. (2004). "The Role of the Physical Environment in the Hospital of the 21st Century: A Once-in-a-Lifetime Opportunity." Center for Health Design.

Ulrich, R., Zimring, C., Zhu, X., DuBose, J., Seo, H., Choi, Y., Quan, X., and Joseph, A. (2008). "A Review of the Research Literature on Evidence-Based Healthcare Design." *Health Environments Research and Design Journal* 1(3): 61–125.

Underhill, P. (1999). *Why We Buy: The Science of Shopping.* New York: Simon and Schuster.

Valdez, P., and Mehrabian, A. (1994). "Effects of Color on Emotions." *Journal of Experimental Psychology: General* 123(4): 394–409.

Vallance, B., Heffernan, T., and Moss, M. (2007). "The Enhancement of Everyday Prospective Memory by Rosemary Essential Oils." Proceedings of the Annual Conference of the British Psychological Society, http://www.bps.org.uk/publications/proceedings.

Vanderak, S., and Ely, D. (1993). "Cortisol, Biochemical and Galvanic Skin Responses to Musical Stimuli of Different Preference Value by College Students in Biology and Music." *Perceptual Motor Skills* 77: 227–234.

Van Meel, J. (2000). *The European Office: Office Design and National Context.* Rotterdam, The Netherlands: 010 Publishers. (S)

Van Meel, J., De Jonge, H., and Dewulf, G. (1997). "Workplace Design: Global or Tribal?" In J. Worthington (ed.), *Reinventing the Workplace.* York, England: Architectural Press, 50–63.

Veitch, J., Charles, K., Farley, K., and Newsham, G. (2007). "A Model of Satisfaction with Open Plan Office Conditions: COPE Field Findings." *Journal of Environmental Psychology* 27(3): 177–189.

Veitch, J., and Gifford, R. (1996). "Choice, Perceived Control and Performance." *Journal of Environmental Psychology* 16: 269–276.

Vinsel, A., Brown, B., Altman, I., and Foss, C. (1980). "Privacy Regulation, Territorial Displays, and Effectiveness of Individual Functioning." *Journal of Personality and Social Psychology* 39(7): 1104–1115.

Vischer, J. (1996). *Workspace Strategies: Environment as a Tool for Work.* New York: Chapman and Hall.

Vischer, J. (2005). *Space Meets Status: Designing Workplace Performance.* New York: Routledge. (S)

Vischer, J. (2007a). "The Effects of the Physical Environment on Job Performance: Towards a Theoretical Model of Workplace Stress." *Stress and Health* 23(3): 175–184.

Vischer, J. (2007b). "Workplace Performance and Its Value to Managers." *California Management Review* 49(2): 62–79.

Vithayathawornwong, S., Danko, S., and Tolbert, P. (2003). "The Role of the Physical Environment in Supporting Organizational Creativity." *Journal of Interior Design* 29(1–2): 1–16.

Von Bergen, J. (2006). "Mastering ADHD on the Job." *Philadelphia Inquirer* (November 12), http:www.go.philly.com/adhd.

Vroon, P. (1997). *Smell.* New York: Farrar, Straus and Giroux.

Wachs, T. (1978). "The Relationship of Infants' Physical Environment to Their Binet Performance at 2½ Years." *International Journal of Behavioral Development* 1: 51–65.

Wachs, T. (1979). "Proximal Experience and Early Cognitive-Intellectual Development: The Physical Environment." *Merrill-Palmer Quarterly* 25: 3–41.

Wachs, T., and Gruen, G. (1982). *Early Experience and Human Development.* New York: Plenum.

Wachs, T., Uzigiris, I., and Hunt, J. (1971). "Cognitive Development in Infants of Different Age Levels and from Different Environmental Backgrounds: An Exploratory Investigation." *Merrill-Palmer Quarterly* 17: 283–317.

Wall, E., and Berry, L. (2007). "The Combined Effects of the Physical Environment and Employee Behavior on Customer Perception of Restaurant Service Quality." *Cornell Hotel and Restaurant Administration Quarterly* 48(1): 59–69.

Ward, J., and Barnes, J. (2001). "Control and Affect: The Influence of Feeling in Control of the Retail Environment on Affect, Involvement, Attitude, and Behavior." *Journal of Business Research* 54: 139–144.

Waxman, L. (2006). "The Coffee Shop: Social and Physical Factors Influencing Place Attachment." *Journal of Interior Design* 31(3): 35–53. (S)

Webb, J., and Weber, M. (2003). "Influence of Sensory Abilities on the Interpersonal Distance of the Elderly." *Environment and Behavior* 35(5): 689–711.

Weinstein, C. (1981). "Classroom Design as an External Condition for Learning." *Educational Technology* 21: 12–19.

Weinstein, C., and Wookfolk, A. (1981). "The Classroom Setting as a Source of Expectations About Teachers and Pupils." *Journal of Environmental Psychology* 1(2): 117–129.

Weisman, J. (1981). "Evaluating Architectural Legibility." *Environment and Behavior* 13(2): 189–204.

Wells, M. (2000). "Office Clutter or Meaningful Personal Displays: The Role of Office Personalization in Employee and Organizational Well-Being." *Journal of Environmental Psychology* 20(3): 239–255.

Wells, M., Thelen, L., and Ruark, J. (2007). "Workplace Personalization and Organizational Culture: Does Your Workplace Reflect You or Your Company?" *Environment and Behavior* 30(5): 616–634.

West, A., and Wind, Y. (2007). "Putting the Organization on Wheels." *California Management Review* 49(2): 138–153.

Wheeler, S., and Berger, J. (2007). "When the Same Prime Leads to Different Effects." *Journal of Consumer Research* 34: 357–368.

Whitfield, T. (1983). "Predicting Preference for Familiar, Everyday Objects: An Experimental Confrontation Between Two Theories of Aesthetic Behaviour." *Journal of Environmental Psychology* 3(3): 221–237.

Williams, C. (2004). "A Lifestyle Choice? Evaluating the Motives of Do-It-Yourself (DIY) Consumers." *International Journal of Retail and Distribution Management* 32(5): 270–278.

Williams, C., Armstrong, D., and Malcolm, C. (1990). *The Negotiable Environment: People, White-Collar Work, and the Office.* Ann Arbor, MI: Facility Management Institute.

Wilson, E. (1984). *Biophilia.* Cambridge, MA: Harvard University Press.

Wilson, E. (2008). "The Nature of Human Nature." In S. Kellert, J. Heerwagen, and M. Mador (eds.), *Biophilic Design.* Hoboken, NJ: John Wiley & Sons, 21–25.

Wilson, M. (1996). "The Socialization of Architectural Preference." *Journal of Environmental Psychology* 16(1): 33–44.

Wilson, M., and MacKenzie, N. (2000). "Social Attributions Based on Domestic Interiors." *Journal of Environmental Psychology* 20(4): 343–354.

Winawer, J., Witthoft, N., Frank, M., Wu, L., Wade, A., and Boroditsky, L. (2007). "Russian Blues Reveal Effects of Language on Color Discrimination." Proceedings of the National Academy of Sciences 104(19), http://www.pnas.org.

Wineman, J. (1982). "Office Design and Evaluation." *Environment and Behavior* 14(2): 271–298.

Wineman, J., and Serrato, M. (1999). "Facility Design for High-Performance Teams." In E. Sundstrom et al. (eds.), *Work Team Effectiveness*. San Francisco: Jossey-Bass, 271–298.

Wise, J., and Hazzard, T. (2000). "Green Buildings, Benefits and Bionomic Design." *Arch-Tech* (Winter): 24–30.

Wise, J., and Hazzard, T. (2002). "Fractals: What Nature Can Teach Design." *ICON* (March): 2–9.

Wohlwill, J. (1966). "The Physical Environment: A Problem for a Psychology of Stimulation." *Journal of Social Issues* 22(4): 29–30.

Wohlwill, J., and Heft, H. (1987). "The Physical Environment and the Development of the Child." In D. Stokols and I. Altman (eds.), *Handbook of Environmental Psychology, Volume 1*. New York: John Wiley & Sons, 281–328.

Wong, C., Sommer, R., and Cook, E. (1992). "The Soft Classroom 17 Years Later." *Journal of Environmental Psychology* 12(4): 336–343.

Wrzencewski, A., McCauley, C., and Rozun, P. (1999). "Odor and Affect: Individual Differences in the Impact of Odor on Liking for Places, Things, and People." *Chemical Sense* 24: 713–721.

Yalch, R., and Spangenberg, E. (1990). "Effects of Store Music on Shopping Behavior." *The Journal of Services Marketing* 4(1): 31–39.

Yildrim, K., Akalin-Baskaya, A., and Celebi, M. (2007). "The Effects of Window Proximity, Partition Height, and Gender on Perceptions of Open-Plan Offices." *Journal of Environmental Psychology* 27: 154–165.

"Young Children Rely on One Sense or Another, Not a Combination, Studies Find." (2008). Press Release, Cell Press, http://www.current-biology.com.

Zakay, D. (1989). "Subjective Time and Attitudinal Resource Allocation." In L. Levin and D. Zakay (eds.), *Time and Human Cognition*. Amsterdam, The Netherlands: Elsevier.

Zalesny, M., and Farace, R. (1987). "Traditional Versus Open Offices." *Academy of Management* 30: 240–259.

Zaltman, G. (2003). *How Customers Think: Essential Insights Into the Mind of the Market.* Boston: Harvard Business School Press.

Zeisel, J. (2006). *Inquiry by Design.* New York: W.W. Norton. (S)

Zentell, S. (1983). "Learning Environments." *EEQ* 4: 90–115.

Zhang, Y., Feick, L., and Price, L. (2006). "The Impact of Self-Construal on Aesthetic Preference for Angular versus Rounded Shapes." *Personality and Social Psychology Bulletin* 32: 794–805.

Zimring, C., and Peatross, D. (1997). "Cultural Aspects of Workplace Organization and Space." In G. Moore and R. Marans (eds.), *Advances in Environment, Behavior, and Design.* New York: Plenum Press, 195–221. (S)

Zoladz, P. and Raudenbush, B. (2005) "Cognitive Enhancement Through Stimulation of the Chemical Senses." *North American Journal of Psychology* 7(1): 1–16.

INDEX

Acceptance, basic human need and place design, 18
Activity and place design, 6, 135–137
Adaptation, 136
Adjacencies, workplace environments, 201–202
  design implication, 202
Aesthetics, *see* Design experience and place responses
Affordances, *see* Complying, function of a well-designed space
Age-related design concerns, 175–176. *See also* Children and place design
Almond scent, 42
Ambient environment. *See also* Hearing; Scents; Touch; Vision
  learning environments, 222–223
  residential environments, 171
  retail environments, 211–218
  workplace environments, 184–185
Appropriateness, *see* Well-designed space
Aquarium, *see* Fish tank
Architectural determinism, 181–182
Architectural evolution, 26. *See also* Future
Art
  healthcare environments, 234–236
    appropriate images, 234–236
    appropriate placement, 236
    pediatric areas, 235–236
    personal/perceived control and, 236
  labeling, 188
  workplace environments, 188
Artisan living, 144–145
Assessments, *see* Research methods
Attention deficit disorder/attention deficit hyperactivity disorder and place design, 174–175
Attention restoration theory, 31–32
Attention to others (personality factor) and place design, 97–98
Autism and place design
  learning environments, 227
  residential environments, 174–175

Baby powder scent, 43
Balance, visual, and response to, 60
Bariatric factors and design, 179
Barriers, furniture, 76

Basic human needs satisfied through place design, 15–19
  acceptance, 18
  curiosity, 16
  eating, 18
  family, 18
  honor, 17
  idealism,17–18
  independence, 16
  order, 18
  physical exercise, 18
  power, 16
  romance, 18
  saving, 18
  social contact, 17
  status, 17
  tranquility, 18
  vengeance, 17
Basil scent, 43
Bergamot scent, 42
Biophilic design, 84–87
  definition of, 84–85
  design implication, 86
  principles of, 85–87
Boundary, *see* Territory

Cedar scent, 42
Ceiling
  color and response to, 54
  height and response to, 71–72
Challenging, aspect of well-designed space, 22, 35
  national culture and, 130–131
  residential environments, 176
  workplace environments, 204–205
Chamomile scent, 42
Change management, 150
Children and place design, 29, 173–174
  healthcare environments
    adolescent patients, 240
    pediatric areas and art, 235–236
Cinnamon-vanilla scent, 42, 43
Circulation routes, workplace environments, 192–194
Classroom, *see* Learning environments
Clove scent, 43